GOVERNMENT AND POLITICS IN JAPAN

The Road to Democracy

GOVERNMENT AND POLITICS IN JAPAN

The Road to Democracy

J~OHN~ M. M~AKI~

F~REDERICK~ A. P~RAEGER~

Publisher • New York

BOOKS THAT MATTER

First published in the United States of America in 1962 by
Frederick A. Praeger, Inc., Publisher
64 University Place, New York 3, N.Y.

© 1962 by Frederick A. Praeger, Inc.

All rights reserved

Library of Congress Catalog Card Number: 62-13735

GOVERNMENT AND POLITICS IN JAPAN
is published in two editions:

A paperback edition (U-512)
A clothbound edition

Manufactured in the United States of America

Foreword

This study of democracy in Japan originated with my sudden realization in 1955 that Japanese democracy was not simply in prospect, but in existence. That realization grew out of an analysis of several developments in early post-occupation Japanese government and politics that were interpreted by many observers, including myself, as signs either of a "reverse course" away from democracy or of a still considerable immaturity of democracy itself. My examination of these phenomena convinced me that although the manifestations of backtracking and immaturity were real enough, they were also only a part of a broader picture of a democratic political society in operation. Later events, even the disquieting ones of 1960, confirmed my analysis.

I had been a student of Japanese government and politics for some years and, as a civilian with the American occupation forces, had had the opportunity of observing Japan during the fascinating and exciting period between February and August of 1946. I had believed, as did virtually all other observers, that the integration of democracy into Japanese society would be a difficult and lengthy process. Thus, it was clearly not enough simply to recognize that Japanese democracy had come into existence in the short decade between 1945 and 1955. There had to be explanations: of how democracy had become a reality and been integrated so rapidly into the society, and of why the new democracy gave the appearance of being permanent. The search for reasons forced me into a reconsideration and fresh analysis of contemporary

v

Japanese society, the concept of democracy itself, the nature of the occupation and its interaction with Japan, and the history of Japan between 1945 and 1960. The result is this study.

Parts of this book have appeared in different form in such journals as the *Western Political Quarterly, United Asia, India Quarterly, Far Eastern Survey*, and *The New Leader*. Other material has come from my unpublished papers read at annual meetings of the Association for Asian Studies and the American Historical Association.

After the completion of an earlier version of the manuscript, I was particularly fortunate in being able to enjoy a sabbatical leave in 1958–59, during which I revisited Japan on a Fulbright research professorship. Although I was engaged in research only tangentially related to this study, I was able to observe firsthand the new Japan and to check empirically the validity of certain conclusions I had arrived at as a result of reading and reflection. I am particularly grateful to the Board of Regents of the University of Washington for granting my sabbatical leave, to the International Education Program of the United States Government for the Fulbright research professorship, and to Mr. Iwao Nishimura, Executive Secretary, and his staff of the United States Educational Commission in Tokyo for their assistance, always rendered with kindness, courtesy, and cheerfulness, which contributed so much to the pleasure and profit of my stay in Japan.

I also wish to express my gratitude to the members of the Modern Japan Project of the Far Eastern and Russian Institute of the University of Washington, who gave me the benefit of their comments in the Project's research colloquium during discussions of preliminary versions of several chapters. My colleague, Professor Herbert Passin, was also kind enough to read and comment on several chapters. My special thanks are due to Professor Cecil Cody of the University of Massachusetts, Professor Robert Sakai of the University of Nebraska, Professor Robert Scalapino of the University of California (Berkeley), and my colleague Professor George E. Taylor, who took the time and trouble, as only true friends would, to read in its entirety an earlier version of the manuscript and to comment in detail on it. I am deeply indebted also to my colleague Professor Robert J. C. Butow, for reading and commenting on the final draft. All who commented on the manuscript at any stage have helped to eliminate errors and to clarify the language and the ideas, but I alone am fully responsible for all shortcomings in the book as it now stands.

My appreciation is also due Miss Grace Brewer, Mrs. Helen Vitous, and several unknown members of the stenographic pool of the University of Washington for excellent work in the typing of the manuscript.

I am most grateful to the Far Eastern and Russian Institute and its Director, Professor Taylor, for two grants-in-aid that came at critical periods in the preparation of the manuscript and enabled me to complete the study in considerably less time than otherwise would have been the case.

Finally, a note about two usages—one followed, one abandoned. The Japanese usage regarding personal names is followed, i.e., the surname first and the given name second. However, macrons to indicate long vowels in romanized Japanese words are omitted.

JOHN M. MAKI

University of Washington
November, 1961

Contents

GOVERNMENT AND POLITICS IN JAPAN

The Road to Democracy

Prologue: The Problem

The emergence of democracy in Japan was one of the most significant political developments of the mid-twentieth century; it was also one of the least noted. It was significant because Japan became the first non-Western society to develop a strong and viable democracy, and also because it offered a striking example of a rapid transition from an authoritarian to a democratic system of government and politics. It remained largely unnoted because it was unattended by bloodshed and tension, and because it was overshadowed by far more spectacular events: the Cold War, the triumph of Communism in China, and the collapse of colonialism in Asia and Africa.

This book is a study of democracy in Japan. It addresses itself to the problem of how democracy, a Western-created and Western-developed concept of government and politics, could become rapidly and firmly rooted in a nation that not only had no democratic history and tradition of its own but had developed a modern governmental system of an authoritarian character. To understand more precisely the nature of the problem, it is necessary to examine briefly its two main components, Japan and democracy.

Japan is an old nation, although it does not rank among the oldest. Its earliest historical chronicles date from the beginning of the eighth century A.D. The best informed historical guess is that the islands were peopled as early as 5000 B.C. and that there was probably an identifiably Japanese society in the islands by the beginning of the Christian Era. The society is an Asian one, located in the area, though on the eastern periphery of Asia, and having for centuries been influenced by its neighbors, especially China. In its entire history Japanese society has never duplicated the peculiar economic, political, and social conditions characteristic of Western civilization that over a period of centuries contributed to the growth of modern democracy. The Japanese system of government and politics was thoroughly nondemocratic in nature and without any elements that might have led to the growth of an indigenous democracy, yet there is no evidence that the Japanese ever believed its authoritarian character to be inconsistent with the social and political values they regarded as good.

In the middle of the nineteenth century, when Japan was forced to drop its self-imposed policy of seclusion and for the first time in its history found itself fully in the current of world affairs, it developed a political and governmental system consistent with its own past and in tune with the authoritarian stream of modern Western government. By the mid–1930's, Japan had developed a characteristic form of twentieth-century authoritarian government that, though it may have fallen considerably short of being totalitarian, was still the antithesis of democratic government.

Therefore, when Japan started out on the road toward democracy, amid the ruins of defeat and the crisis of occupation in 1945, the country seemed confronted with two great obstacles that, if not actually insurmountable, would take some years to overcome: the inert mass of a nondemocratic history and tradition and the oppressive weight of authoritarianism. Our search to understand why these obstacles were swept away so easily and why the goal of democracy was reached so soon requires first a brief examination of the nature of modern democracy.

I shall not attempt here the extremely difficult task of defining democracy. Rather, I shall simply describe the working concept of democracy that has been used in this study and state briefly its principal implications. A true democracy must have three characteristics: the guarantee of freedom, free elections, and a representative and responsible government.

The freedoms guaranteed include those that are tradition-
ally associated with a democratic political society: the freedoms
of thought, religion, conscience, association, assembly, residence,
travel, and person, as well as speech, press, and all other forms of
expression. In most democracies, these freedoms are closely allied
with certain fundamental rights, especially the right of the individual to be secure in the enjoyment of life, liberty, and property
against the arbitrary action of government; the right to a fair
trial; and the right to petition the government for redress of
grievances. The freedoms and the related rights imply certain
important considerations that must be made explicit.

In the first place, freedom under democracy has meaning only
if it is guaranteed to the individual without qualifications relating
to his particular social, political, or economic role in the general
community. Stated negatively, the guarantee of freedom cannot
be limited to any one group at the expense of the general community of individuals. It is only through the enforcement of
such a broad guarantee of the freedom of the individual that
existing and undesirable limitations on freedom can be removed
and the real be made to square with the ideal.

Second, the freedom of the individual is not absolute. As the
philosophers of modern democracy have unceasingly pointed out,
the individual, in the exercise of his freedom, must not interfere
with the freedom of his fellows or impair the general well-being
of his society. How to strike a balance between the guarantee
of freedom and its necessary restriction is one of the most difficult
problems confronting a democracy.

Third, the guarantee of freedom and of rights is, in essence,
a guarantee against arbitrary or tyrannical action by the government toward the individual. A government, by definition, has
the force at its command to control the lives of all who live under
it. It is the democratic system that has succeeded in creating
limitations on the power of the state vis-à-vis the individual. But
even under democracy the individual is never free from the threat
of the application of force by his government; his only defense,
albeit a powerful one, is that such application can be made only
under certain conditions and in accordance with certain procedures.

This raises the final consideration—that in spite of the strictures on its power to control enjoyment of freedom, only the government can act to control the exercise of freedom by the individual when such exercise threatens the freedom of others or the well-being of society. Thus, in the area of relations between the individual and his democratic government we have another delicate problem of balance: to restrain the government generally from infringing on the freedom of the individual, but to empower it to do so in certain instances.

Any objective observer can easily perceive the existence of a general air of freedom in a democracy, even in the presence of obvious strictures on its enjoyment, a situation we shall note on a number of occasions in this study. Such an observer can also quickly perceive the absence of this air of freedom and the oppressive presence of only the strictures in a nondemocratic political society, such as Japan in the recent past.

The second characteristic of democracy, free elections, is a special application in the vital area of politics of the general guarantee of freedom. At least three major considerations are involved: (1) the freedom of individuals, parties, and factions to express as they wish their own programs and qualifications and to attack or oppose those of their opponents or the government; (2) the freedom of the individual to vote in secret for the candidate, party, or policies he has decided to support; and (3) the absence of governmental control or interference—as distinct from influence—in either campaigns or elections.

Free elections are intimately intertwined with the third characteristic of democracy. For it is through representative and responsible government that citizens of a democracy are able to exercise a degree of control over and influence on the machinery of state that is impossible under a nondemocratic system. The nature of representative and responsible government under a system of free elections can best be made clear by listing its principal features: open and unrestricted competition for political power among individuals, parties, and factions; periodic exposure of individuals and parties in power to the judgment of the general electorate (or, in other words, impermanence and insecurity of the tenure of power); provision for the peaceful and open transfer of power from one group to another; responsiveness on the part of the government to the reactions of voters, rivals, and pressure groups; and the inability of the government and those controlling it to maintain themselves in power through a monopoly of the instruments of force and mass persuasion. In each of these, the fundamental issue is the relationship between the government and those who live under it.

The whole complex structure of modern democracy was the product of centuries of political, social, and philosophical thought peculiar to the stream of Western civilization. I cannot attempt to outline the history of this development, nor can I describe in detail the essential institutional framework that makes possible the existence of the guarantees of freedom, free elections, and representative and responsible government. But I should point out that this framework must include: an industrialized economy providing a reasonable degree of economic well-being for the population, a system of universal education, the media of mass communication, political parties, a functioning central government, a national legislature, a judicial and legal system, and a shared system of values supporting the worth and desirability of democracy itself. Much of this study deals with the vital issue of the institutional framework for democracy in the particular case of Japan.

Another issue that must be examined if we are to understand democracy in Japan is the relationship between the governing and the governed. The growth of modern democracy in the Western world was characterized by two simultaneous, interacting developments: the emergence of the institutional framework of the modern nation-state and the creation of the features of modern democracy itself. Most nations today have the requisite institutional framework, but they have not all followed the democratic pattern. In general, the two prevailing types of modern government and politics have been the democratic and the authoritarian (with the latter merging into the totalitarian, especially during the middle decades of the twentieth century). Both types have the same basic institutional framework; the critical difference between them lies in the governed-governing relationship. Under democracy the balance is in favor of the governed;

under authoritarianism and totalitarianism, of the governing. As we shall see in the discussion of democracy in Japan, this difference accounts for significant variations in the structure of governments.

Democracy in Japan did not undergo evolutionary growth, as in the West. The essential issue was one of changing the governed-governing relationship from an authoritarian to a democratic one within the institutions of the modern nation-state, the essentials of which Japan had developed by the beginning of the twentieth century. It was then necessary to adjust, modify, and redirect the working of the existing framework of Japanese society so that the three basic features of democracy could become operative.

What made possible the successful execution of this complex task was a set of extremely special circumstances. A lost war, the chaos and dislocations of defeat, an enlightened occupation acting in the name of a government determined to establish the conditions for democracy inside the country, a society equipped with the basic institutions of the modern nation-state, and a population generally willing to reject the discredited authoritarianism and to embark on the construction of a new democracy—all these combined to make possible a peaceful democratic revolution that succeeded in an astonishingly short period of time.

What is more, the democratic revolution, either immediately or within the space of a few years, brought tangible, desirable, and apparently enduring gains to millions of individuals and to important social, economic, and political groups without simultaneously creating classes or groups of the dispossessed with grievances against the new order. The elimination of militarism, aggression, and authoritarianism was welcomed widely throughout Japanese society as a positive benefit. And more important, new rights and freedoms, new relationships, new positions of leadership, new opportunities for advancement and achievement, and a new level of economic well-being throughout the society gave millions of persons a direct stake in the maintenance and strengthening of the new democracy. How this came about is another principal theme of this study.

Finally, the strength and viability of the new democracy were vividly demonstrated during the 1950's. That the nation enjoyed all the basic freedoms was demonstrated daily, for example, in the media of mass communication. The country witnessed the smooth operation of free elections. And there was responsible and representative government, although on occasion it showed signs of irresponsibility. Equally important, the new democracy survived a number of negative tests. Although limitations, some of which appeared threatening indeed, were placed on the enjoyment of freedom, none undermined the foundations of the structure of liberty itself. On occasion, the control of the government over the instruments of force—the police and the military—seemed to bode ill for the maintenance of the balance of the democratic governed-governing relationship. But the threat did not materialize. The new system also survived crises marked by a disregard of the parliamentary procedures deemed essential for democracy, a halting operation of the party system, and the resort to mass violence as a form of political action. The older democracies of the West have witnessed and survived similar crises of their own. Perhaps the conclusion to be drawn from both Japanese and Western experience is not that such crises are necessarily fatal to democracy, but that both their appearance and their resolution are attributes of the democratic process itself, manifestations of the existence of freedom. In Japan, the crises followed the pattern that they did because they occurred within the general context of democracy, and Japanese democracy outlived them because they were resolved by the very operation of democracy.

1

The Prelude to Democracy

Japan's long, twisting road to democracy first ran through territory utterly alien to democracy and then moved toward a thoroughly antidemocratic destination. Japanese history before the end of the feudal state in about 1870 did not provide a foundation for the independent development of a Japanese variation on the theme of modern democracy; after 1870, the leaders of Japan were not interested in democracy, and Japanese society did not develop in that direction. But what took place between 1870 and 1945 constituted the essential prelude to the new democracy. Social, economic, and political institutions were created and developed for the purpose of furthering the authoritarian type of society that was in conformity with the past and with the desires, policies, and actions of the leaders of Japan; the individual was so nurtured as to be an effective unit in his society. Yet, the molding of such institutions and individuals necessarily resulted in the construction of the foundation required for the rapid growth of democracy following the crisis of defeat in war and a military occupation.

The fundamental processes of Japanese history between 1850 and 1945 can be roughly dated and described as follows: 1850–70, the disintegration and final collapse of the centuries-old patterns of feudal society; 1870–95, the founding of a national society and the consequent emergence of a new structure of government and new patterns of politics; 1895–1945, the development, temporary success, and final collapse of authoritarianism.

The Structure of Tokugawa Power

To perceive clearly the problems of Japan in the century from 1850 to 1950, it is necessary to go back about two and a half centuries to the time when Japan had just emerged from an earlier and different crisis in its history. The leaders of the great and powerful Tokugawa family dominated Japan from about 1600 to 1867, nominally as the deputies of the emperor, but actually as the unchallenged rulers of the country. Through a combination of military power, statesmanship, and brilliant political tactics and strategy, they not only brought to a successful conclusion a long period of internal chaos, confusion, and civil war, but also firmly established their family in power. The Tokugawa regime also brought to its highest point of development —and at the same time demonstrated that it could go no further —the Japanese system of feudalism. Tokugawa feudalism was as nondemocratic as its earlier Japanese counterpart and its European equivalent.

In simplified form, the characteristic features of Japan during this period were: (1) domination of the society by the Tokugawa family, in reality responsible neither to the emperor nor to anyone else and ruling through a semicentralized but highly effective government; (2) a strictly hierarchical society, with a warrior class at the top in terms of power, prestige, and authority; (3) a large number of independent feudal lords, in control of their own estates, but loyal to, under the control of, or in a state of armed neutrality toward the Tokugawa government; (4) a basically agricultural economy controlled by the warrior class and built on the labor of the peasants, but with a growingly important commercial sector operated by a merchant class without political power or influence; and (5) a structure of controls, formal and informal, over the lives, livelihood, activities, and movements of virtually all members of the society. There was nothing to encourage the independent development of democracy. The individual had no rights and privileges. Government as exercised by either the Tokugawa family or the feudal lords was not responsible to the people and rested ultimately on the warrior monopoly of arms. However, this society in all its aspects was thoroughly

Japanese. That the system operated successfully—if success can be measured by the continuation of Tokugawa rule and the maintenance of a reasonable degree of law and order and of economic well-being—indicates that it was not inconsistent with either the realities or the values of Japanese society at the time.

For the post–1870 future of Japan, the heritage of the Tokugawa period was of great significance. Although the Tokugawa family fell from power, Japan's feudalism almost simultaneously came to an end, and the nation apparently embarked on a new and strange course in its history, the nondemocratic elements of the Tokugawa system had a great influence on the new Japan. The old feudalism vanished, yet its spirit infused the new nation-state. Here was, indeed, the beginning of the authoritarianism that was to be characteristic of most of the first century of modern Japan.

The early heads of the Tokugawa family and their advisers were brilliant politicians and statesmen. This was clearly demonstrated by their creation of a system of government and politics that kept the family in power for more than 250 years. The greatest strength of the system, however, proved to be its greatest weakness. Its strength lay in its static nature, designed to maintain an unchanging relationship between the omnipotent Tokugawa family on the one hand and the rest of Japan on the other.

Social Change and Tokugawa Collapse

Overtly, Japanese society was static during the Tokugawa period. The continued domination of one family, the absence of significant alteration in the structure and operation of government, the maintenance of the strict division among the warrior, peasant, artisan, and merchant classes (in that descending order), and the basic role of agriculture in the feudal economy distinguished what seemed to be an immutable, perdurable society. Yet, there were at least two fundamentally important socio-economic developments that were undermining not only the Tokugawa structure of power but the whole foundation of feudalism on which it was erected. One was the growth, on the continuing base of agriculture, of a money economy that by its mere existence was altering the economic positions of the warrior feudal families, the merchants, and the peasants, and was consequently creating new political and social problems. The second, closely related, was the growth of a new urban society, most conspicuously in what are now the modern cities of Tokyo and Osaka, but also throughout the country in the towns being built up around the castles of the feudal lords. The Tokugawa government was not blind to these important developments, but, generally speaking, the policies it devised to deal with them were designed to cushion their impact on the existing order, thereby maintaining the status quo, rather than to accept them as the facts of change they were and thereby open the way to incorporating them into a new order of society that would still be under Tokugawa control.

In this new situation, land and its principal product, rice, could no longer serve adequately as the exclusive foundation of the economy. Feudal lords and their retainers now needed money not just for day-to-day existence, but to maintain themselves and their class in power. This need created economic tensions as well as political discontent among them. Merchants, though unable to use their control over money as a means of access to political power, became increasingly venturesome—as they saw Tokugawa power declining—and willing to provide the funds required by the anti-Tokugawa lords. As the warrior lords tried futilely to solve their economic difficulties by demanding payment of taxes in cash, increasingly heavy economic demands were made on the peasants. As a result, the strength of the Tokugawa regime was further undermined by a general situation of political disorder and social unrest. The growth of cities placed an increasing emphasis on the use of money, as more and more peasants were pulled away from the land, more opportunities for monetary transactions among the merchants were created, and warriors (leaders and followers alike) were saddled with new expenditures. These unplanned, uncontrolled developments wrought such a transformation that the structure of feudalism no longer corresponded to the new structure of Japanese society, in which the restricted range of new elements outweighed the solid core of the old.

In the mid-nineteenth century, political and military challenges to Tokugawa authority developed increasingly as the impact of the internal social crisis on the Tokugawa fabric of power widened. To this situation was added a new crisis: the demand, first by the United States and then in rapid succession by the other Western powers, that Japan end her policy of seclusion from the Western world (another element in the Tokugawa system of control) and establish formal treaty relations with them. Japan's first modern treaty with a Western power, the Treaty of Kanagawa concluded with the United States in 1854, set in train a series of events that led to the Tokugawas' fall from power in 1867.

Before turning to the question of the founding of the new national society, it is necessary to examine the peculiar characteristics of the shift of power from the hands of the Tokugawas to their enemies, who became the molders of the new society—a pattern that had a direct bearing on the nature of the change that began in about 1870. Although the shift was fundamental and far-reaching, it was made without widespread political turmoil or disorder, in contrast with what was happening at the same time in China and with what was to happen almost a century later as Western colonialism gave way to nationalism in Southeast Asia. There was no revolution in the proper sense of the term, and there was no true civil war, although there was limited civil strife. Sporadic fighting broke out before and after 1867 (not actually ending until 1877), but it never resulted in real chaos. The Tokugawas were ejected from power by what was essentially a *coup d'état* rather than a revolutionary attack on the government or governing class by the governed. The dramatic upheaval was not of a nature to challenge the basic political concepts of Japanese society or to undermine its over-all stability. Actually, within three years, the domestic political situation was stable enough to permit a rapid attack on the problem of modernization.

Another important additional clue to the nature of the changes that took place in Japan in the late 1860's and early 1870's is found in the composition of the leadership that brought Tokugawa power and feudalism to an end and began the great task of the construction of Japan as a modern national society. The vast majority of the men who directed and manned the machinery of government and politics in the new Japan came from the former warrior class. They were not merchants, nor were they of the people. The merchants during the Tokugawa period had developed increasingly great economic strength, but they had never been able to break through the barriers—legal, social, and political—that lay between them and political power. Some of them worked with the new leaders in their successful attack on the fortress of Tokugawa might, and some were of great financial assistance to the new regime, but in no sense was their role revolutionary. They did not attain political leadership, and they were not in a position to develop institutional devices that would give them a formal share of power and control in the new system of government. Nor was the voice of the people heard—or even represented—in this critical period. Peasant dissatisfaction and unrest had undermined the Tokugawa position, but peasant violence had not overthrown the government. The new leaders of Japan did not find themselves in the position of having to appeal for popular support either to crush the Tokugawas or to protect themselves against a resurgence of Tokugawa strength. In the crisis of the mid-nineteenth century, it was only among the merchants and the peasants that there might have developed a revolutionary spirit, a surge of revolutionary action to break the continuity between the feudal past and the emergent society. Both the structure of Tokugawa society and the nature of the *coup d'état* prevented the development of such a trend.

The End of Feudalism and the New Society

Once the issue of political supremacy had been decided against the Tokugawa regime, the way was clear to attack the solution of the two far more fundamental problems: the internal crisis posed by the process of social change, which the Tokugawa government had been unable to control or direct; and the external crisis posed by the coming of the Western powers. With the benefit of historical hindsight, it is easy to see that both crises could have been handled by a single broad course of action: the conversion of a feudal society, purely Japanese in both externals and internals, to a modern national society, with all the external characteristics of the modern nation-state, but infused with the traditional and unique Japanese ethos. Such a conversion would have solved the internal crisis, for the only alternative would have been an attempt, foredoomed to failure, to strengthen and revitalize feudalism. And since it was modern nation-states with their new forms of economic, political, diplomatic, and military power that had created the external crisis, Japan could hold them off only by becoming as much like them as possible. There is no evidence that the problem appeared to the Japanese leaders of that time in such explicit terms. Yet, what they did conformed in every respect to the ideal course of action.

Between 1870, when the major attack on the feudal society began, and 1895, when war against China ended in victory—a convincing demonstration of her mastery of the new forms of power—Japan had either established or started to develop such essential features of the modern nation-state as an industrial economy, a centralized and bureaucratic government, an army and navy, a national system of education, newspapers (the forerunners of a broad system of mass communication), a railroad system, a telegraph system, political unification, a modern system of law, and a sentiment of national unity spread widely among the people. But all of this had been erected on an unshakable Japanese foundation: the imperial throne, deeply rooted in history and tradition and considerably reinforced by being made the pillar around which the new national unity was built; the tradition of the subservience of the ruled to the ruling; the domination of government and politics by an oligarchy; an authoritarian family system; and a moral and ethical system based on the subordination of the individual to the requirements of society, and especially of the state. Thus, the new Japanese nation-state as it had emerged by the end of the nineteenth century could be described as a substantial modern structure of new political, social, and economic institutions, held together by a tough and resilient web of traditional, nondemocratic social and cultural ideas and attitudes.

The initial problem confronting the new leaders of Japan was the destruction of the loosely centralized structure of government left by the Tokugawas and the elimination of all the "local governments" under the several hundred feudal lords who possessed a considerable degree of autonomy within their individual estates. Such a structure had served Tokugawa and pre-Tokugawa requirements well, but it was completely at variance with the governmental needs of a modern nation.

The abolition of the old system was carried out rapidly, and equally rapidly a new system was instituted—centering, of course, around a strong executive branch that could direct and accomplish those things necessary for the creation of the new state. Although a true cabinet system was not created until 1885, a quasi-cabinet form of government was established as early as 1868. As an indication of the speed with which the new governmental edifice was built, the Finance and Foreign Ministries were created in 1869, the Education Ministry in 1871, and the War and Navy Ministries in 1872. The important consideration is not that these and other ministries functioned perfectly from the beginning, but that their creation and even halting operation meant that at no time in the critical initial decades of nation-building was Japan confronted with a situation of administrative collapse or chaos. The concentration on the executive branch meant that the most essential things were either done or at least effectively worked on from the beginning.

It is significant that the second major branch of government created was the judiciary. The first court system was established in 1875 and administered by the executive branch through a Ministry of Justice, which had been established in 1871. Under the strong executive system, the administration of justice was closely controlled by the cabinet. In addition, it should be added, the Japanese Government was anxious to push ahead rapidly on the creation of a modern system of law and courts. This was absolutely necessary if extraterritoriality and, beyond that, the unequal treaty system were to be abolished and Japan was to win full equality in the comity of nations.

Although there were experiments in the establishment of a legislative branch in the early years, it is significant that no true national legislature, even narrowly representative, was created until 1890, under the provisions of the 1889 Constitution.

Thus, we see an emergent pattern of government in which responsibility and power were centered in the hands of a strong executive, which the history of the Tokugawa period had pre-disposed the leaders of Japan to adopt and which the current situation required. Such an executive was also ideally suited for the use of the restricted leadership group that successfully maintained a monopoly of power.

The Constitution of 1889

In little more than twenty years after the Tokugawa collapse, Japan also had its first modern constitution. Actually, it became clear by 1880 that the new state required a written fundamental law. Yielding unwillingly to the irresistible pressure and agitation for a constitution, the oligarchy retained full control over the drafting process and consequently over the content of the document. In 1881, it was announced in an Imperial rescript that a system of representative government would be established by 1890. There followed several years of careful preparation, principally involving on-the-spot investigation of the Prussian and Austrian constitutions. Because of their autocratic and monarchical features, these were deemed the ideal models for Japan's first constitution. Between 1886 and 1888, under conditions of great secrecy and absolute control by a small group, the constitution was drafted.

On February 11, 1889, this constitution was bestowed on the Japanese nation as a gracious gift from the Emperor Meiji, and from then until 1947, it was Japan's fundamental law. Like all constitutions, it dealt with the problem of sovereignty, the general structure of government, and the relation between the government and the people. It was within this framework that Japan's authoritarianism developed. It might have been possible for democracy to grow under the Meiji Constitution without a significant alteration in its content, but the course of events in the country prevented such a development.

The fundamental principle around which the 1889 constitution was built was that of absolute imperial sovereignty. This meant governmental power and authority were vested solely in the emperor—not in any arm of the government, not in a class, not in the people, not in a political party—and were not to be shared in any manner. Prince Ito Hirobumi, the principal drafter of the document, made this abundantly clear in his authoritative commentary, issued immediately after the promulgation of the constitution. The persistent and unchanged character of this concept is strikingly demonstrated by a comment in 1940, more than half a century after the promulgation, by Professor Fujii Shinichi, an eminent Japanese professor of constitutional law:

> The supreme power of the Tenno [Emperor] over state affairs covers, in its broad sense, the same sphere as His sovereign power, comprising the fields of legislation, administration, and judicature. The judicial power exercised by courts of justice in the name of the Tenno, the executive power exercised by various administrative organs outside of matters personally attended to by the Tenno, and the legislative power exercised with the consent of the Imperial Diet—all merge in the supreme power of the Tenno. Although these powers are not personally wielded by the Tenno, the courts of justice and administrative organs possess their respective rights as entrusted to them by the Tenno, so that, it may be said, they all emanate from the supreme power of the Tenno. As to the exercise of the legislative power, the consent of the Imperial Diet is needed, which consent means only that the Diet gives its consent to the legislative act of the Tenno and nothing more. The Tenno exercises it personally over His subjects.

Here is clearly described a form of government characterized not by a democratic separation of powers with its consequent checks and balances, but by the concentration of all powers of government in a single source. The omnipotent emperor simply wielded his unitary sovereign power in the three areas of government. The 1889 Constitution was explicit and detailed in its listing of the imperial powers of government. Yet, it was obviously impossible for the emperor as an individual to exercise these powers personally and directly; they had to be delegated to others who were actually charged with the responsibility of seeing to it that they were exercised properly, so that the country might be well and truly governed under the emperor.

As might be anticipated, in view of the role of the executive, the cabinet was the dominant organ of Japanese government until the end of World War II. The constitution, however, devoted only one article to the cabinet, not even actually using the term, but referring simply to the "ministers of state" who were "to give advice to the emperor and be responsible for it." The responsibility, as Prince Ito was careful to point out, was only upward to the emperor, not lateral to the other branches of the government and not downward to the people or their representatives. This casual, nonspecific handling of the problem of the role and powers of the cabinet was undoubtedly purposeful, in order to permit the broadest possible interpretation. At any rate, the powers of government were effectively centered in the hands of the cabinet.

The five most important ministries were those of War, Navy, Education, Home Affairs, and Justice. Their roles were crucial in both government and politics. For reasons to be dealt with later, the War and Navy ministries came to predominate in Japan. In the first place, by custom and by ordinance only a general or an admiral could serve as a Minister of War or the Navy. This placed effective control over policy, both domestic and foreign, in the hands of the services. For if either the army or the navy disagreed with government policy, the service minister would either resign or threaten to resign, thus bringing about the fall of a cabinet. In addition, a new minister would not be nominated until the services were given assurance that the offensive item of policy would be altered or dropped. In the second place, the army and navy enjoyed the "right of direct access." This meant that they could go directly to the emperor with their advice and receive imperial sanction for their policies. There was no foundation for this in either the constitution or law. However, the constitutional provision that the emperor was the commander-in-chief of the army and navy was sufficient to provide a basis for the argument that, as specialists in the field of military affairs who were likewise responsible for administering them, the services had the right of direct access to the emperor on military matters without hindrance from the nonexpert civilian members of the cabinet. This dominant role of the military in the government contributed greatly to the development of Japanese authoritarianism from 1930 onward.

The Education Ministry also played a major role in the growth of authoritarianism. It created the national, government-controlled system of universal education, which led to mass literacy but was also used as a powerful and effective instrument of mass indoctrination. Reverence toward the emperor, the supremacy of the state, the subordination of the individual to the requirements not only of the state but of the family, the glorification of military tradition, chauvinism, and the acceptance of aggression were some of the themes of the singularly successful indoctrination program carried out through the schools.

Another state organ that contributed greatly to authoritarianism was the Home Affairs Ministry, especially through its key function of operation of the national police system. Prior to 1945, the police were used as a means of controlling the activities of candidates of opposition parties, of censoring the press, of controlling individuals and organizations suspected of being even remotely subversive, and in general of keeping the people subjected to the will of the state.

In an area in which there was considerably less direct involvement in the daily life of the people, the Ministry of Justice also played an important part in the authoritarian structure. It had direct administrative control over the judicial system. Although judges were to administer the law impartially, their positions as bureaucrats under the control of the Ministry—making them dependent on it for both salary and advancement—hardly guaranteed independence for the judicial branch.

The Imperial Diet, the legislative and representative branch of the government, was a decided innovation in Japanese government when it was formally inaugurated in 1890. But it never succeeded in fighting free of the controls of the executive. It suffered from one crippling constitutional restriction—the absence of the power to control the purse strings. The Diet could reduce no item in the budget without the consent of the cabinet and, in the event the Diet refused to approve a new budget, the existing budget was automatically continued in force for a new fiscal year. This meant, of course, that there was not available the standard means of fiscal control to keep the cabinet under legislative curb.

The special bicameral nature of the Imperial Diet also restricted its effectiveness as a brake on authoritarianism. The House of Peers, the upper house, was composed of members of the royal family, peers of the different orders (elected by their fellows), imperial appointees honored for their distinguished contributions to the state, and representatives of the highest taxpayers of each prefecture (also elected by their fellows). Such a membership guaranteed that the upper house would be extremely conservative. The House of Representatives suffered from at least two crippling defects as a representative body: First of all, the right of suffrage was severely limited, with women never possessing it and men enjoying it universally only after 1925, when financial qualifications were finally eliminated. Secondly, political parties never operated effectively as an institutional device to ensure the operation of representative government in the lower house.

In the early 1890's, just after its establishment, the Imperial Diet did struggle to achieve power and influence in its own right, but it failed because of the strength inherent in the executive, the political astuteness of the leaders of the government, and the Diet's own institutional immaturity. However, courageous individual Diet members, especially in the lower house, did on later occasions attack the government and its leaders bitterly over issues of policy, both domestic and foreign, that seemed—as they actually were—to be leading Japan toward disaster. Nevertheless, the Diet—the one branch of government that had a representative and at least quasi-democratic flavor—was never able either to shift the course of government and politics in a solidly democratic direction or to withstand the rising tide of authoritarianism.

The final aspect of the 1889 Constitution that must be considered is the relationship between the people and the government. Significantly, the people were termed "subjects." In the chapter dealing with the rights and duties of subjects, there was an enumeration of all the basic freedoms, such as freedom of thought, speech, religion, assembly, association, press, and property. That these were even enumerated was a significant innovation. However, there was no effective guarantee of these freedoms, for, with the exception of that of property, all were qualified by provisions to the effect that they could be enjoyed according to the law or within the limits of the law. This included not only duly enacted legislation but also an extensive body of regulations and ordinances issued by the cabinet without reference to the Imperial Diet. In effect, what was guaranteed was not the enjoyment of freedoms by the people, but the right of the government to limit their exercise. This reflected what had been happening prior to the constitution—the first regulations controlling the content and publication of books dated from 1869—and foreshadowed later developments. At no time in modern Japan, from the early 1870's until 1945, were the people free of restrictions on the exercise of freedoms.

Thus, two concepts molded the structure and operation of government and the course of politics under the 1889 Constitution: absolute sovereignty in the hands of the emperor, to be exercised at the discretion of the cabinet; and the subservient position of his loyal subjects. Both in theory and in practice, the government was able to exert a maximum of control over the lives of the people, who naturally enjoyed only a minimum of freedom. The constitution did not stand in the way of certain abortive attempts in the direction of democracy, particularly in the decade or so following World War I, but on the other hand there was nothing in the constitution or the theory behind it that was conducive to such development.

War and Authoritarianism

The authoritarian tendencies in this governmental system were strengthened by the series of wars that Japan became involved in between 1895 and 1945. War anywhere inevitably increases the domestic power of the governments involved; not only are all positive steps taken to strengthen the military potential of the warring society, but every negative step is taken to eliminate anything that might stand in the way of successful prosecution of the war. It is not strange that there was mutual reinforcement between recurring war and authoritarian government in Japan.

In 1894–95, Japan easily vanquished China, its only potential Asiatic rival in the Far East. In 1904–5, with considerably more difficulty, Japan defeated Imperial Russia, a world power and, because of its own territory in the area, Japan's only serious rival for hegemony over Northeast Asia. Japan's military involvement in World War I was relatively minor, yet the returns were considerable: Germany was eliminated as a rival in China; a great expansion of both economic and military strength took place; and the country was finally accepted without question as one of the world's great powers. In 1931–32, through military aggression but without resort to formal war, Japan seized from China control over strategically and economically important Manchuria. From 1937 to 1945, Japan carried on major military operations against China that resulted in her gaining control over China's most important areas. In 1941–42, after the attack on Pearl Harbor— only a key tactical element in a grand strategic plan—Japan carried out military operations that gave her control over all the vast area from the Aleutian Islands in the north and east to the borders of India in the south and west.

Only once between 1895 and 1945 did Japan appear to veer away from the parallel roads of authoritarianism at home and aggression abroad, striking out in new and democratic directions. Partly because of the late flowering of democratic ideas and institutions (the desire for the seriously circumscribed freedoms that had been only nominally recognized, the development of political parties, etc.) that had been planted as early as the 1870's, partly as a result of the wave of hopeful democratic liberalism that swept through much of the world in the years immediately following World War I, partly because of the revulsion against militarism produced by the then unparalleled tragedy of the war, and partly because of the early onset of the postwar depression in Japan, the army was pushed into the background, and it seemed as if democratic processes had finally and effectively been set in motion. Universal male suffrage was instituted, political parties were active as never before, and the civilian agencies of the government gained control in the formulation of domestic and foreign policy. Also, Japan seemed to be cooperating wholeheartedly in efforts to establish a system of collective security under the League of Nations, a clear indication of both the domination of foreign policy by civilians and the apparent abandonment of war as an instrument of national policy. Many observers, Japanese and foreign alike, felt that Japan was moving in the direction of a liberal, democratic, constitutional monarchy, if, indeed, it had not already arrived there.

But Japan was brought abruptly back to the authoritarian course by the Manchurian crisis of 1931–32, which had a great impact on Japan's internal policies and on Far Eastern international affairs, in addition to being a major preliminary to World War II. The crisis put the army back into a dominant position in the government and set Japan off on the major phase of its overseas aggression. On September 18, 1931, Japan's Kwantung Army, based on the Kwantung Leased Territory, a Japanese possession in the Liaotung Peninsula (the southern tip of Manchuria), engineered an explosion on the South Manchurian Railway just outside Mukden. Using this as a pretext, the Kwantung Army, supported by army authorities in Tokyo, moved rapidly in what was obviously a very carefully planned and well-prepared series of actions. Soon all of Manchuria was occupied. In the initial stages, the Japanese cabinet decided that the incident would be settled through diplomatic channels by peaceful means. On this crucial issue, the army in Tokyo challenged the cabinet and emerged from the brief political struggle not only with Manchuria in its hands, but also in a secure position from which it could directly or indirectly control all important government policies. From the army success in this crucial internal struggle dates the progress of Japan toward its truly authoritarian system.

Between 1932 and 1937, Japan did not wage war against China, but intensified its armaments build-up in anticipation of the major struggle that was to come. On the domestic scene, this was the period of "government by assassination," during which the military, supported by like-minded civilians and chauvinistic organizations, steadily encroached on all areas of government at the expense of the moderates, the political parties, and the press— which had played an important role in curtailing the influence of the military in the 1920's and had been initially critical of its actions both in Manchuria and at home. Japan's authoritarianism never reached the heights of ruthless efficiency or the depths of inhumanity characteristic of similar systems in Nazi Germany and the Soviet Union, to mention only two examples. In its way, however, it was just as nondemocratic, undemocratic, and anti-democratic as any of its counterparts.

But the military establishment, despite its domination of Japanese society, did not monopolize power; it was first among a triumvirate. The two other members of the power elite were the bureaucracy and the *zaibatsu* (literally, "financial clique"), the great combines that dominated the economy. The creation of a strong bureaucracy was implicit in the establishment of an effective central government and in the existence of a strong executive. Japan's modern bureaucracy developed rapidly into an efficient, tightly organized, cohesive body of civil servants with an unshakable *esprit de corps*. It controlled the executive branch of government because it was, in essence, that branch itself; yet, like other bureaucracies, it did not enter directly into the arena of politics to compete openly for political power for its own sake. However, particularly because of its control over education and the police, the bureaucracy played a key role in the authoritarian system. Secure both in its position and in its sense of authority, it collaborated willingly with the military.

The position of the *zaibatsu* as the third member of the triumvirate was less obviously that of a power group. Unlike the other two, it had under its control none of the obvious instruments of force. Yet its power role was great. The families controlling the great firms that made up the *zaibatsu* structure came from either the socially despised and politically impotent but economically dominant merchant class, or from a few of the great feudal families that had profited from the settlement made by the government in return for the surrender of their feudal estates. The government, as we have seen, had concentrated on the rapid development of industrialization, through the establishment and operation of such enterprises as arsenals, railroads, and steel mills, and through the encouragement of private enterprises, mainly by assisting those organizations that soon developed into the *zaibatsu*. Thus, from the beginning there was a close working relationship between government and private capital. The *zaibatsu* firms were established and in effective operation in the early twentieth century, but their great period of growth came as a result of the phenomenal expansion of Japan's economy during World War I and the 1920's, when they were able to strengthen their monopoly position in the economy through their ability, because of the very size and complexity of their operations, to withstand the shock of the depression and to absorb smaller organizations that sought refuge under the wing of the *zaibatsu* as the only means of survival. From roughly 1930 onward, they dominated the Japanese economy in every respect.

Initially, the *zaibatsu* attempted to strengthen their position in relation to the government and to develop their political influence by working closely with the political parties, especially during the 1920's and into the 1930's. But this working relationship did not serve the interests of the *zaibatsu* and, indeed, proved fatal to the political parties. Both came under devastating attack from the military and their ultranationalist civilian allies. The *zaibatsu* were alleged to be interested in profits to the exclusion of the national welfare, while the parties were accused of being un-Japanese because they represented a foreign, Western institution and, even more, a liberalism that was incompatible with the unique structure of Japanese politics. Since they were not strong as a political institution and did not enjoy a broad base of popular support, the parties collapsed. The *zaibatsu*, however, survived. They were both unable and unwilling to resist and thus to make themselves the object of terroristic pressure. Besides, their control over industry made them indispensable to the successful prosecution of the plans, both domestic and foreign, of the military.

Within the triumvirate, only among the *zaibatsu* was there a significant amount of liberalism. Education at home and abroad and a certain amount of cosmopolitan experience, not widely shared by the others, contributed to a strong liberal strain in the thinking of some *zaibatsu* leaders. But self-protection and self-interest outweighed this inclination. In the early 1930's, the *zaibatsu* were targets of bitter propaganda attacks, and even assassination, by the military and its supporters. These, of course, had the desired effect of silencing or eliminating the current of liberalism. Self-interest required taking a strong stand against a labor-union movement, for example, in concert with the government, and also contributed to the readiness of the *zaibatsu* to provide the sinews of war for the military. As Japanese aggression in the late 1930's and the closing of world markets resulting from the outbreak of World War II created more and more problems in the international market for the *zaibatsu*, so it seemed more and more reasonable for them to act in concert with the military in Asia in the establishment of a Japanese hegemony that would result, it was hoped, in a vast expansion of Japanese economic opportunities in the area.

Thus, in spite of their different characters and different motivations, there was abundant reason for the military, the bureaucracy, and the *zaibatsu* to stand together and to serve as the driving forces of Japan's authoritarianism and aggression.

I should like to review here the principal features of this authoritarianism, both because they were the logical culmination of the Japanese political and governmental system that emerged after the fall of the Tokugawa regime and because they had to be eliminated before Japan could have a democratic society.

(1) The denial of freedom in all its forms. Bitter experience in this century has taught us that freedom and authoritarianism cannot exist in the same society, that the authoritarian state through its control over and exercise of the instruments of force inevitably throttles freedom. In addition, in the Japanese case, freedom in any form was both superfluous and irrelevant under a system in which the supreme political value was unquestioning loyalty and obedience to the sovereign and divine emperor.

(2) The system of strict censorship. The government, through the police, did everything in its power to keep from the people anything in any form that might subvert the authoritarian system —ideas, information, customs, books, motion pictures, or news.

(3) The twofold program of indoctrination. Positive indoctrination, for both young and old, was designed to create the absolute virtue of loyalty to the emperor, subservience to the state representing him, and acceptance of the glories of militarism both in its manifestations in history, tradition, and folklore and in the current wartime exploits of the Imperial Army and Navy and their individual heroes. Negative indoctrination included consistent attacks on socialism, Communism, democracy—any-

thing that might conceivably run counter to the stream of positive indoctrination.

(4) The dominant role of militarism. Not only was war or the imminence of war ever-present before modern Japanese society, but military activities in one form or another touched closely on the life of every Japanese. The program of universal male conscription, instituted in the early 1870's, meant that if every man had not been directly involved in Japan's armed forces, then certainly almost every Japanese family had at least one member who had been in the service. This was regarded not as a distasteful duty but as a glorious contribution to the emperor and to the state. Military service and war, with its sacrifices and fleeting glories, were accepted as normal, admirable, and rewarding activities of society and individual alike.

(5) The authoritarian nature of the government itself. The activities of the War, Navy, Education, Home, and Justice Ministries were the most obvious expression of the whole system. No individual and no opposition group could challenge the supremacy of the omnipotent and omnipresent state.

(6) The police state (an extension of the preceding point). It was the police who brought directly to bear the whole force of the state on the lives of the people, suppressing, controlling, and attempting to extirpate all that could conceivably undermine authoritarianism.

(7) The extremely circumscribed area of permissible political activity. In a society in which the supreme political duties were loyalty to the emperor and subservience to the will of the state, there was no room for political parties, free elections, a responsible executive, or the freedoms of thought, expression, association, and assembly—all of which were necessary for broad and vigorous popular political action.

To turn to the negative features of the system in 1945 is to bring home to the democratic reader its real nature, as well as to indicate the changes that had to be wrought if Japan were to become democratic. There were no political parties. There were no free elections. There was no responsible government. There was no equality for half the population, the women, who had no political, economic, or social rights. There were no labor unions.

There was no equitable return for all the people for their labor. There was no enjoyment of fundamental human rights. There was no due process to protect the citizen from the naked force of the law.

Japan, it is true, had no bloody purges, no genocide, no prison camps full of political prisoners, no single all-powerful political party, and no charismatic leaders of the Hitler stripe. It can be said that Japanese authoritarianism was not characterized by such excesses because it fitted so well into the historical and social matrix of the country that they were not needed.

The Institutional Substructure

_ When World War II ended with defeat for Japan, its people, the occupation, and the governments the latter represented were almost exclusively preoccupied with the problems created by the nature and course of authoritarianism and aggression and by the mutually agreed-upon necessity to eliminate them. Few, if any, gave thought to the all-important substructure on which both had been erected and which was all but buried under the debris of defeat. It was this foundation, however, that persisted through defeat and through the complicated democratic revolution, and which made possible the phenomenally rapid emergence of an operable Japanese democracy. Stated in the most general terms, the substructure was the national society that had replaced the old feudalism during the last quarter of the nineteenth century and that had become the vehicle for both authoritarianism and aggression.

What animated and made effective the basic national substructure was, of course, the Japanese people, who had lived the lives of the population of a modern nation-state. Most of them enjoyed (until the war fell heavily upon them in the early 1940's) a sufficiency of the basic necessities of life—food, clothing, and shelter; some even enjoyed luxuries. They had benefited from an adequate system of public health, which had guarded them effectively, if not completely, against the depredations of epidemics and had contributed to the development of stronger and larger physiques among the younger generation. As parents, soldiers, skilled and unskilled workers, and highly productive farmers, they enjoyed the foods and the freedom from disease that gave them the sheer physical strength and endurance required for the successful operation of a national society. In addition, they also had the mechanical skills, the intellectual training, and the discipline that are the basis of the varied talents required in an operative nation. In 1945, Japan was confronted with no problem of educating and training its population—a problem whose importance and magnitude have been demonstrated in every new nation that has become independent since 1945.

Another indispensable part of the substructure was a broad leadership corps. Here the important consideration was neither charisma nor the prosaic and more tangible qualities that make for greatness in leadership, but the existence of a large, well-trained, and experienced body of men in government, politics, education, industry, agriculture, science, technology, business, finance, and all other professions who could plan and manage the multifarious activities of a contemporary national society.

Japan's essential structure of government was not destroyed by the war and it continued to function after the defeat, even in the face of great difficulties. Political unification, as expressed in its broadest sense of a consensus on the critical issue of the nature of an acceptable political system, also never disappeared in defeat. Certainly, there was great political controversy among a much greater number of political organizations and much more discussion of the nature of the new government than ever before in Japanese history. Yet, there was never a split on the issue deep enough to paralyze governmental action, to say nothing of becoming a civil war. In the areas of government and politics, Japan did not suffer the fate of internal collapse or dissension that has characterized the rest of Asia since 1945.

Neither was Japan confronted with the difficult problem of building a completely new and different economy. It is true that reconstruction and rehabilitation were needed. But the basic problem was the comparatively simple one of doing certain things for and to a viable, though badly damaged, industry and a basically strong agriculture. The same was true of the systems of education and of mass communication, which were both to play new and major roles in the creation and operation of the democracy to come.

The changes that took place in Japan during the second half of the nineteenth century were native ones—that is, they were instituted and executed by the Japanese themselves. There was Western assistance, but the tasks, major and minor, were done by the Japanese themselves in a highly effective working combination of foresighted and able leaders and hard-working, obedient, disciplined, and adept followers. What emerged was also essentially Japanese, of its time and as the product of history, even if many of the externals were clearly of Western origin. The changes that have been inaugurated in the second half of the twentieth century have been of a far different nature. Instituted and prosecuted by a military occupation—by definition an external force in the society—the changes were rapidly taken over by the Japanese and incorporated into the web of a new pattern of society, strikingly divorced not only from the recent authoritarianism but, more significantly, from the flow of tradition. Yet, even the new pattern of society remained essentially Japanese. It was not forced on the Japanese by a ruthless and brutal military occupation, although on the surface that was what seemed to be happening. Nor was it copied exactly by the Japanese from Western or American models, although many of the externals are clearly of such foreign origin.

The necessary prelude to Japanese democracy consisted of two parts: the creation of a modern national society and the casting of that society in an authoritarian mold. The former gave Japan the social, political, and economic institutions that served the needs of the authoritarian state well, but also required only modification and adaptation to serve the new democratic order. The latter not only led to the disaster of military defeat, a necessary preliminary for the democratic revolution, but also—and this was a matter of far greater significance—filled a major segment of Japan's leadership and people with a revulsion against authoritarianism as well as a desire for freedom. These were the sources for what rapidly became an unmistakable Japanese will to build and to make viable a new web of political, social, and economic relationships that constitutes the pattern of the new democracy.

2

The Role of the Occupation
in the Democratic Revolution

Japan's peaceful democratic revolution was born of a lost war. It originated in a military occupation dominated by the United States, which was determined that fundamental changes had to be brought about inside Japan. The revolution ran a course fixed by a complex interplay between the occupation forces and the Japanese Government and people. It became rooted in Japan because the general social environment turned out to be unexpectedly congenial to democracy.

From the beginning, the United States was resolved to bring about revolutionary changes in Japan, although the terms "revolution" and "revolutionary" were never a part of the American policy vocabulary. From the standpoint of the U.S. Government, such changes were necessary because, it was believed, they would prevent Japan from ever embarking on military aggression again, they would be welcomed by the Japanese, and the result would be a society more desirable not only in Japanese terms but in broad human terms as well. American policy clearly outlined the changes needed to achieve this better society. The nature of the occupation was such that it was possible simultaneously to force and induce the changes envisaged. Of fundamental importance, however, was the fact that what American policy conceived and what American action accomplished found an immediate response in the Japanese—one that arose either from acceptance of the fact of Japan's temporary inability to resist the occupation or from a more positive welcome for the changes inspired by it.

The Course of the War and the Occupation

The revolution had its origin in the later developments of the war, involving the successful attack on Japan itself, as well as the devising of political means for bringing the war to an end—that is, through negotiation instead of a costly invasion. As the offensive against Japan gathered strength during the latter part of 1943 and the early part of 1944 and reached an initial climax in the summer of 1944 with the attack on Guam, Saipan, and Tinian, followed in early autumn by the invasion of the Philippines, it became clear that the United States would have to carry the principal burden almost alone, even though the war was being waged by a broad coalition of major and minor powers. Commitments in other theaters of war and limitations on manpower or war matériel prevented other nations from sharing equally in the Pacific operations. The Chinese continued to keep their armies in the field at home, waging the stubborn defensive warfare that had typified their military efforts against Japan in the long years since the summer of 1937. The European Allies naturally centered their attention and strength on the assault against Nazi Germany until V-E Day, just over three months before Japan's surrender. Australia and New Zealand, also heavily committed to assist the total British Commonwealth war effort, had neither the manpower nor the industrial capacity to assume a position of full and equal partnership in the war against Japan. The Soviet Union, both unable and unwilling to go to war in Asia until the last minute, fought against Japan for only a week.

This military situation—the almost exclusively American offensive against Japan in the closing stages of the war—meant that the United States inevitably took the lead also in the surrender negotiations, the initiation of the occupation, and the formulation of occupation policy. When the Japanese finally accepted the Allied surrender terms (also largely of American composition), only the United States was both ready and willing to assume the major responsibility for the occupation. The United States alone among the Allies had the manpower available in the western

Pacific and the sea and air transport necessary to move an army of occupation into position rapidly. Again, the European Allies were not vitally interested in this operation and, more importantly, were not in a physical position to contribute to it. The Chinese had enough manpower, but no means of getting it into Japan. The Soviet Union also had abundant military personnel operating against the Japanese, some of whom might have been used for occupation duty. At any rate, Stalin and his government indicated an interest in occupying only the northern half of the island of Hokkaido. A suggestion to this effect was firmly rejected by President Truman during the difficult and confused period immediately following the Japanese capitulation and before the beginning of the occupation a little more than two weeks later. Consequently, the operation began as one completely dominated by the United States and almost completely manned by American military and civilian personnel; and it continued for six years and eight months to be an occupation legally Allied but in fact American. Even when, late in 1945, Allied machinery for the occupation was set up—consisting of a Far Eastern Commission, sitting in Washington and responsible on paper for the formulation of Allied policy for occupied Japan, and an Allied Council for Japan sitting in Tokyo and serving as a consultative and advisory body for the occupation headquarters—the U.S. Government made sure that neither would be able to intervene effectively in the occupation. And their roles remained insignificant as far as the substance of the occupation was concerned.

Evolution of American Occupation Policy

Another factor of great importance at the start was that only the United States had devised anything that could be described as an occupation policy. The American policy actually grew out of the military operations against Japan, and although it only began to develop quite late in the war and was then formulated very quickly, it emerged finally as one of the soundest policies in the history of American foreign relations.

Throughout the war against Japan, until the spring of 1945, Allied and American policy toward Japan, as toward Germany, was simply that of unconditional surrender—a policy that was no policy. Certainly, its enunciation by the major Allied powers early in 1942 indicated a determination to fight through to complete victory; it also constituted a pledge among themselves not to stop short of such victory by taking the easier course of a negotiated peace, an eventuality more likely to develop in respect to Nazi Germany than to Japan. But this was not the sort of policy likely to induce either German or Japanese leaders to sue for peace. Indeed, it provided both governments with an excellent device for whipping up and maintaining the civilian will to fight, and they took advantage of it in their domestic propaganda by equating unconditional surrender with either enslavement or extermination—an easy task, given the uncompromising nature of the phrase and the initial failure of the Allied governments to define its meaning.

There was a slight expansion of the meaning of unconditional surrender for Japan in the Cairo Declaration of December, 1943, issued by Chiang Kai-shek, Winston Churchill, and Franklin D. Roosevelt in the names of the Republic of China, the United Kingdom, and the United States. However, the nub of this declaration was simply that Japan would be deprived of all territory it had seized "by violence and greed" since 1895. This certainly marked no progress either in the formulation of the terms of unconditional surrender or in the application of political pressure on the Japanese Government to bring the war to an end. If anything, it merely served to reinforce the interpretation of unconditional surrender that was being so industriously spread by Japanese propaganda.

The first indication of what the Japanese Government—and people—might expect if it surrendered unconditionally came in the form of a statement by President Truman, released significantly enough on May 8, 1945, V-E Day, as if it had been timed to be buried in the momentous news from Europe. The U.S. Government was faced with the difficult problem of maintaining both civilian and military morale for the effort still to come against Japan, at a time when what was regarded as the major enemy had surrendered. Truman's words are worth repeating here, not because they represented a major policy shift, but because they revealed the still extremely cautious approach to the issue of unconditional surrender and also because they foreshadowed actual policy as it appeared only a few weeks later:

Nazi Germany has been defeated.

The Japanese people have felt the weight of our land, air, and naval attacks. So long as their leaders and the armed forces continue the war, the striking power and intensity of our blows will steadily increase and will bring utter destruction to Japan's industrial production, to its shipping, and to everything that supports its military activity.

The longer the war lasts, the greater will be the suffering and hardships which the people of Japan will undergo—all in vain. Our blows will not cease until the Japanese military and naval forces lay down their arms in unconditional surrender.

Just what does the unconditional surrender of the armed forces mean for the Japanese people?

It means the end of the war.

It means the termination of the influence of the military leaders who have brought Japan to the present brink of disaster.

It means provision for the return of soldiers and sailors to their families, their farms, their jobs.

It means not prolonging the present agony and suffering of the Japanese in the vain hope of victory.

Unconditional surrender does not mean the extermination or enslavement of the Japanese people.

The last sentence, a direct answer to Japanese propaganda, was probably the most important element in the whole statement. It should be noted that, with the exception of the sentence referring to the return to Japan of soldiers and sailors, the statement was cast in negative terms; it was a description of what unconditional surrender did not mean and of the conditions to which it would put an end. There was no reference to what might be done to Japan in the event that the Japanese forces did lay down their arms unconditionally. Thus, the statement was not a real advance toward a positive policy for a defeated Japan.

However, within the U.S. Government a broad policy was being secretly drafted. The main responsibility for this seems to have been centered in what was called the State, War, and Navy Coordinating Committee (SWNCC). Unfortunately, no account of this organization, its personnel, responsibilities, and operations has yet been written. SWNCC was a completely American organization, designed to coordinate the formulation of U.S. policy on matters related to military operations carried out by American armed forces. It had been discovered as early as 1942, in the African and European theaters of war, that there were few purely military problems; almost every campaign automatically created complex diplomatic and political problems that were beyond the powers (and sometimes the skill) of the military command to handle and at the same time could not be dealt with in isolation from military operations. These problems might range from the political attitudes and actions to be taken by commanders in the field following the end of tactical military operations and during the administration of civil affairs by the army, to the manner in which relations with governments-in-exile should be handled. SWNCC's Subcommittee for the Far East was responsible for the drafting of policy papers dealing with Japan. Apparently, the Department of State began to concern itself as early as 1942 with the problem of a policy for a defeated Japan, but toward the end of 1943 or the beginning of 1944, the main burden of the drafting of policy was shifted to SWNCC. The original objective of SWNCC seemed to have been the drafting of a political policy to be followed during the invasion of Japan, and particularly during the period of postoperational military administration.

However, in the spring of 1945, a new aspect of the planning of the war against Japan began to emerge. The successful invasions of Iwo Jima in February, 1945, and of Okinawa in April, 1945—climaxing a long series of difficult attacks on island strongholds—had been extremely costly in both casualties and matériel. The American Joint Chiefs of Staff expected the invasion of Kyushu, scheduled for the fall of 1945, and of Honshu, scheduled for the spring of 1946, to be even more difficult and costly. It was estimated that the invasion and conquest of Japan proper would result in a million American casualties (killed, wounded, and missing) and that the consumption of matériel would be proportionately high. This, of course, gave rise to consideration by the U.S. Government of other means of bringing the war to a victorious conclusion. It had also become clear by this time that Japan's only real hope of escaping complete and crushing defeat was to inflict such high casualties on American forces that it might be possible to negotiate a cessation of hostilities on terms well short of unconditional surrender. Japan's entire military situation was so desperate that there seemed to be no hope at all for victory. The defeat of Nazi Germany had deprived Japan of the psychological prop of having a fighting ally; it also meant that Allied forces in Europe could, at least in part, be deployed for the attack on Japan. And the massive fire raids of the spring of 1945, the destruction of Japanese shipping, and the extensive damage to Japanese industry had already dealt heavy blows to the nation's strength. The combination of all these factors made a negotiated surrender, which might or might not be unconditional, a realistic alternative to the continuation of the fighting.

The first serious posing of the alternative came early in July, 1945, in the form of a memorandum to President Truman from Henry L. Stimson, the Secretary of War. However, this memorandum was apparently based on an earlier one prepared in the Department of State in the summer of 1944 and later approved by SWNCC. It concentrated on the problem of an alternative to the "forceful occupation of Japan," and Stimson recommended that the Allies call on Japan to surrender and outlined what terms could be offered to the Japanese Government. Approved by the cabinet and the President on July 2, 1945, the memorandum was the basis of the more significant Potsdam Declaration, issued a few weeks later.

Two factors of considerable importance governed the subsequent development of the policy that was sketched in the Stimson memorandum. The first was that the heads of state of the major Allies were scheduled to meet at Potsdam in mid-July, 1945, to discuss the future prosecution of the war against Japan, as well as the already pressing political problems arising out of the defeat of Nazi Germany. Secondly, the top conferees at Potsdam knew that the first detonation of an atomic bomb had taken place at Alamogordo, New Mexico, on July 16, 1945. Even before this first test, the decision had been made to use the bomb against Japan if the war were still going on when the weapon became a reality. At this point, the possibility of using the atomic bomb and the decision to attempt to bring the war to a close prior to an invasion converged. The result was the issuing of the Potsdam Declaration on July 26, 1945, in the names of Chiang, Truman, and Clement Attlee (who had just succeeded Churchill). Joseph Stalin, who was present at Potsdam, was of course fully informed of the contents of the declaration and subscribed to it two weeks later when the Soviet Union declared war on Japan. Thus, the declaration represented the policy of the major Allies fighting against Japan.

The Potsdam Declaration

Briefly, it warned Japan to cease fighting at once and outlined what the Japanese Government and people might expect if they did surrender unconditionally (i.e., accept the conditions stated in the declaration). There was no mention of the atomic bomb. The declaration stated simply: "The full application of our military power, backed by our resolve, *will* mean the inevitable and complete destruction of the Japanese armed forces and just as inevitably the utter devastation of the Japanese homeland." This and other references to the armed might of the Allies were taken to mean that the kind of attack that had been carried on against Japan would be continued. The only deviation from the normal in this pronouncement was the device, unusual in policy statements, of italicizing one word, "will." The Japanese—and the world—were given no other warning that an unconventional weapon that would result in a new kind of "utter devastation" was ready for use. At any rate, the Japanese Government saw fit at the time not to accept the conditions set forth.

The Potsdam terms of surrender are of sufficient importance to be quoted in full here:

> There must be eliminated for all time the authority and influence of those who have deceived and misled the people of Japan into embarking on world conquest, for we insist that a new order of peace, security, and justice will be impossible until irresponsible militarism is driven from the world.
>
> Until such a new order is established *and* until there is convincing proof that Japan's war-making power is destroyed, points in

Japanese territory to be designated by the Allies shall be occupied to secure the achievement of the basic objectives we are here setting forth.

The terms of the Cairo Declaration shall be carried out and Japanese sovereignty shall be limited to the islands of Honshu, Hokkaido, Kyushu, Shikoku, and such minor islands as we determine.

The Japanese military forces, after being completely disarmed, shall be permitted to return to their homes with the opportunity to lead peaceful and productive lives.

We do not intend that the Japanese shall be enslaved as a race or destroyed as a nation, but stern justice shall be meted out to all war criminals, including those who have visited cruelties upon our prisoners. The Japanese Government shall remove all obstacles to the revival and strengthening of democratic tendencies among the Japanese people. Freedom of speech, of religion, and of thought, as well as respect for the fundamental human rights, shall be established.

Japan shall be permitted to maintain such industries as will sustain her economy and permit the exaction of just reparations in kind, but not those which would enable her to rearm for war. To this end, access to, as distinguished from control of, raw materials shall be permitted. Eventual Japanese participation in world trade relations shall be permitted.

The occupying forces of the Allies shall be withdrawn from Japan as soon as these objectives have been accomplished and there has been established in accordance with the freely expressed will of the Japanese people a peacefully inclined and responsible government.

As a statement of policy, the Potsdam Declaration went far beyond any earlier pronouncement, though it was essentially a further development of the Stimson memorandum rather than a fundamentally new policy devised at Potsdam. In general, its terms can be divided into two categories: negative (or punitive) and positive (or constructive). In the first category were: the elimination of the militarists and their followers, a punitive Allied occupation, the limitation of the territory of Japan, disarmament, punishment of war criminals, elimination of obstacles to democracy, and economic disarmament. The shorter but much more important list of positive terms included: the return of military personnel to their homes, the establishment of basic freedoms and respect for fundamental human rights, the guarantee of access to raw materials necessary for the operation of a peaceful economy, and the establishment in accordance with the will of the people of a peaceful, responsible government.

Narrowly speaking, these conditions did not represent a policy for a defeated Japan, but rather a statement of the terms that the Japanese must accept in order to end the war. The Japanese Government, however, did not begin negotiations for surrender until after the crushing blows of the atomic bombs and the Soviet declaration of war. Within the government, the terms were debated at length, especially the relatively unimportant issues of the punishment of war criminals and the occupation, to both of which the military leaders were obviously opposed. However, the greatest stumbling block to acceptance was the absence of any mention of the one matter that apparently gave Japan's leaders the greatest concern—the future of the Emperor, both as a person and as an institution.

The first offer of the Japanese to accept the Potsdam terms, delivered through the Swiss Government on August 10, 1945, was made "with the understanding that the said declaration does not comprise any demand which prejudices the prerogatives of His Majesty as a Sovereign Ruler." The reply, sent in the names of the four major Allies on August 11, but drafted by the U.S. Government, dealt with the problem somewhat indirectly in the following terms:

> From the moment of surrender the Authority of the Emperor and the Japanese Government to rule the state shall be subject to the Supreme Commander of the Allied Powers who will take such steps as he deems proper to effectuate the surrender terms. . . .
>
> The ultimate form of government of Japan shall, in accordance with the Potsdam Declaration, be established by the freely expressed will of the Japanese people.

The clear implication of the Allied answer was that the Emperor would continue to reign and that the Japanese Government would continue in existence, both subject to the authority of the Supreme Commander, while the future form of government, presumably including the role of the Emperor therein, would be determined by the Japanese people themselves. This formulation proved acceptable to the Japanese leaders, and the terms of unconditional surrender were accepted.

U.S. Initial Postsurrender Policy

While the Potsdam Conference was going on, and particularly after the tremendous events of the first two weeks of August, 1945, another highly important development in the area of policy formulation for a defeated Japanese enemy was taking place inside the U.S. Government. The Far Eastern Subcommittee of SWNCC began and pushed to rapid conclusion the task of formulating a detailed plan to cover the entire range of the coming occupation. SWNCC produced a policy paper entitled "United States Initial Postsurrender Policy for Japan"; it was approved by the White House on August 29, 1945, just two weeks after the Japanese acceptance of the surrender terms, and immediately radioed to General Douglas MacArthur, who had been appointed Supreme Commander for the Allied Powers (SCAP) to direct the occupation. This became the policy of the U.S. Government that General MacArthur was to execute so brilliantly in the field. Slightly more than two months later, early in November, 1945, the policy paper was converted into directive language and transmitted to General MacArthur by the Joint Chiefs of Staff. It thereby constituted the official orders under which he was operating. In the summer of 1947, the essence of this policy paper—the only changes being those necessitated by the flow of events in the two years since the surrender—was formally approved by the Far Eastern Commission, and it thus became Allied policy for the occupation.

"United States Initial Postsurrender Policy for Japan" is certainly one of the truly great state papers of American foreign policy. Composed before the first occupation soldier set foot on Japanese soil, it dealt with every major issue that was to confront the occupation forces; there were no gaps to create delay in the operation or to impede the implementation of the policy. No part of the program outlined turned out to be significantly unrealistic or unworkable, as far as the course of the occupation was concerned. The paper gave direction and order to the whole intricate process. It gained the acceptance of the Japanese Government—grudging at times, but nevertheless sufficient. It was approved by a diverse collection of other governments with an interest in what was happening in Japan. It stated both definite policy goals and effective means by which those goals were to be achieved. Though changing circumstances completely external to Japan later cut the ground out from under certain aspects of it, the policy continued to be sound in terms of the end for which it was conceived—the revolutionary shift from the old authoritarianism to the new democracy. Moreover—and this must be the key test of any policy paper—it effectively served the national interests of the United States.

The greatness of this document lies in the fact that it did provide broad policy direction, giving the occupation a purpose and a consistency of action. It did not guarantee a solution of all the problems, nor did it prevent errors and false starts; these things no policy can do. To gauge the excellence of the postsurrender policy, one need only compare it with what was tantamount to a complete absence of U.S. policy toward Korea in the summer and fall of 1945, or with the absence of clear purpose and consistency in our policy toward China that was being evolved in the closing months of 1945.

Our policy for the occupation was directed to the achievement of only two basic objectives:

(a) To insure that Japan will not again become a menace to the United States or to the peace and security of the world.

(b) To bring about the eventual establishment of a peaceful and responsible government which will respect the rights of other states and will support the objectives of the United States as reflected in the ideals and principles of the Charter of the United Nations. The United States desires that this government should conform as closely as may be to principles of democratic self-government, but it is not the responsibility of the Allied Powers to impose upon Japan any form of government not supported by the freely expressed will of the people.

The first objective, a negative one, clearly implied that certain things would be done in order to limit the Japanese ability to do what it had done in the past. The second objective, a positive one, that of bringing about the development of a new, democratic government in Japan, was, of course, directly related to the problem of the elimination of the old authoritarian system.

These chief aims were to be achieved by four basic means:

(a) Japan's sovereignty will be limited to the islands of Honshu, Hokkaido, Kyushu, Shikoku, and such minor outlying islands as may be determined, in accordance with the Cairo Declaration and other agreements to which the United States is or may be a party.

(b) Japan will be completely disarmed and demilitarized. The authority of the militarists and the influence of militarism will be totally eliminated from her political, economic, and social life. Institutions expressive of the spirit of militarism and aggression will be vigorously suppressed.

(c) The Japanese people shall be encouraged to develop a desire for individual liberties and respect for fundamental human rights, particularly the freedoms of religion, assembly, speech, and the press. They shall also be encouraged to form democratic and representative organizations.

(d) The Japanese people shall be afforded opportunity to develop for themselves an economy which will permit the peacetime requirements of the population to be met.

The remainder of the paper consisted of a detailed description of the steps to be taken to carry out the policy. To summarize them, they dealt with: an Allied occupation of indeterminate length under an American commander; the subjection of the authority of the Emperor and the Japanese Government to that of the Supreme Commander for the Allied Powers, who was to utilize and to act through the existing machinery of the Japanese Government; complete disarmament and demilitarization, including the barring of military men from public office and the dissolution of ultranationalistic societies; trial of war criminals; encouragement of the desire for individual liberties and democratic processes, including the granting of all freedoms, the opportunity to learn about democracy and democratic processes in other countries, encouragement of political parties, suspension of all discriminatory and oppressive laws, release of political prisoners, and reform of the judicial, legal, and police systems; destruction of the economic basis of Japanese military strength; transfer of Japanese industrial installations as reparations; development of democratic organizations in labor, industry, and agriculture in order to widen the distribution of income and of ownership of the means of production and trade; barring from economic activity of individuals not directing their energies toward the peaceful development of the Japanese economy; the dissolution of the large industrial and banking combinations (*zaibatsu*); the development of an economy that would permit the peaceful requirements of the population to be met; a reparations policy based on payment in kind that would "not interfere with or prejudice the program for Japan's demilitarization"; a promise that Japan would eventually be permitted to resume normal trade relations with the rest of the world; and the inclusion of Imperial Household property in any program that involved the achievement of the objectives of the occupation.

Even this skeleton outline of the basic postsurrender policy indicates the breadth of the operation envisaged by the planners in Washington. Directly or indirectly, almost every aspect of Japanese life was to be covered in the program of the three D's—demilitarization, disarmament, and democratization. The result could be nothing short of a revolution.

Unfortunately, no record exists of the assumptions on which the policy was based. However, they can be easily and, I believe, accurately inferred from both the wording of the policy and the manner in which the occupation itself later unfolded. These must have been the principal assumptions: that there could be little opposition or obstruction from the Japanese Government because of the concentration of a maximum of control and influence in the hands of the occupation; that it was possible to achieve by the mechanical means of disarmament and demilitarization the elimination of Japan as a threat to the peace and security of the world; that all individuals, groups, laws, and institutions that had impeded democratic developments in Japan and had been props to the old authoritarian system had to be eliminated by the occupation; that the Japanese people, if given the proper opportunity and encouragement, would opt for a democratic government or at least a government that would "conform as closely as may be to principles of democratic self-government"; that any form of government not "supported by the freely expressed will of the Japanese people" could be neither democratic nor permanent; that certain possible and desirable economic changes were required in order to achieve the political goal of democratization; and finally, that changes in social structure and relationships were also desirable and possible. The over-all success of the occupation constituted a striking demonstration of the soundness of these assumptions. It is clear that what was envisaged was a thorough-going—and revolutionary—change in the whole framework of Japanese government, politics, economy, and society. Not only were certain things to be eliminated—in itself a great change—but the plan was to provide something new and different to fill the resulting gaps.

The Occupation and the Japanese Government

The peculiar relationship between the occupation and the Japanese Government requires some comment, because it had a considerable influence on the manner in which the changes envisaged in U.S. policy were actually carried forward. The basis of the relationship was the decision to permit the Japanese Government to continue to function; thus, although the occupation was supreme, it never ruled Japan directly. The reasons for this basic decision were that the Japanese Government at the end of the war was still in operation, not having been overwhelmed by a military invasion as in the case of Germany, and that the United States was incapable of establishing a true military government simply because there were too few Americans who knew Japan and its language well enough to administer the affairs of the country. Though the source of some misgivings at the time, the decision turned out to be a wise one.

The U.S. Government was keenly aware of the potential difficulties involved in having the military occupation work through the existing machinery of government. The formula for the relationship as stated in "United States Initial Postsurrender Policy for Japan" was:

> The authority of the Emperor and the Japanese Government will be subject to the Supreme Commander, who will possess all powers necessary to effectuate the surrender terms and to carry out the policies established for the conduct of the occupation and the control of Japan.
>
> In view of the present character of Japanese society and the desire of the United States to attain its objectives with a minimum commitment of its forces and resources, the Supreme Commander will exercise his authority through Japanese government machinery and agencies, including the Emperor, to the extent that this satisfactorily furthers United States objectives. The Japanese Government will be permitted, under his instructions, to exercise the normal powers of government in matters of domestic administration. This policy, however, will be subject to the right and duty of the Supreme Commander to require changes in governmental machinery or personnel or to act directly if the Emperor or other Japanese authority does not satisfactorily meet the requirements of the Supreme Commander in effectuating the surrender terms. This policy, moreover, does not commit the Supreme Commander to support the Emperor or any other Japanese governmental authority in opposition to evolutionary changes looking toward the attainment of United States objectives. The policy is to use the existing form of Government in Japan, not to support it. Changes in the form of Government initiated by the Japanese people or government in the direction of modifying its feudal and authoritarian tendencies are to be permitted and favored. In the event that the effectuation of such changes involves the use of force by the Japanese people or government against persons opposed thereto, the Supreme Commander should intervene only where necessary to ensure the security of his forces and the attainment of all other objectives of the occupation.

In greatly simplified terms, the formal pattern of the operation of the occupation can be summarized as follows: The occupation, by means of directives issued under the authority of the Supreme Commander, ordered the Japanese Government to do certain things designed to achieve the objectives of the occupation; the Japanese Government then instituted the required action. The occupation also kept as careful a check as possible on the actions of Japanese authorities, central or local, in following occupation directives. Of almost equal significance were the informal aspects of the relationship between the government and the occupation, ranging from "suggestions" from General Mac-Arthur to Japan's prime ministers, through conferences between occupation authorities and Japanese bureaucrats, to private, after-hours conversations between Japanese and Americans who found a common interest in solving the problems created by the peaceful revolution.

The Occupation in Operation

U.S. policy for the occupation was converted from paper to reality with speed and effectiveness. It took about a month for the occupation forces to get settled after the surrender, the terms of which were signed on September 2, 1945. Men, supplies, and equipment had to be gotten into the country; offices and living quarters had to be set up for occupation personnel; a working relationship with the Japanese Government had to be created; and the necessary intelligence data had to be collected. It was early in October, 1945, that the occupation began to swing into full operation.

Perhaps the real beginning of the occupation can be dated from the issuance on October 4, 1945, of the first of a series of fundamental directives. It was entitled "Removal of Restrictions on Political, Civil, and Religious Liberties," and its great importance is clearly shown in its opening sentences:

> In order to remove restrictions on political, civil, and religious liberties and discrimination on grounds of race, nationality, creed, or political opinion, the Imperial Japanese Government will:
> a. Abrogate and immediately suspend the operation of all provisions of all laws, decrees, orders, ordinances, and regulations which:
> (1) Establish or maintain restrictions on freedom of thought, of religion, of assembly and of speech, including the unrestricted discussion of the Emperor, the Imperial Institution, and the Japanese Imperial Government.

(2) Establish or maintain restrictions on the collection and dissemination of information.

(3) By their terms or their application, operate unequally in favor of or against any person by reasons of race, nationality, creed, or political opinion.

The directive also ordered the Japanese Government to release all political prisoners, to abolish all agencies of government responsible for maintaining the restrictions and discriminations mentioned above, and to remove and bar from similar positions in the future all individuals serving in those agencies in important capacities.

A week later, on October 11, 1945, General MacArthur issued a statement to the Japanese Government requiring additional fundamental reforms. The general said that he expected the government to institute "as rapidly as they can be assimilated" the following reforms: the emancipation of women through their enfranchisement; the encouragement of labor unions; the opening of the schools to more liberal education; the abolition of "systems which through secret inquisition and abuse have held the people in constant fear—substituting therefor a system of justice designed to afford the people protection against despotic, arbitrary, and unjust methods"; and the democratization of economic institutions. The directive and the statement initiated a period of orders and action that constituted the core of the democratic revolution.

At the apex of Japanese society, the Emperor was converted from an absolute ruler with allegedly divine attributes to a mere mortal who serves as the symbol of the nation and of the people's unity. Although U.S. policy regarding the Emperor was not specific, his central position in the constitution, government, politics, propaganda, indoctrination, and religion of the old authoritarianism meant that an inevitable and drastic change would follow in the wake of the implementation of other aspects of the occupation's policy. His new position, as it has evolved, is that of a limited constitutional monarch whose role and powers are perfectly consistent with the new democracy.

The major occupation objective of disarmament and demilitarization was achieved with great rapidity, primarily because it was an almost completely mechanical task. Military losses had already carried disarmament well along among Japanese forces stationed at home or abroad. The destruction of fortifications, arsenals, and stocks of weapons and the demobilization of the armed forces were carried out quickly and effectively in the first few months of the occupation. By mid–1946, Japan's former military machine had ceased to exist. Even the process of demilitarization—of eliminating the Japanese will to war—was off to a good start. Defeat and its consequences had already gone far to disabuse the great bulk of the population of the idea that militarism was a paying proposition. The elimination of military propaganda, training, and doctrines from the schools also contributed much to the process. With demobilization of the armed forces and the resulting dissolution of the military command and removal of various governmental organs from military control or direction, the military was ejected from its key position in the state. Thus, in the space of a few months, the occupation eliminated from government, politics, and even the daily life of the people the military men, attitudes, propaganda, policies, and organs of government that had dominated so much of Japanese life for so long.

Paralleling demilitarization and disarmament was the attack on the civilian arms of government that had created and made effective the Japanese brand of authoritarianism. The powers of the cabinet were drastically reduced, especially those involving control of the people. Government controls over the police, the educational system, local government, and the organs of information and opinion were speedily removed. The Privy Council and the influential but informal council of former prime ministers, both advisory organs to the Emperor, were abolished.

In place of the authoritarian structure, the occupation fostered a system consisting of an executive branch with greatly reduced powers, a legislative branch supreme within the government, and a judicial branch created to protect the rights and freedoms of the people. The occupation also helped to develop an extensive network of local government, designed not only to give the Japanese people additional direct control over the administration of their own affairs, but also to form a permanent barrier to the reassumption of the powers of control over local affairs that had grown up under the old system.

The single political party, the Great Japan Political Association, which had been created in the spring of 1945 in the vain hope of putting into operation a political organization more effective than the Imperial Rule Assistance Association, was dissolved. Almost overnight, with occupation blessing, a whole new lineup of political parties sprang into existence. Some were singularly—and fortunately—short-lived, but in the course of a few years Japan had developed the type of party system indispensable for the operation of representative government.

Also in its very early stages, the occupation directed the Japanese Government to suspend or to eliminate a wide range of laws, ordinances, and regulations (in addition to those falling under the October 4 directive) that had been used to build up the authoritarian system and to prevent the development of opposition or even criticism. Foremost in this legal revolution was the occupation's successful attempt to replace the Constitution of 1889 with a new and democratic fundamental law. This highly controversial revision (described in detail in Chapter 4) has continued to be one of the fundamental issues in Japanese politics.

In the economic sphere, the occupation moved rapidly to eliminate the *zaibatsu*. The great firms were dissolved, and individuals high in their councils were temporarily purged from the world of business. But the capitalist system was by no means uprooted; what Japan has now is a system of relatively free enterprise, still basically capitalistic. It was clear, however, that the elimination of *zaibatsu* domination would not alone be sufficient to provide a solid economic foundation for the democratic order. Therefore, the farmer and the worker were placed in positions in which they both enjoyed a greater economic return for their labor and played a far more influential role in politics. The union movement prospered, and a substantial proportion (by far the highest in Asia) of farmers became owners of the land they tilled.

In addition to these drastic alterations in the structure of government, politics, and economics, the occupation also moved ahead in the broad area of social reform. The outstanding action in this field was the emancipation of women. The abolition of the social, political, and legal inferiority of women, which had been based on tradition, history, and cultural attitudes, was a major contribution to the democratization of Japanese society. Also of great social significance were the changes that the occupation brought about in the educational system, resulting in a revolution in the concept, content, and administration of education, and changes in the information media that led to the free flow of information and opinion so vital to the effective operation of a democratic society. (The impact of these social changes on the role of the individual in the new democracy is discussed in Chapter 6.)

The occupation also undertook a highly controversial purge program designed to eliminate from public life all the militarists, their active supporters or collaborators, and high civilian officials, policy-makers, and others who had been actively involved in the promotion of foreign aggression and domestic authoritarianism from 1931 to 1945. All told, about 200,000 individuals (about 0.25 per cent of the population at that time) were purged, although all were "depurged" by the end of the occupation in 1952. Perhaps the most important consequence of this measure was a temporary scrambling of the leadership corps of the country, with the resulting creation of opportunities for potential leaders who had not yet had a chance to rise to the top.

The occupation was responsible for the elimination of only one social class, the court nobility. Although disarmament and demilitarization resulted in the barring of career military officers from public life—and, of course, from following their careers—these officers constituted not a class but a profession. However, the new constitution definitely eliminated the peerage and prohibited its revival. Thus, the ancient aristocracy of the blood and the new modern peerage created by imperial appointment for achievement were both dissolved. But it should be noted that the members of this class, who constituted only a small percentage of the population, were neither liquidated nor deprived of the opportunity to pursue careers.

Let us now turn to the structure of the occupation and analyze some of the factors that contributed to the effectiveness of its operation. Because of the dominant American role in the final offensive, because the forces under his command had carried the principal burden of the American land operations against the Japanese, and because he was the senior American Army commander in the field, General MacArthur was appointed Supreme Commander for the Allied Powers (SCAP) to direct the occupation. His nomination by the U.S. Government was immediately approved by the other Allies. He remained in office until his dramatic dismissal in April, 1951. It should be noted that he was the Supreme Commander *for* the Allied powers, not *of* the Allied powers—an American general in command of American forces, acting for the other Allied powers, not a commander of a force consisting of troops of the Allied powers. This is an important distinction, since a general responsible only to his own government could act rapidly and directly, avoiding the frustrations and stagnations arising from a multilateral Allied occupation, such as that in Germany.

At the apex of the occupation structure was General Headquarters, Supreme Commander for the Allied powers (GHQ, SCAP). The nerve center of the entire occupation, it was the main channel for communication with the Japanese Government. Indeed, it was the government *over* the government of Japan. In addition to the General himself, the core of GHQ, SCAP, consisted of a dozen staff sections, each of which was responsible for a particular segment of the occupation. A partial listing of the titles of these staff sections will indicate their scope: Government Section, Economic and Scientific Section, Civil Information and Education Section, Public Health and Welfare, and Natural Resources. In these various sections, detailed plans for the implementation of the broad policies outlined by the U.S. Government were drafted.

It was from GHQ, SCAP, that the orders went forth to the Japanese Government to take certain actions or to refrain from others. It was also the principal source of the inspiration for Japanese individuals and groups to make efforts to establish and to operate the institutions of democracy, such as the new national legislature and the judicial system. Its role was of major importance during the first years of the occupation, particularly the first two, but from 1948 on its importance steadily diminished, for its major tasks had been completed by then.

The other main element of the occupation consisted of the tactical forces scattered throughout Japan. These forces, too, were all American, with the exception of British Commonwealth units stationed in and around Hiroshima. As military-government units, their primary concern was with problems on the local level: the implementation of broad occupation policies at the grass roots, relations between the population and the occupation forces, and Japanese compliance with occupation commands, government orders, and legislation.

The sprawling mass of the occupation was the machine through which the Supreme Commander and his government worked to achieve the goal of democracy for Japan. As an organization and as a collection of individuals, it was the machine that converted policy into action, the means by which the United States had its greatest impact on Japanese government, society, and people.

The occupation labored under some handicaps, one of the greatest being its foreign nature. It was manned by aliens, racially different from the Japanese, who were doing un-Japanese things to Japan. And yet its very foreignness was one of the most significant elements in its whole approach to the problem of the nurturing of democracy. The militaristic authoritarianism of Japan was the product of old and powerful streams that had flowed through Japanese history, culture, and society. The abortive attempts to introduce democracy into Japan from the 1870's to the 1930's had ended in failure because they found no favorable environment. The people were unreceptive, and the government took the action necessary to rid the country of potentially democratic developments. Thus, it was clear that if the course of history were to be shifted and democracy ever firmly planted in Japan, it would have to be done by foreign hands. Thus, in spite of the resistance that its foreign nature naturally inspired, the occupation was also the bearer of a political system that was to receive a warm and unexpected welcome from the Japanese.

Another handicap was the fact that the occupation was military. Although civilians played an important role in GHQ, SCAP, their presence was not sufficient to change its military nature. Authority rested fully in the hands of the military command. All occupation personnel lived and worked under military control. The hierarchy, authority, and discipline upon which any military organization must be based are clearly the antithesis of democratic practice, action, and theory. To many of its members —as well as to many observers, American, Japanese, and otherwise—the military nature of the occupation seemed an insuperable barrier to its efforts to institute any kind of a democratic program. But it turned out not to be.

A psychological difficulty confronting the occupation was that it was the representative of a victorious government. From the very beginning, this created problems. Obviously, there was on the one hand at least a certain overbearing attitude, and on the other, a spirit of resentful subservience. Yet, despite this unfortunate situation, the power and prestige arising from victory contributed to the occupation's ability to drive forward over any Japanese opposition to the successful achievement of its goals. There was never any question, especially in the key years from 1945 to 1947, of negotiation between equals, of compromise, adjustment, or accommodation of views.

The arbitrary nature of the occupation was another issue. Since it was both military and victorious, the occupation was in the happy position of being able to order the Japanese Government to do anything it wished. Again, this situation might have been expected to hinder the achievement of a democratic order. But it did not. Rather, it hastened Japanese compliance.

Not to be ignored is the fact that the occupation enjoyed a monopoly of force. It was sovereign. For Japanese to defy the orders of their government, even though those orders were merely being relayed from the omnipotent occupation, would have been defiance of a power that could not be resisted. No one could say "no" to the occupation, much less resist overtly its actions. The new Japanese democrats had no battles to fight. They were operating under the aegis of a victorious army of occupation that controlled all power and authority.

Thus, the foreign, military, victorious, and arbitrary nature of the occupation, plus its ultimate foundation on force, did not prevent it from bringing about the "establishment of a peaceful and responsible government." Indeed, these apparently unfavorable factors had the effect, in part, of guaranteeing the acceptance of occupation policy and its execution by the Japanese.

Of even greater importance were the more constructive aspects of the occupation, which contributed to its success. The first was a psychological factor of high value: the favorable reaction of the Japanese to the good conduct of the occupation troops. Partly as a normal expression of the enmity and hatred engendered in war, partly as a means to whip up and maintain civilian morale, and partly as a device to steel civilians to resist to the bitter end the anticipated invasion of the country, Japanese official propaganda during most of the war had assiduously developed the "Americans are beasts" theme. By the time the hostilities ended, the Japanese population was apparently convinced that the American armed forces were made up almost exclusively of brutes, sadists, desecrators of the dead, rapists, thieves, and murderers.

However, it soon became apparent that the vast majority of the American troops were quite the reverse. For the most part—exceptions were certainly not lacking—they turned out to be almost ridiculously nonmilitary in bearing, kind, generous, helpful, understanding, and eager to learn about Japan and its people. These virtues compensated for the deficiencies of an occasional overbearing attitude, signs of material well-being too obviously displayed, the desire to profit in the black market, and high and loose living. It also became evident that the small minority of Americans who did behave according to the worst anticipations by resorting to crimes of violence were dealt with harshly by their own authorities.

Because of the obvious contrast between average American behavior and the propaganda picture that had been created and accepted as accurate, the vast majority of the Japanese either welcomed or tolerated the American occupation forces. This, of course, meant that they were predisposed to accept many of the steps that the occupation was taking in order to achieve democracy.

Another positive aspect, closely allied to the above, was the untold thousands of cases of individual kindness of Americans to

Japanese. Food, clothing, medicine, books, magazines, and many other things that the Japanese needed to satisfy physical or psychological needs were provided by members of the occupation, sometimes in violation of military orders. In addition, a substantial amount of official aid was extended to the Japanese population in the form of surplus supplies of food and other necessities of life. These and other manifestations of private and official kindness served as a powerful means to dispose the Japanese favorably toward the occupation and its works.

Violence, terror, forced labor, and mass executions were not a part of the picture. The contrast with totalitarian occupations, both Communist and non-Communist, in recent years is striking. The very absence of these gave the Japanese reason not to resist.

Its relationship to the U.S. Government and the existence of a firm and effective policy were two other elements in the eventual success of the occupation. Perfectly obvious from the beginning, yet obscured by geographical distance and the degree of apparent autonomy granted to GHQ, SCAP, was the fact that it was the instrument of the American Government, an instrument that did an outstanding job of implementing its government's policy. The role of the government in relation to the occupation has still not received the emphasis that it deserves.

In the first place, the concentration of control in American hands meant, as has been noted before, that it was physically and politically impossible for any other government to interfere with the undertaking. It should be added that the majority of the Allies, critical though they were of certain aspects of U.S. policy and its execution, refrained from actions that would have disrupted the occupation.

In the second place, the U.S. Government, being democratic, naturally devised a policy based on the eventual creation of a democratic government in Japan. As obvious as this point seems to be, it was one that was not as clearly perceived and frequently stated as it should have been during the occupation and afterward. The government and American individuals have been singularly hesitant about stressing their contribution to the creation of a new postwar democracy.

Actually, as already noted, U.S. policy for the occupation

should be regarded as one of the most brilliant achievements in the history of American foreign policy. It was sound in conception, comprehensive in scope, clear in formulation, and, for all its complexity, relatively easy to execute. At no time from the very beginning in September, 1945, did the occupation have to function in a policy vacuum. There were no gaps to prevent effective action. There were no unmentioned issues, crying for clarification from far-off Washington, to cause friction between the United States and its allies or to create opportunities for confusion within Japan. The initial impetus and momentum of the policy enabled the occupation to apply unremitting pressure on the Japanese Government to get on with the job as fast as possible. The Japanese found precious little in the way of open area for evasive maneuvering. In fact, there was remarkably little discrepancy between the goals as originally stated and the achievements of the occupation, even though certain details were fumbled or not fully developed.

The Role of General MacArthur

A final factor of a far different order contributing to the ultimate success of the occupation was the personality of the Supreme Commander for the Allied Powers. In all his dealings with the Japanese, General MacArthur never gave any indication that he was anything other than absolutely supreme. He listened to and advised the Japanese leaders who came or were summoned to him, but he never became involved in argument or detailed discussion. In Japan, as he was not in the United States, MacArthur was above controversy. He consistently gave the impression that he was unswerving in his purpose, unshakably confident of his power, and devoted to the single aim of achieving what he considered to be the objectives of the occupation. During the first five years of his stay in Japan—from his dramatic landing at Atsugi Airfield, west of Yokohama, late in August, 1945, to the outbreak of the Korean conflict in late June, 1950—he left Japan only twice, once to go to Manila to be present at the independence ceremonies on July 4, 1946, and once to go to Seoul for the establishment of the Republic of Korea on August 15, 1948. During all that period, too, he never traveled through Japan, keeping himself in virtual isolation in his quarters in the American Embassy and his office in the Dai-Ichi Building.

During the period of the occupation's major work, mid–1945 to mid–1947, the General never deviated from the task of carrying out his government's policy. Indeed, his great accomplishment in the occupation lay in his singleminded pursuit of the broad objectives of his government as laid down in the "United States Initial Postsurrender Policy for Japan" paper and in the subsequent directives of his superiors, the Joint Chiefs of Staff. A fine soldier, he was able in this critical situation to push through to completion the vast and complicated task set by that policy and those orders. Perhaps the great tragedy of the General's career grew from the fact that when the occupation was virtually ended he was confronted by a vastly different situation in which he felt impelled to act counter to the stated policy of his government and to challenge the orders of his commander-in-chief. During his tenure as Supreme Commander, MacArthur did and said many things that were and have been subjected to criticism by Japanese, Americans, and others. However, the verdict of posterity must be that he did not commit a single major error in his command of the occupation.

Viewed within the centuries-old sweep of Japanese history, the occupation was only a fleeting and adventitious circumstance. But its revolutionary achievements were enormous. It brought to the country popular sovereignty, fundamental human rights, free elections, responsible government, and respect for the worth of the individual. These are the essence not only of democracy, but of Japan's new society as well.

Yet, this achievement could never have endured had it not been for the favorable circumstances on the Japanese side. It was the Japanese response during the occupation that provided the necessary condition for the successful democratic revolution; it was the Japanese will and ability to build into their own society all that the occupation brought that have made the new democracy viable.

3

Japan's Response

As U.S. policy for Japan arose out of circumstances born of the strategy of the war, so were the conditions for the Japanese response to it created by the impact of the war on Japanese society. To understand Japan's own role in the democratic revolution, it is necessary to examine the temporarily shattering effect of the war on Japan, the reaction of the Japanese Government and its leaders to the occupation, the reaction of the Japanese to war and the new democracy, and, finally, the readiness of the country to undergo the war-born revolution.

The Impact of War on Japanese Society

The tide of war had turned inexorably against the Japanese in the summer of 1944, and it was clear by early 1945 that defeat was merely a question of time and method. By then, Japan was feeling for the first time in its history the devastating impact of a war visited on its land by a foreign enemy. No Japanese could avoid seeing before his eyes the failure of the policy of aggression. In Japan itself, there was death, destruction, and devastation of an unprecedented order, wrought first by the great incendiary, carpet-bombing raids of the spring of 1945 and climaxed by the horror of the atomic bombs. Loss of life and destruction of property were perhaps only the most obvious consequences of defeat. In addition, there were the shortages of food, clothing, fuel, and shelter, and the breaking up of families as the result of mobilization, fatalities, and the evacuation and demolition of cities. If not at the time, then later on, it became abundantly clear that Japan's plight was due not only to the armed might of the United States, but to the fundamental miscalculations of the Japanese military. The defeat was too clean and crushing ever to be explained away by some future apologist.

Yet, in this hopeless situation, the Japanese Government was urging the people to fight to the death as the only alternative to unconditional surrender. After the two atomic bombs and the Soviet declaration of war—all three coming between August 6 and 9, 1945—the Government was finally forced into accepting Allied surrender terms. Earlier, it had made a few highly secret and tentative gestures toward a negotiated peace, but nothing had come of them. Significantly, even the final negotiations were conducted with the utmost secrecy inside the government. No more than a mere handful of high officials were privy to the discussions and the final decision. The Government, desperate as its position was, still controlled the population without fear of challenge.

In a dramatic conference on the morning of August 14, the Emperor made clear his view that the hostilities should be brought to an end as rapidly as possible. At the moment, the leaders of Japan, as events immediately thereafter were to demonstrate conclusively, wished only for an end to the fighting, not for the kind of change already envisaged in the American policy then being formulated. On the other hand, the Japanese people neither revolted against the military nor toppled the authoritarian regime under which they had lived for so long. It was foreign armed might that defeated the Japanese war machine on the field of battle; it was to be a foreign military occupation, acting under orders from its government, that was to follow up the victory by bringing about a bloodless revolution. Blood had been spilled aplenty, but in defense of the old system against external attack, not as a part of the construction of a new one.

Japan in the summer of 1945 was open for the process of change triggered by the defeat and the occupation and its policy. In short, Japan at the end of World War II was an organized, operating, and basically stable society—in grave difficulties. To Japanese society as a whole, the country seemed, at first, on the very brink of collapse. There were acute shortages of everything. Substantial portions of virtually all the cities had been leveled. Travel was disrupted. Families were scattered. Unemployment was high. Demobilization and repatriation of civilians and military personnel from overseas were creating serious personal and family problems. Communications facilities had been badly disorganized. Factories of all kinds had been destroyed or had ground to a halt because of the inability of workers to get to their jobs, the unavailability of raw materials, or the abrupt cessation of war production. Inflation was setting in. The overseas empire had been lost. The world-wide network of economic activities (trade, shipping, and banking) had been shattered. Government administration was highly inefficient, mainly because of the communications breakdown. All these tribulations and others created a dismal picture indeed for the Japanese. As the history of the next few years was to prove, however, they were only surface difficulties, although to the Japanese people, their government, and the occupation as well they seemed fundamental ones at the time.

Yet, it must be remembered that the Japan that was experiencing these troubles was able to handle them because years earlier it had become an operative national society. Its problem was one of reconstruction, rehabilitation, and reformation—a huge undertaking, indeed, but certainly not as overwhelming as the problem of creating a national society, the problem that soon was to confront almost all of Asia.

When the occupation took its potentially revolutionary program into Japan late in the summer of 1945, therefore, conditions were such as to ensure a minimum of opposition to its punitive measures and a maximum of receptivity to its constructive policies. However, there were no indications that the Japanese Government had lost or was even threatened with the loss of control over the population, or that the Japanese people were able, ready, or willing to challenge the authority of the government. After the war some Japanese leaders expressed apprehension that a truly revolutionary situation might have developed, had the conditions of the summer of 1945 continued. But the facts of the situation were that the Japanese Government was not subjected to any internal political pressure, organized or unorganized, to bring the war to an end or to institute significant changes in the fabric of the society. Nevertheless, at the war's end, both the government and its leaders had been discredited, if not dispossessed. The government was functioning only under the greatest stress and without its normal effectiveness. Except for the still great influence of the Emperor, the old political system was unpopular and virtually inoperative. On the other hand, the grave economic and social dislocations rendered the people and the society ripe for a change. Consequently, the Japanese, people and government alike, responded positively—sometimes willingly, sometimes unwillingly—to both the policies and the actions of the occupation.

The Emperor

Of great importance in the development of the democratic revolution was the role played by the Emperor of Japan, Hirohito. Initially, it must be clearly kept in mind what his role was not: It was not that of a great charismatic leader; it was not that of a strong chief executive who made crucial decisions and saw that they were carried out; nor was it that of a statesmanlike monarch working closely with his ministers to rule his people. The active element in his role was slight, most of it coming at the critical time when Japan made the decision to accept Allied surrender terms. Actually, the passive aspect of Hirohito's role was of far greater significance. His mere presence on the throne gave the people a sense of continuity that helped them go through the upheaval of transition from one system to another with a minimum of disorder.

At the time of the surrender negotiations, as we have seen, the single issue of most concern to Japan's leaders was the fate of the Emperor. The enemy press and government spokesmen during the war had made critical and in many instances intemperate statements about the Emperor. They touched on his possible personal responsibility for Japanese aggression and consequently his presumed guilt as a war criminal, his role in the creation of the fanatical fighting spirit of the Japanese, and the necessity for the elimination of the imperial institution as a part of the program of making the Japanese a peace-loving people. Such statements and the opinions they reflected were known to the Japanese. Thus, the government had abundant reason to fear for the safety of Hirohito's person following the end of the war, to say nothing of the fate of his throne. But the somewhat equivocal answer of the American Government as to the future of the Emperor (that the ultimate form of government "be established by the freely expressed will" of the people) seemed sufficient to reassure the Japanese negotiators. Although there was no clear guarantee of his future, it was obvious that the United States Government and, hence, the Allies had no intention of making the Emperor an immediate target of their vengeance.

On the Japanese side, there developed in the closing stages of the war and at the time of the surrender still another facet of the Emperor's role. During the tense conferences, held in the strictest secrecy in an air-raid shelter on the Imperial Palace grounds in Tokyo, the Emperor, according to what must be accepted as reliable eyewitness reports, broke the deadlock over acceptance of the Allied terms by stating decisively that in his opinion the war should be brought to an end as soon as possible. Very shortly after the conclusion of the war, this bit of information was spread throughout Japan. As a result, the people felt that he had contributed enormously to their welfare and happiness.

It was decided that the news of the acceptance of the surrender terms should be delivered to the Japanese people by the Emperor himself in a history-making radio broadcast (recorded rather than live). The recording was made on August 14 (Japan time), also in the greatest secrecy, but the news somehow leaked out. Early on the morning of August 15, a few hours before the scheduled noon broadcast, a group of soldiers went into the Imperial Palace grounds and searched diligently but unsuccessfully for the record before they were persuaded to leave.

The Japanese nation was alerted that morning by radio and newspapers that an extremely important broadcast would be made at noon, but still with no hint as to the identity of the speaker. The impact of the broadcast on the Japanese people was tremendous. Once the initial shock of the Emperor's words had worn off, the people accepted the surrender with apparent relief and gratitude.

The most important part of this historic broadcast was the Emperor's statement concerning the actions of the people after the surrender. Here are the concluding sentences:

> However, it is according to the dictates of time and fate that We have resolved to pave the way for a grand peace for all generations to come by enduring the unendurable and suffering what is insufferable.
>
> Having been able to safeguard and maintain the structure of the Imperial State, We are always with ye, Our good and loyal subjects, relying upon your sincerity and integrity. Beware most strictly of any outbursts of emotion which may engender needless complications, or any fraternal contention and strife which may create confusion, lead ye astray, and cause ye to lose the confidence of the world. Let the entire nation continue as one family from generation to generation, ever firm in its faith of the imperishableness of its divine land, and mindful of its heavy burden of responsibilities and the long road before it.
>
> Unite your total strength to be devoted to the construction for the future. Cultivate the ways of rectitude; foster nobility of spirit; and work with resolution so as ye may embrace the innate glory of the Imperial State and keep pace with the progress of the world.

The significance of this pronouncement was that it came from the head of the state, who had been revered and worshiped by all, that it was related to the end of wartime suffering and privation, and that it was also a general guide for future conduct. These rather vague generalizations constituted not an order for the Japanese people to obey slavishly, but rather an admonition, a statement of hope for the future that must have been reassuring to many of his listeners both then and later on. Perhaps the true value of the speech was its reassurance that there would be a reasonable continuity between the past and the future.

A few months after the surrender, the Emperor issued, on January 1, 1946, his famous renunciation-of-divinity Imperial Rescript, allegedly drafted inside GHQ, SCAP, and designed to encourage the Japanese to work through their present difficulties and build for the future. "The ties between us and our people," the document states, "have always stood upon mutual trust and affection. They do not depend upon mere legends and myths. They are not predicated on the false conception that the Emperor is divine and that the Japanese people are superior to other races and fated to rule the world." These sentences were hailed, outside Japan particularly, as representing a renunciation of the myth of divinity and as marking the beginning of a new role for the Emperor in Japanese society.

There was also initiated early in 1946 an even more meaningful campaign involving the Emperor, the one sometimes referred to as his "humanization." We still do not know what lay behind this campaign and how and why it was decided upon. It is a reasonable assumption, however, that the decision to embark on it was made at the highest levels of the Japanese Government. What began at that time and has continued to the present was a deliberate effort to bring the Emperor as close to his people as possible, to make concrete the renunciation of divinity. As a result of the insistence of the occupation, and also of the demilitarization aspect of occupation policy, the Emperor completely abandoned the military uniforms in which he had formerly appeared so frequently and had almost invariably been photographed. His "uniform" since 1946 has been standard Western civilian clothing, mostly business suits. Thus, in outward appearance, he is now no different from millions of other Japanese men.

Also in 1946, the Emperor initiated a long series of public appearances that have continued to the present as part of his routine. He has gone into all parts of Japan and has been in far closer contact with his people than any other Japanese monarch. He has inspected farms, factories, schools, and nurseries. He has attended baseball games and other athletic events. In 1948, after the Emperor had toured northern Japan, a publisher released a fascinating book of photographs of the imperial trip. Some of the pictures show people, especially older folk, in tears, obviously overcome by emotion at such close observation of a man whom they had long regarded as a semidivine, if not actually divine, ruler. Others show farmers, workers, or minor officials conversing with the monarch on what seems to be a footing of perfect equality. Some show expressions of frank and open curiosity. In others, people are demonstrating simple and enthusiastic welcome for a personage whom they obviously regard with affection. What is most striking about these reactions toward the Emperor is the contrast between them and the situation that existed during and before the war. First of all, such contact simply did not take place. For example, during the great fire raids on Tokyo in the spring of 1945, the Emperor toured the devastated districts for the obvious purpose of raising the morale of the people. But pictures merely show him walking down the streets, followed by respectful aides and advisers, through the ruins of destroyed homes and buildings; none of his subjects, the victims, are visible. Prior to the surrender, too, his subjects were expected to keep their eyes off him, bowing respectfully in the imperial presence.

Constitutionally, the Emperor is now "the symbol of the state and of the unity of the Japanese people"; politically, although he is without governmental and political powers, he is the monarch of a constitutional democracy; culturally, he is a link with the historical past—not the unhappy decades of militarism, but the centuries of valued and honored tradition. No longer a god on earth, no longer the object of awe and veneration, he is a human ruler regarded with respect, admiration, and apparent affection by his people. Because of the barriers created by court protocol and the apparent nature of his own temperament, this gentle, dignified, and studious monarch will, beyond a doubt, never write his memoirs. His nation and its history—and, indeed, the world— will be the poorer for not having in his own words the record of the experiences, the thoughts, and the feelings of the ruler who, as a quasi deity and as an individual lived through an age of militarism, a devastating defeat, and a democratic rebirth of his people.

It is safe to say that the life of Hirohito is a watershed in the history of Japan's imperial institution. His successor, Crown Prince Akihito, has already entered into a life far different from that of his father. His marriage in April, 1959, to his Crown Princess, Michiko, born a commoner, provided a measure of the new role of the imperial institution under democracy. Television covered the activities of the bride and groom from early morning before the wedding ceremony until the return to the Imperial

Palace after a procession witnessed by millions. About the only aspect that remained cloaked in the former air of mysterious awe and reverence was the ancient imperial marriage ceremony itself, which was described though in newspapers and magazines. The great outpouring of public affection and curiosity constituted another demonstration of the extent to which the imperial institution itself has been transformed under democracy.

The Bureaucracy

The second major Japanese institution that contributed to an easy transition from the old system to the new was the bureaucracy. The occupation was attempting a thoroughgoing reform of Japanese government, economic structure, and society. Yet, it depended for the successful forwarding of this program on a government still manned by career bureaucrats, trained and experienced under the old regime and, in many instances, obviously out of sympathy with the essentials of the occupation's program. Indeed, not a single one of the major reforms of the occupation, with the exception of the original version of the land reform, originated inside the Japanese Government; all came from the occupation, but the bureaucracy provided the necessary machinery for carrying out these reforms.

A very small percentage of the bureaucrats were involved in the purge, and those included were on the ministerial level or in the top career ranks. The vast majority, however, continued to carry out their responsibilities and to maintain the discipline and procedures that were the essence of their activities. Here was an outstanding example of the "neutralism" of the modern bureaucrat. It is accurate to state that the Japanese bureaucracy served its new foreign master, the occupation, as it had served its old master, the Japanese military.

The primary functions of the Japanese Government in the early stages of the occupation were: (1) to administer the affairs of Japanese society, with particular reference to the economic and social problems arising out of the war and the near chaos of defeat and the early occupation; (2) to carry out the orders of the occupation, especially those involving the destruction of those things in Japanese life that the occupation held to be positively harmful or undesirable; and (3) to draft ordinances, laws, and orders that would create or encourage the positive democratic elements that occupation policy envisaged for the new Japan. All these functions the bureaucracy carried out effectively, though not always voluntarily, happily, quickly, or efficiently. But the net results were impressive. Despite Japan's difficulties during the critical years of 1945–47, the nation did not collapse economically, it was not visited by bloody revolution, nor did the social order disintegrate, although the strains of black-market activity, crime, and delinquency were severe. In addition, the old evils and malpractices of government and politics were eliminated, and the new system was built.

The bureaucracy made significant contributions to these accomplishments, for it was the prime source of continuity between the old and the new in Japanese government. The simple fact that it continued to operate helped to keep within reasonable bounds the impact of the war and the defeat on Japanese society. For example, bad as the food shortage was, and inefficient as were the rationing and distribution systems in the hard winter of 1945–46, the very existence of systems operated and controlled by the government prevented a critical situation from becoming possibly catastrophic. In the same trying period, law violations, crime, and delinquency were widespread, and police operations were in many respects inefficient. Nevertheless, the existence of a police system meant that life and property were reasonably secure.

Again, the bureaucracy created a legal basis for many of the occupation's moves. Everyone knew that the acts of the Japanese Government were dictated by the occupation, but it was also true that almost all occupation action was based on the orderly procedures of the Japanese Government. Even the highly controversial and inequitable purge was carried out under government auspices. While, in many instances, the arbitrariness of the actions of the occupation was only thinly disguised, if at all, these acts did take place within the framework of accepted executive and legislative procedure. The net effect, therefore, was that the occupation's acts were set in Japanese soil and given the opportunity to take root.

Although the bureaucracy should be given credit for its contributions to the revolution, any praise should be kept as impersonal as the operations of a modern bureaucracy usually are. It was not necessarily a burning zeal for democracy that led the Japanese officials to obey the orders of the occupation and to be the instruments of reform. It was discipline and a sense of responsibility to the job assigned that proved to be the major motivations. Thus, the Japanese executive branch, as a going bureaucracy, and the Japanese official, as an obedient civil servant, constituted the main working connection between the occupation and Japanese society, as well as the principal means by which the imported reforms were first injected into the society's fabric.

Great emphasis has been placed on the role of U.S. policy. A consideration of the part played by the bureaucracy in the revolution, and of the broader issue of the relationship between the occupation and the Japanese Government, raises the interesting question as to whether or not the latter had a policy of its own to guide its course after the war. With the possible exception of the humanization of the Emperor, there is no indication that such a policy, secret or otherwise, was adopted, but a number of the items already discussed seem to add up to what was, in effect, a working formula. In the first place, the acceptance of the surrender terms—including the statement on the position of the Emperor and the special relationship between the occupation and the Japanese Government—constituted in itself a policy of considerable importance. It meant that the basic intention of the Japanese Government was to submit to the occupation and to do its bidding. The portion of the Emperor's end-of-the-war broadcast quoted above could also be taken as part of the government's intentions. The Emperor was possessed of sovereign power under the old constitution, and he spoke not only as an individual but as the absolute ruler of his country. It is clear that the Japanese Government adhered to the course that the Emperor laid down for all his subjects in that memorable broadcast.

During the occupation, it was widely felt that an obviously unstated policy of the Japanese Government and many of its leaders was to sit out the occupation and then bring to naught as soon as possible much of what the foreigners had accomplished. In view of the nature of the occupation, its relations with the government and with Japanese society in general, and the changes for which it was responsible (not all of which were universally popular), it was natural that the fear of a rapid reversion to the old would be prevalent both inside and outside the occupation. But if such a plan ever existed, it was never executed. As will be pointed out in subsequent chapters, there has been some regression or incomplete realization of a number of the reforms, but in no case has there been a return to the previous situation. What has happened could be described as a swing away from the extremes of the occupation to a state of affairs more normal for an independent, sovereign state.

Antimilitarism and Antiauthoritarianism

The roles of the Emperor and the bureaucracy and the existence of a possible Japanese policy toward the occupation are only narrow aspects of the total involvement of Japanese society in the democratic revolution. Of great importance were the psychological attitudes of the people toward their immediate past and their emergent future: their revulsion against war and militarism, their rejection of authoritarianism, and the immediate welcome extended to the freedom that came as a part of both occupation policy and the democratic revolution.

Perhaps the most important political and social aspect of Japan after 1945 was the complete revulsion against all things military. This has been one of the main currents running through Japanese politics: It has been a key issue in the development of the new constitutionalism and the controversy over constitutional revision; it has colored Japan's diplomacy; it has been one of the most important elements in the view the Japanese have taken of world affairs in general and of Japan's position therein; and it has been a major motivating factor in the greatest controversies the country has witnessed since the end of the occupation. The reality of its existence has been measured by numerous public-opinion polls; it is manifested in the statements of Japanese leaders in all fields; it is a consistent theme to be found in the many journals of opinion; it is given expression by individuals in such forms as letters to the editor, school compositions, and daily conversation; and it is the subject of large numbers of meetings and demonstrations sponsored and carried out by both interested and disinterested private and political organizations.

It is important to note that this reaction is far more than adherence to pacifism as an ideal; it is based on the bitter reality experienced and vividly remembered by almost every adult Japanese. Of course, pacifism is a current, and a strong one, in the antiwar and antimilitary attitudes of the Japanese, but to them war and its sufferings are to be avoided not on grounds of principle but on grounds of their demonstrated past effect. The suffering, death, dislocation, destruction, deprivation, worry, and strain that were the fruits of war were the source not only of the antimilitarism directed toward the old order, but of the persistent fear of any recurrence of it in postwar, postoccupation society.

Paralleling this, but by no means as widespread, was a reaction against authoritarianism. Perhaps its principal manifestation is the persistent memory of the rude and arrogant conduct of the former police. Only a small portion of the population suffered from torture or physical violence at the hands of the police, but a very high percentage of them still have vivid recollections of humiliations or subservience forced on them. Again, personal experience was significant in fostering rejection of the old order.

The almost immediate appearance of both antimilitarism and antiauthoritarianism among the attitudes of the Japanese public at the end of the war made the people receptive to what the occupation would bring. When the occupation began, there was the widespread feeling that it would be some time before the world could be sure that the Japanese had really renounced militarism and authoritarianism. There was even greater doubt, and with good reason, that they would welcome the freedom that the occupation was bound to introduce. The weight of history, tradition, and culture and the effects of two generations of powerful indoctrination seemed to be immediate and almost insuperable barriers between the Japanese and an understanding and appreciation of democracy.

That these barriers were speedily surmounted was due to the massive and positive response of the Japanese to freedom itself.

Some individuals, especially the intellectuals, welcomed this freedom enthusiastically. It was something many of them had longed for and had been denied. They were experiencing for the first time the all-important absence of the restraints and constraints of the vanishing authoritarian system; instead, they had freedom of expression and thought and the opportunity to act as individuals free from the oppressive weight of authority. Many other Japanese, unaware of the blessings of freedom, were to experience solid and positive advantages from the new atmosphere being created. Power, influence, privileges, concrete rights, greater income, more goods, wider opportunities, and more leisure— these were some of the gains won by both individuals and groups throughout Japanese society and found to be desirable and worth defending. And it was these gains that provided the positive foundation for the general acceptance of the new system.

The Institutional Substructure for Democracy

The final reason for the country's readiness for change lay in the basic strength of the institutional substructure of Japanese society as it existed on the eve of the democratic revolution. As far as the society was concerned, the problem of the revolution was not to build new institutions, but to make it possible for the existing institutions to function in new ways. Japan did not have to recapitulate the history of the development of modern democracy. Many observers, including this one, mistakenly assumed during and immediately after World War II that recapitulation was the core of the problem of democracy in Japan. Modern democracy has evolved in certain Western societies that were simultaneously going through the process of developing the institutions characteristic of the modern nation. Japan, by contrast, developed the institutions of the modern nation first and then turned to the problem of democratization. That the one task was completely successfully made it unnecessary to spend years and years on the other.

Thus, the occupation created no new institutions in Japan. All the essential ones involved in the democratic revolution had existed for some decades. Some had been suppressed, some stunted, and others distorted; some were authoritarian, and none was truly democratic in conception or operation. There was a central government, an emperor, and a bureaucracy. There had been political parties, and though the party system had gone out of existence in 1940, hundreds of persons had been involved in party operations. A constitution and a modern system of law had operated effectively, though nondemocratically, for more than half a century. The existence of rights and freedoms had been acknowledged, although their enjoyment had been curtailed to the extent that they were virtually nonexistent. Japan had modern industry, modern finance, and modern science and technology, but all were directed primarily to the satisfaction of the military demands of the state. Unions had existed, though barely and in the face of determined private and official opposition. The farmers, though poverty-stricken and living under a burden of debt, were not the forgotten men they have been in other contemporary societies. Women, still to be emancipated, were playing important roles in the authoritarian society as mothers, workers, and loyal subjects. The individual had been unwittingly prepared to play a new and democratic role in his society.

To understand democracy in Japan, it is necessary to observe, therefore, the confluence of many factors: a lost war, a wise occupation policy, the qualities of the personalities of a general and an emperor, the apparently contradictory characteristics of the occupation, the business-as-usual attitude of the Japanese bureaucracy, the revulsion against militarism and authoritarianism, the appeal of freedom, and, above all, the strong institutional foundation of Japanese society. There is no way of determining precisely what or how much each of these contributed to the success of the revolution. Some were clearly more important than others; yet, had any been missing or significantly different, the course of events would inevitably have shifted.

Most of the initial actions of the occupation can be interpreted as nonmilitary blows delivered by the victor on the vanquished; there was little room for true interplay between GHQ, SCAP, and the Japanese Government on such issues as disarmament, demilitarization, the purge, the suspension of authoritarian laws, and the dissolution or modification of authoritarian governmental agencies. The issue of constitutional revision was probably the first major item of reform on which interaction appeared, even though the Japanese had little room to maneuver. The basic law that emerged was the foundation not only for the revolution, but for the viable system of democracy that resulted from it. Indeed, the question of the constitution, of major importance at the time, has continued to dominate much of Japanese government and politics.

4

Origins and Principles of
Constitutional Government

Japan's 1947 constitution is one of the most interesting fundamental laws in the history of modern constitutional government.
Forced on the nation by a military occupation, it is nevertheless
warmly supported by a substantial majority of the people as a
highly desirable, indeed indispensable, foundation for a going
system of democracy. Drafted in deep secrecy and with great
rapidity by a group of foreigners, few if any of whom could be
regarded as statesmen capable of devising a fundamental law for
a nation of some 75 million people at the time, it has proved
to have no defect serious enough to require immediate amendment or to create crippling inhibitions on the operation of government or politics. Though it is filled with ideas and concepts
almost completely foreign to Japanese history, tradition, and
values, the constitution has fitted rapidly and easily into the
patterns of contemporary Japanese society. Utilizing a completely non-Japanese concept of sovereignty, creating a radically
different relationship between the government and the people, and
erecting a new structure of government based almost entirely on
foreign models, it has provided Japan with a workable governmental system that, in all but a few unessential details, is admirably suited to the country's needs.

The resolution of these seeming paradoxes lies in two simple
facts: In spite of its foreign origin and its foundation on foreign

concepts and institutions, the 1947 constitution brought rights and freedoms to which the Japanese immediately responded and which they welcomed as essential aspects of their new system of politics. And the basic law was predicated not on the establishment of a new system of government *ab initio*, but on the realignment of intragovernmental relationships and of the relationship between the government and the people that had been in existence for many decades.

The Origins of the 1947 Constitution

The issue of constitutional revision became a critical one almost from the moment that the occupation took the first step to eliminate the old order and to create conditions for the emergence of the new. The basic problem was that every move made against the old system either involved direct or indirect attack on some aspect of the old constitution or lacked basis in that instrument. As long as this situation persisted, every act of the occupation, welcome or unwelcome, could only be interpreted as one forced on Japan by a foreign occupation and with no legal or constitutional foundation. It is still debatable whether the course embarked upon—the forcing of a new constitution on the Japanese—was a wise one or not. At least, it did have the positive virtue of providing a firm foundation for the drastic changes that were being carried out. The alternatives, perhaps sounder in the long run but certainly less attractive in the immediate circumstances, would have been to permit the indefinite continuation of the unhappily contradictory situation between the reforms and the existing constitution, to suspend the Meiji constitution and thus eliminate the contradiction, or to permit the Japanese to develop their own basic law eventually under occupation tutelage. Perhaps the real reason that none of these measures was adopted is to be found in the first and abortive attempts to bring about a change in the Meiji constitution.

Early in October, 1945, General MacArthur summoned Prime Minister Shidehara Kijuro and informed him that the Japanese Government would have to give first priority to the problem of revising the Meiji constitution. Between then and February, 1946, a seriocomic political drama was enacted that clearly revealed the unwillingness or, perhaps, complete inability of the Government and its leaders to respond to the challenge. Although the Government established committees and commissions to work on revision, these were all necessarily composed of men who had lived and acted under the old constitution. They had known no other fundamental law; its principles, particularly the concept of imperial sovereignty, seemed perfectly natural to them. There were plenty of individuals in Japan, especially members of the newly active Communist Party, who would have been glad to draft a new and revolutionary—in more senses than one—instrument. But the Government could not be expected to call on them as long as it held the responsibility for producing the required draft.

After four months of labor had produced no results acceptable to General MacArthur and his advisers, GHQ, SCAP suddenly took the matter into its own hands, and its Government Section set to work secretly. A combined crew of army and navy officers and civilians of varied backgrounds—lawyers, writers, professors, civil servants, and a few without any professional experience who had gone into the services directly from college—was given the responsibility of drafting what was technically to be only a revision of the existing constitution, but actually was a completely new one. Working with great speed, the Government Section finished its draft in the space of a few weeks. The draft was extremely rough in many respects, but it is a tribute to all who were involved in that curious "constitutional convention" that what they produced did serve as a sound point of departure for an organic law that outlasted the end of the occupation and, though certainly not perfect, provided a working foundation for a democratic system of government and politics.

General MacArthur decided that the existing constitutional proprieties should be observed, and the Japanese Government was informed that it would have to act as the sponsor of the draft. On March 6, 1946, the Government released the document as its own, along with both an imperial rescript proclaiming it to be a revision (actually an extended amendment) of the Meiji constitution and a message from General MacArthur giving it his blessing.

Though SCAP had attempted to maintain absolute secrecy around the circumstances of the drafting in order to establish the fiction of its Japanese origin, it was obvious that the document was a product of SCAP itself. As a number of Japanese expressed it at the time, it "sounded as if it had been translated from a foreign language." Needless to say, the appearance of the draft created a sensation. Not only was it clearly of occupation origin, but it was thoroughly democratic and completely out of tune with the existing constitution. It was published in newspapers throughout the land, was the occasion for a flood of books and pamphlets, and became the object of wide public discussion.

After undergoing some rewriting and minor revisions by the government, in close collaboration with the occupation, the draft was submitted to the old Imperial Diet in the early summer of 1946, in accordance with the amendment provisions of the 1889 constitution. For many weeks, the House of Representatives and the House of Peers debated the instrument, always honoring the fiction that it was of Japanese origin. The Diet did make a number of alterations (all with the approval of the occupation), but these dealt with relatively minor details. For example, although the original draft called for a unicameral legislature, the House of Peers succeeded in having the present bicameral system adopted. This was a change of considerable significance, but it did not touch at all on the far more important issue of the power of the legislative branch or its relations with the executive and judicial branches. The Diet discussed all aspects of the draft, but was not permitted to tinker with any of the really fundamental principles set forth. The constitution was approved by the Diet on October 7, 1946, and promulgated on May 3, 1947.

It was the occupation that originated, directed, and obviously controlled the drafting, the content, and the process of approval of the new constitution. But it must also be noted that the Japanese role was active, however restricted. This point should be kept in mind, for the proponents of revision have argued that revision is necessary because the document was "forced" on the country without reference to Japanese desires.

The new constitution consists of 103 articles in 11 chapters. Both in broad principle and in specific detail, it differs completely from the constitution it supplanted. Japanese constitutional theorists are generally agreed that the document's three basic principles are: (1) the renunciation of war, (2) the sovereignty of the people, and (3) the guarantee of fundamental human rights. All three flowed directly or indirectly from occupation policy, a circumstance that has not resulted in their rejection as broad principles, but has led to an outcry among conservatives for modifications that could potentially vitiate them.

The Renunciation of War

The renunciation of war, set forth in the famous Article 9 (see Appendix, p. 247), is undoubtedly the most dramatic provision of the constitution and has become the center of the country's greatest constitutional controversy—that over rearmament. Nevertheless, the fact remains that from the narrow, constitutional point of view, it is by far the least important of the three principles. It could be stricken from the document without affecting in the least the truly fundamental issues of the locus of sovereignty, the structure of government, the relation of the people to the government, the issue of freedom, and the pattern of political activity. Touching none of these issues directly, its presence in the constitution is a manifestation of the impact of the occupation policy of disarmament and demilitarization on Japan. Yet, such a narrow approach to the renunciation of war completely ignores its transcendent political importance, which arises from its key role in postwar, post-occupation controversies over issues of both domestic and foreign policy (see Chapter 9).

The link between the occupation policy of disarmament and the renunciation of war in Article 9 is perfectly clear. However, the responsibility for the insertion of the renunciation into the constitution has never been unequivocally ascertained. Sound evidence points to the Japanese; equally sound but perhaps less direct evidence points to the occupation. The ultimate verdict of history may well be that the circumstances surrounding the original inclusion of the clause are relatively unimportant and that what really counts is that occupation policy on disarmament happened to coincide with the views of individual Japanese leaders and with the desires of a significant portion of the population—a situation typical of other aspects of occupation policy.

The lost war and the occupation policy led to the constitutional renunciation of war and all military forces; but the Cold War created a serious dilemma for the U.S. Government and the Japanese Government and people: strict adherence to the letter and spirit of Article 9, which might invite aggressive attack; or the satisfaction of the requirements of national defense, which might nullify a basic constitutional principle.

In late 1945 and early 1946, not only was it U.S. policy that Japan be permanently disarmed, but it was also the American expectation that disarmament would be feasible. The assumptions on which this expectation must have been based can be summarized as follows: Japan would never again be permitted to act as it had in the past, particularly from 1931 to 1945; Nationalist China would be the dominant power in Asia; the United Nations would operate effectively to guarantee international peace and security; and the major powers would band together to maintain orderly relations among themselves and all the nations of the world, primarily by wielding their influence through the United Nations. Yet, in less than the five years between the end of World War II and the outbreak of the Korean conflict, it became apparent that only the first of these assumptions was to become a reality. The development of the major power struggle between the Soviet Union and the United States, the division of the world into the opposing camps of democracy and Communism, the accession to power of the Communists in China, and military aggression in Korea all created a situation in which the exposure of an unarmed Japan to the threat of Communist military attack from the Asiatic continent seemed unwise from the official points of view of both the Japanese and the U.S. governments. Thus, the policy of disarmament and demilitarization, no matter how wise it had seemed in 1945–46, had come to be regarded, even before 1950, as increasingly unrealistic and dangerous to the national interests of both Japan and the United States.

The formal and official abandonment of disarmament was embodied in both the peace treaty and the U.S.-Japan Security Treaty of 1951. What ensued was a process of gradual, defensive rearmament that, however limited, aroused massive controversy. The source of the controversy was the conflict between Japanese government policy and popular attitudes. The great majority of the people not only welcomed Article 9 from the time it first appeared, but also took great pride in it, then and later. They felt that it represented a complete rejection of the policies that had won Japan so much hatred and had brought disaster to the nation, while it simultaneously opened the way to a peaceful future. Many also hoped that this thoroughgoing renunciation of war would be a good example to the rest of the world. Consequently, it is little wonder that many Japanese have consistently defended Article 9 and have bitterly contested every governmental action that has seemed to undermine it.

The formation of the Defense Agency and the Self Defense Forces under it (see Chapter 5) was the means by which the government hoped to handle its problems of national defense. The forces are charged with the responsibility of preserving the nation's security, but their existence is in apparent violation of the letter and the spirit of the constitution. Their status has been rationalized by resort to the extraconstitutional principle of the inherent right of any nation to defend itself against outside attack. Constitutional theorists have advocated this principle, but its most authoritative statement has come from the Supreme Court in an important judgment in 1959 (the Sunakawa decision) upholding the constitutionality of U.S. military bases in Japan. Although the decision did not involve the issue of the constitutionality of the Self Defense Forces, it seems reasonable to assume that, if a case dealing with that issue ever does reach the court, the justices will lean heavily on the self-defense doctrine.

Perhaps the most important political consequence of Article 9 is that it serves as a powerful motivating force for those who wish to revise the Constitution. Their principal arguments are that this provision was forced on Japan by the occupation; that, given the state of international tension and the existence of large Soviet and Chinese Communist forces in the immediate vicinity of Japan, the country must have a defensive military arm; and that the constitution should recognize the generally accepted principle of self-defense. Singly and in combination, these arguments appeal to many Japanese and seem to them at least to serve as ample justification for revision. If only Article 9 were involved in the move for revision, the problem, though still controversial, would be a relatively minor one. The greatest danger, though, is that revision of that article might be tied to an alteration of the entire constitution, which would entail tampering with far more important provisions.

However undesirable the conflict between Article 9 and the Self-Defense Forces may be, the forces do not in themselves represent a return to the old military domination of the government, and their potential for political interference is fully contained by a number of factors, constitutional and otherwise. The conflict has also not produced any threat to the fundamental rights guaranteed by the constitution. It seems that perhaps the most desirable solution to the problem is to continue the present ambiguous situation indefinitely. The basic causes, after all, lie outside Japan itself. Should a general relaxation of international tensions occur, the problem would then be resolved without recourse to constitutional amendment.

The Sovereignty of the People

The concept of the sovereignty of the people is undoubtedly the most important of the constitution's three basic principles, because by supplanting the old concept of imperial sovereignty it became the motivating spirit of the entire instrument. However, in view of its great importance, it is surprising that the constitution deals so casually with this principle. In the body of the constitution, no article is devoted solely to the sovereignty of the people. The only reference to it comes in Article 1, which is concerned with the position of the Emperor and which reads: "The Emperor shall be the symbol of the State and of the unity of the people, deriving his position from the will of the people, with whom resides sovereign power." However, the preamble—strictly speaking, merely an introduction with no necessary binding force—contains this statement: "We, the Japanese people, acting through our duly elected representatives in the National Diet . . . do proclaim that sovereign power resides with the people and do firmly establish this Constitution. Government is a sacred trust of the people, the authority for which is derived from the people, the powers of which are exercised by the representatives of the people, and the benefits of which are enjoyed by the people." (This, incidentally, was one of the principal passages in the constitution that sounded as if it had been translated from a foreign language, so alien did it seem in the light of traditional Japanese political thought.)

The principle of popular sovereignty does not mean direct popular government, an obvious impossibility in a complex modern society. It means simply that the ultimate authority in government is "derived from the people." Government under this principle must be both representative and responsible—representative because the general electorate freely chooses men and women to serve as the makers of law, and responsible because the electorate is able to control directly or indirectly the actions of the branches of government.

The principle of popular sovereignty manifests itself throughout the instrument. It lies behind the articles relating to the supremacy of the legislature, the limitations on the executive, the guarantee of extensive rights before the law for all the people, the popular review of justices of the Supreme Court, the close link between the National Diet and the cabinet, and the guarantee of autonomy in local government. The consequences of the establishment of this principle are dealt with in the remainder of this chapter and in the next in relation to the guarantee of rights and freedoms and the structure and operation of the government.

The establishment of popular sovereignty resulted in the destruction of the old principle of imperial sovereignty. To understand the extent of the drastic change that took place it is necessary to examine briefly the new constitutional position of the Emperor. Although Chapter I of the constitution, consisting of eight articles, is devoted to the position of the Emperor, it is characterized almost entirely by the establishment of limitations on his role. Article 1 states that the Emperor is now only "the symbol of the State and of the unity of the people," deriving his position from their will. In addition, to make perfectly clear his symbolic role, Article 4 declares that the Emperor shall perform only certain "acts in matters of state" and that "he shall not have powers related to government." Articles 6 and 7 list specifically those acts that the Emperor may carry out, such as the promulgation of laws, proclamation of general elections, attestation, appointment, and dismissal of ministers of state and certain other public officials, awarding of honors, reception of foreign ambassadors, and various ceremonial functions. Even these he may not perform on his own initiative; all require the advice and approval of the cabinet.

This narrow delimitation of the powers of the Emperor was designed to achieve two goals: to eliminate the peculiar and excessive powers that had formerly centered on the throne and to ensure that the throne would never again be used politically. However, the symbolic position of the Emperor has become the center of one mild controversy within the broader one over constitutional revision. Some conservatives are anxious to eliminate the Emperor's role as only a symbol and to make him the constitutional "head of state." They argue principally that every nation has a head of state and that "symbol," as applied to the Emperor, is meaningless, making him indistinguishable from, for example, the national flag. However, no serious proponent of this change argues in favor of the restoration of imperial sovereignty, and all declare that the throne should be kept free from politics. As for the opponents of this change, they argue that it might possibly lead to a recurrence of past abuses.

The Guarantee of Fundamental Human Rights

The third basic principle of the new constitution is the guarantee of fundamental human rights. Article 11 provides that the people "shall not be prevented from enjoying any of the fundamental human rights . . . conferred . . . as eternal and inviolate rights." Although that guarantee is unconditional, Article 12 establishes that certain responsibilities for fundamental human rights lie with the people, who are to maintain them through their constant endeavor, refrain from any abuse of them, and be "responsible for utilizing them for the public welfare." And Article 13 reads: "All of the people shall be respected as individuals. Their right to life, liberty, and the pursuit of happiness shall, to the extent that it does not interfere with the public welfare, be the supreme consideration in legislation and other governmental affairs." This raises the highly important point of the relationship between the freedom of the individual and public welfare as a limitation on the enjoyment of rights. It also makes the government responsible for serving the people's right "to life, liberty, and the pursuit of happiness."

On the basis of these provisions, the constitution bestows on the individual Japanese citizen a truly imposing list of rights. Summarized, they are: the freedoms of thought, conscience, religion, assembly, association, speech, press, and all forms of expression, choice of residence and employment, and academic activity; freedom from discrimination "in political, economic, or social relations because of race, creed, sex, social status, or family origin"; equality under the law; the "inalienable right" to choose public officials and to dismiss them; universal adult suffrage; the right of peaceful petition "for the redress of damage, for the removal of public officials, for the enactment, repeal or amendment of law, ordinances or regulations or for other matters"; the right to sue the state or other government body for redress for damage resulting from an illegal act of any public official; marriage on the basis of mutual consent; equal rights for husband and wife; the right "to maintain the minimum standards of wholesome and cultured living"; the right of all individuals to an equal education "correspondent to their ability"; the right to work; the right of workers to organize and to bargain and act collectively; the right to own or hold property; and the right to due process of law. Balanced against this array of rights and freedoms is a small but significant list of duties and responsibilities, including: refraining from the abuse of any freedom or right; the responsibility for utilizing rights and freedoms for the public welfare; the constant endeavor to maintain rights and freedoms; the obligation (as well as the right) to work; and liability to taxation.

It should be noted that this list of freedoms and rights includes the important concept of equality—not the thorny issue of "natural equality," but that of "practical equality," meaning equality under the law, equality of the sexes, the right to equal education, and equality of the rights of husband and wife.

The rights of the individual before the law are given great

emphasis in the constitution. Ten articles out of the total of 103 deal specifically with this matter, reflecting the desire to eliminate the abuses of the old judicial and legal system. The Japanese citizen now enjoys these legal privileges: equality under the law; freedom from deprivation of life or liberty or the imposition of other criminal penalty except "according to procedure established by law"; freedom of access to the courts; no arrest except upon warrant; no arrest or detention without immediate notification of the nature of the charges; privilege of counsel; security of home, papers, and effects except under warrant; security against torture or cruel punishments; the right to "speedy and public trial by an impartial tribunal"; right of examination of witnesses and of "compulsory process for obtaining witnesses in his behalf at public expense"; freedom from compulsion to testify against himself; freedom from being criminally liable "for an act which was lawful at the time it was committed, or of which he has been acquitted," and from double jeopardy; and the right to sue the state for redress after acquittal following arrest or detention. Virtually none of these privileges had existed under the former legal system. They have all become firmly integrated into the new one.

Although there have been threats to, and abuses of, some of the wide range of constitutionally guaranteed freedoms, on balance, the abstractions of the constitution have been successfully converted into reality. However, some issues of serious concern have arisen concerning these rights.

The first is the sociological problem of the role of the individual as established by the recognition of respect for the individual, equal rights for marriage partners, elimination of discrimination on the basis of sex or social status, and marriage on the basis of mutual consent. These constitutional provisions and the subsequent laws bearing on them have resulted in a shifting, if not a fundamental reorganization, of basic social and family relationships. In itself, this would be a disturbing phenomenon to many individuals in any society, let alone Japan's, in which the weight of traditional social relations has been so great. In addition, Japanese society has also been the scene of such contemporary phenomena (apparently common to all industrialized and urban societies, especially those that have also gone through the traumatic experience of extensive wartime damage and dislocation) as a sharp rise in all types of crime and juvenile delinquency and an apparent loosening of family ties. As a result, many Japanese feel that perhaps the constitutional emphasis on the role of the individual is excessive and should be modified somehow. Significantly, however, these same people apparently feel that there can be no return to the former inferior status of women. Nor do they desire a restoration of the former patriarchal system, with its extreme concentration of authority in the hands of the male head of the family.

A more concrete constitutional problem is that arising out of the so-called "three rights of labor"—to organize, to act, and to bargain collectively. Since the establishment of the union movement under the aegis of the occupation, union activities (in addition to their positive aspects) have been characterized by strikes resulting in public inconvenience; slowdowns; violence, sometimes in connection with strikes and sometimes not; participation in mass demonstrations, also on occasion accompanied by violence; and involvement in political questions unrelated to labor problems. The result has been that many Japanese have begun to feel the need for a more explicit statement in the constitution of labor's responsibilities as well as its rights—for example, the qualification that the three rights not be used in contravention of the public welfare. The rights themselves, however, are still regarded as being desirable.

By far the most important constitutional question relating to the principle of the guarantee of fundamental rights is that of the nature of the public welfare and its application to rights and freedoms, as put forth in general terms in Articles 12 and 13, and as applied specifically in Article 22—regarding the choice and change of residence and choice of occupation—and in Article 29, which states that property rights "shall be defined by law, in conformity with the public welfare." The issue is an important one in every democracy, because it involves the balance between the enjoyment of freedom by the individual and the good of the entire community. It is important in Japanese democracy because it is the only constitutionally sanctioned source of a possible limitation on freedom. This significance is underscored by the fact that the doctrine of public welfare, because of its stress on the good of the society as a whole at the possible expense of the individual, conforms to the traditional values of Japanese society and also bears a close resemblance to the glorification of the state at the expense of the individual that typified the authoritarianism of the recent past.

Japanese constitutional scholars have been interested in this problem from the beginning. What seems to be the prevailing view can be summed up as follows: Fundamental human rights, necessary as they are to a democratic society, are not given to the people under an absolutely unlimited guarantee; the only limiting factor on their enjoyment is the necessity for respecting the rights of others and acting for the good of the society as a whole; the consequence is that rights do, in fact, carry with them responsibilities, as is explicitly stated in the constitution; limitations are justifiable, but only within the narrowest possible bounds and on the grounds that they will serve or protect the public welfare. No responsible scholar tolerates the abuse of freedom, and all are agreed that abuse can be limited through government action, but only by means of duly enacted legislation. The reasoning behind this position is simple and direct: Sovereignty resides in the people; the National Diet is the highest organ of state power and the sole lawmaking organ of the state; the members of the Diet are the duly elected representatives of the people; therefore, the sovereign people, through their elected representatives, may enact legislation controlling abuses of freedom, even though it may involve possible limitation on fundamental rights. But most experts presenting this view further insist that basic rights and freedoms cannot be infringed upon by law; the only thing that can be limited by law is the abuse of rights and freedoms. Furthermore, such legislation can be justified only on the grounds that abuse impairs the public welfare.

The issue of the guarantee of freedom and the public welfare has also been a live one in the courts. The Supreme Court of Japan has ruled on such questions as obscenity and the public welfare and on the power of local legislative bodies to control the right of assembly in the interests of the public welfare. The

Court has consistently upheld the constitutionality of the application of the test of the maintenance of the public welfare to restrictions on freedom. However, the tribunal has been equally insistent that the doctrine cannot be used by any governing authority as an abstract justification for the limitation of freedom; it can be applied only under duly enacted legislation and under clearly defined circumstances.

Although the majority of Japanese constitutional scholars have been either adversely critical of such "public welfare" decisions or fearful of their consequences, the fact remains that there has been no serious erosion of any constitutionally guaranteed freedom through legislative, executive, or judicial action. It is safe to say that there is no gap between the guarantee in the constitution of a very wide range of rights and freedoms and their actual existence. Despite the circumstances of the drafting of the instrument, the freedoms it guarantees were well and quickly rooted in Japan and are being exercised and defended.

5

The Structure of the Government

As envisaged by occupation policy, the new government of Japan is representative and responsible. The basic provisions are contained in the constitution and in a battery of laws based thereon that govern the organization, functions, and powers of the three branches of the government and all its agencies. This chapter deals only with the mechanical features of government; some major problems of government in action will be considered later.

The National Diet

In accordance with the principle of popular sovereignty, the legislative branch of government, the National Diet, is supreme. Article 41 of the constitution provides that it is "the highest organ of state power" and that it "shall be the sole law-making organ of the State." As will be seen below, the constitution also establishes the system of the separation of powers. However, specific constitutional provisions place the Diet in a position of control over the cabinet. And, although the judiciary is independent, it is also subject to control, in part self-imposed and in part based on law.

The National Diet is representative of all the people, its members being chosen in free elections based on universal suffrage. The House of Councillors, the upper house, has 250 members, 150 elected from local constituencies and 100 from the nation at large. The House of Representatives has 467 members elected from 117 constituencies, each returning from three to five members. Despite the existence of a conservative majority among the electorate, the multiple-member constituency has tended to favor nonconservative candidates because those who run second or third, or even fourth or fifth—depending on the size of the constituency —are also elected. In 1956, the conservative Liberal Democratic Party attempted to establish a system of single-member constituencies, but failed.

The 150 local constituencies represented in the House of Councillors are divided among the forty-six major units of local government on a two-, four-, six-, and eight-member basis according to population, with only Tokyo and Hokkaido (the large northern island) electing eight members. Among the House of Representatives election districts, nine prefectures have only one district, and the two smallest have only four representatives each. Tokyo, with 10 per cent of the population, leads with seven districts and a total of twenty-seven seats, about 6 per cent of the total. Hokkaido has five districts with twenty-two seats. Osaka also has five districts, but only nineteen seats. Members of the upper house serve six-year terms, and elections must be held every third year, with half the seats being contested in each election. Elections for the House of Representatives must be held at least once every four years; however, in the event that the House is dissolved by the Emperor on the advice of the cabinet, a general election must be held within forty days after the date of dissolution (Article 54).

The constitution expressly provides that the House of Representatives is dominant over the House of Councillors. A bill becomes a law when passed by both houses (Article 59). However, in the event that the House of Councillors makes "a decision different from that of the House of Representatives" on a bill passed by the lower house, if the latter passes such a bill a second time by a majority of two-thirds or more of the members present, it automatically becomes a law. It is further provided that if the upper house fails to take final action on a bill within sixty days after receipt from the House of Representatives, the latter can take such failure to constitute a rejection. Another important provision supporting the dominance of the lower house is the stipulation that its approval of the budget becomes Diet approval when no agreement can be reached, when the upper house makes a different decision, or when it fails to take final action within thirty days after receipt of a budget bill approved by the lower house (Article 60). The same provision applies to the ratification of treaties (Article 61).

Chapter IV of the constitution, dealing with the National Diet, has twenty-four articles, but only one of them deals directly with legislative powers; the rest relate to organizational and operational problems. The important principle of Diet supremacy is expressed most clearly in its monopoly of the power of legislation. For example, every executive agency exists by virtue of laws passed by the Diet; executive power itself can be wielded only under Diet-enacted law. Even the exercise by the executive of the right of discretionary action is possible only if authority has been granted under law. On the other hand, legislative supremacy and the monopoly of lawmaking have not given complete supremacy to the Diet. An examination of the role of the executive will make clear the great area of power and influence still open to that branch, despite the constitutional provisions relating to Diet power.

It should be added that the concentration of lawmaking authority in the hands of the Diet was also designed to prevent the resurgence of the old system, under which a wide range of executive-issued orders and decrees, ranging from imperial ordinances to ministerial orders, had the force of law and could be issued at the discretion of the all-powerful executive without either approval or, in many cases, even challenge by the Imperial Diet.

The intricate and all-pervading structure of law that prevails in Japan adds still another dimension to the power of lawmaking. As will be discussed later in more detail, the country has a national system of law with, for example, common codes of criminal and civil law and procedure—all passed by the Diet. In addition, the whole corpus of law covers virtually every social, political, and economic situation in Japanese society. Although a considerable degree of local autonomy has been established by the new constitution, all local legislation in every field must be in accord with national legislation passed by the Diet. The lawmaking power touches directly on the daily life of the people.

Another significant area of Diet power is control over financial affairs, as provided for in Chapter VII (Articles 83 to 91). Such control, essential to a system of representative and responsible government, has also remedied the greatest single weakness of the Imperial Diet under the Meiji constitution. The Diet has the following powers relating to the national finances: determination of the manner in which they are to be administered; modification of existing taxes or imposition of new ones; sole power to authorize expenditure of money and the assumption of obligations by the state; consideration and approval of a budget for each fiscal year to be prepared and submitted by the cabinet; authorization and approval of expenditures from a reserve fund to provide for unforeseen deficiencies in the budget; appropriations for expenses of the Imperial Household; receipt from a Board of Audit, through the cabinet, of an accounting of the expenditures and revenues of the state; and receipt of reports at regular intervals, but at least once a year, from the cabinet on the state of the national finances.

The Diet also has the power to conduct investigations in relation to government and may demand the presence and testimony of witnesses and the production of records (Article 62). Although the prime minister and the cabinet ministers have the right to appear before the Diet to speak on bills before it, they are required to appear whenever they are needed to answer questions relating to legislation.

Both houses are organized along identical lines, with a secretariat to deal with internal administrative affairs, a legislative bureau to draft members' bills, sixteen standing committees, and an indeterminate number of special committees. The standing committees are: Cabinet; Local Administration; Judicial; Foreign Affairs; Finance; Education; Social and Labor; Agriculture, Forestry, and Fisheries; Industry and Commerce; Transportation; Communication; Construction; Budget; Audit; House Management; and Discipline. The Discipline Committee has twenty members; House Management and Audit twenty-five each; and the others thirty, forty, or fifty. Committee members are appointed by the speaker of the house. Every member of the Diet is entitled to sit on one committee, but no member may sit on more than two. Committee membership is proportionate to party strength in the house.

One aspect of the committee system requires comment. The first twelve standing committees listed above are all directly related to the cabinet and the executive ministries. Many Japanese observers believe that this system of close linkage between the legislative and executive branches has tended to strengthen the role of the executive. Typical of the system has been the appointment to the appropriate committee of Diet members with backgrounds, if not careers, in the matching ministry or executive agency. This creates a situation in which the bureaucratic loyalties of the committee members may outweigh their legislative responsibilities and their constitutional position as members of the highest organ of state power.

In formal constitutional terms, the two most important links between the Diet and the cabinet are the procedures for selection of cabinet ministers and for dissolution of the House of Representatives in the event of a political crisis. Article 67 provides that the prime minister shall "be designated from among the members of the Diet by a resolution of the Diet." Article 68 provides further that the prime minister is to appoint his ministers, but that a "majority of their number must be chosen from among the members of the Diet." These provisions mean, in effect, that the prime minister and a majority of his ministers are indirectly elected to their offices. Thus, the majority of the top government executives are representatives of the people, although they have not been directly elected to their posts.

The constitution also provides in Article 69 for the manner in which political disagreement between the House of Representatives and the cabinet can be resolved. The Article specifies that the cabinet must resign when the lower house either passes a nonconfidence resolution or rejects a confidence resolution—but with the added proviso, "unless the House of Representatives is dissolved within ten days." It is a curious fact that the constitution, in view of the great detail with which it treats many matters, does not describe the manner of dissolution in more detail. Apart from this statement, the only other reference appears in Article 7, dealing with the Emperor's acts in matters of state. Here, "dissolution of the House of Representatives" is listed along with other acts of state that he is to carry out "with the advice and approval of the Cabinet . . . on behalf of the people."

However, in the event of dissolution, the constitution also provides (Article 54) that a general election must be held within forty days. In short, dissolution is not an act to be entered into lightly by a prime minister and his cabinet. Since both the prime minister and a majority of his ministers must be members of the Diet, they must, as individuals, try to win re-election and hope that their party will gain the majority necessary for the designation of a new prime minister. The cabinet, incidentally, must resign en masse when the Diet is convoked after a new general election, but it continues to serve until a new prime minister is chosen.

Thus, the constitutional provisions concerning the election of the prime minister, the Diet membership of a majority of his cabinet, the process of dissolution, and the calling of a general election are designed to keep effective control over the cabinet in the hands of the Diet, and especially of the lower house. An additional control exists in Article 66, which provides that the cabinet in the exercise of its executive power "shall be collectively responsible to the Diet." Thus, even though the cabinet is vested with executive power under Article 65, it is held accountable to the Diet. It should be recalled at this point that the Diet also has extensive powers of control over the purse.

The Cabinet

In addition to general administrative functions, the cabinet is constitutionally empowered to handle such matters as administration of the law and conduct of the affairs of state; the management of foreign affairs, including the conclusion of treaties, although the approval of the Diet must be obtained either before or after the act; administration of the civil service, in accordance with standards established by Diet-enacted law; the preparation of the budget and its presentation to the Diet; enactment of cabinet orders in accordance with the constitution and Diet-enacted law; and decisions on matters of general and special amnesty, commutation of punishment, reprieve, and restoration of rights.

The principal administrative agencies of the cabinet are the twelve ministries of Foreign Affairs, Finance, International Trade and Industry, Labor, Welfare, Construction, Education, Justice, Agriculture and Forestry, Transportation, Postal Services, and Autonomy (local government). Each is headed by a minister of state, the total number of whom is limited by law to sixteen (the remaining ones heading important nonministerial government agencies).

In addition to the prime minister, the sixteen ministers of state, and the ministries, the cabinet organization embraces the Prime Minister's Office, the Bureau of Legislation, the National Personnel Agency, the National Defense Council, and the Commission on the Constitution. Although outside the cabinet and completely independent of its control, the Board of Audit with its quasi-executive function could also be included as a part of the over-all executive structure. Under the jurisdiction of the cabinet but separate from the ministries is the National Personnel Agency, which is responsible for administering all matters relating to the civil service and is of key importance. The National Defense Council—composed of the prime minister, a minister of state designated by him to serve as his deputy, the foreign and finance ministers, and the ministers of state heading the Defense Agency and the Economic Planning Board—deliberates on important questions of national defense. The Commission on the Constitution, an *ad hoc* body established by law, is charged with the responsibility of investigating all matters relating to the constitution, including the possibility of revision, and reporting the results to the National Diet through the prime minister. The Bureau of Legislation, originally established in 1885 simultaneously with the cabinet system, has been an organ of prime importance in Japanese Government, for it is responsible for the drafting of and research on legislation, including treaties. Because of its role in the drawing up of cabinet-originated legislation, it is an important link between the executive and legislative branches. The Cabinet Secretariat plays a vital role in the coordination of cabinet business, its administrative affairs, and the compilation of information regarding important policies. The status of this office is attested to by the fact that a minister of state may be appointed to serve as chief cabinet secretary.

The Prime Minister's Office

The Prime Minister's Office (PMO), established by law in 1949, is empowered to handle three categories of national affairs: pensions, statistics, and decorations; the over-all coordination of the policies and business of other executive agencies; and the administration of matters not falling under the jurisdiction of other agencies or that may be placed under its jurisdiction by treaty or law. The first two categories are part of the province of the office proper; the third, by far the most significant, is handled by its extraministerial agencies or bureaus (*gaikyoku*).

The Office proper consists of only the prime minister's secretariat, which has under it the Bureau of Decorations, the Bureau of Pensions, and the Bureau of Statistics. In view of the extent of the pension system in Japan, the Bureau of Pensions is an extremely important organ of the government. The Bureau of Statistics is charged with the compilation and publication of statistics dealing with national affairs. Also responsible to the Office proper are a large number of standing and *ad hoc* commissions and committees that study and report on various national problems, such as juvenile delinquency and other youth problems, tourism, employment, land utilization, emigration, and social security.

Of the eleven external agencies or bureaus in 1960, the seven agencies were Imperial Household, Procurement, Administrative Management, Hokkaido Development, Defense, Economic Planning, and Science and Technics; the four bureaus (or commissions) were Fair Trade, National Public Safety, Land Coordination, and Metropolitan Area Consolidation. All the agencies, except Imperial Household, are important enough to be headed by ministers of state, some of whom serve concurrently as the head of two because of the legal limitation on the number of cabinet ministers. Of the bureaus, by far the most important is the National Public Safety Commission since it holds administrative jurisdiction over the police.

The National Public Safety Commission

Let us examine in some detail the National Public Safety Commission and the Defense Agency, which cover two major areas of executive responsibility, internal and external security. As has already been noted, the police and the military not only dominated the executive but also had a direct impact on the life of the people under the old regime. The origins and operations of these two agencies of the Prime Minister's Office reveal the manner in which the executive branch of the government reacted and adjusted to the occupation.

One of the first acts of the occupation in matters of internal government was to eliminate the police system operated and directed by the Ministry of Home Affairs as a major instrument of authoritarian control. However, it was not until 1947 that the program of police reform was completed. What finally emerged was a network of locally operated law-enforcement systems in which every city, town, or village with a population of 5,000 or more had its own police force. In addition, a so-called National Rural Police Force, not to exceed 30,000 members, was run by the national government in order to maintain law and order in areas without their own police forces. This scheme was extremely expensive because it placed the burden of maintaining a local force on every community. It was also very cumbersome, with the local and national police attempting to operate more or less side by side in many areas. It was also difficult to coordinate the efforts of these numerous, scattered organizations. It was apparent almost from the beginning that the new arrangement represented an exorbitant price to pay in finances and efficiency for getting rid of the old system, no matter how desirable that might be.

In 1954, just over two years after the end of the occupation, a new Police Law that completely revised the 1947 setup was passed—but only after violent controversy both inside and outside the Diet, occasioned, of course, by the fears of those who saw in it a dangerous, retrogressive step toward a police state. Under the new system, police forces organized on the level of the major administrative units of local government—the prefectures, Hokkaido, the metropolis of Tokyo, and the urban prefectures of

Osaka and Kyoto—have replaced the former village, town, and city forces and are responsible for the maintenance of law and order as that is normally understood; and a national administrative organization centering in the National Public Safety Commission is responsible for such matters as national police policy, coordination of police activities, financial assistance to prefectural police offices, operations in connection with natural disasters (typhoons, floods, earthquakes, etc.) or large-scale riots, research in police and criminal affairs, training, and the management of the Imperial Palace guards.

A number of provisions in the law are designed as safeguards against a return to the abuses of centralized control. And there are various general statements of principle governing police operations, of which the following are examples: Article 1—"This law has as its object the guarantee of police operation and management based on democratic ideas . . . so that individual rights and freedoms will be protected and public peace and order maintained"; Article 2—"Police activities . . . must not in the slightest degree abuse authority by such things as interference with the rights and freedoms guaranteed in the Constitution of Japan"; and Article 3—"All personnel who carry out police duties based on this law must take an oath of office to the effect that they will protect the Constitution of Japan and that they will carry out their duties with impartiality, justice and fairness." The conduct of the police has been a highly controversial issue since the enactment of this law. Yet, an impartial foreign observer can only conclude that, on balance, the police have adhered to the principles outlined above. Beyond any question, they have not reverted to the old practices and attitudes, in spite of a number of incidents that can be cited against the record of the present system.

The National Public Safety Commission is composed of a chairman, who must be a minister of state and thus is held responsible to the Diet, and five members appointed by the prime minister with the consent of both houses. Barred from appointment are those with any experience during the previous five years as public officials in police or public prosecutor's activities. Members are also forbidden to take part in political activities, and no political party may be represented on the Commission by more than two members. The prime minister is empowered to proclaim national or local emergencies in the event of natural disasters, riots, or similar situations. He may also issue direct orders to the heads of police boards responsible for the areas involved in emergency proclamations. However, he must submit such proclamations of emergency to the Diet for approval within twenty days after issuance and must cancel them as soon as possible after the emergency ends or if the Diet does not approve his action or votes to suspend the proclamation. No prime minister prior to 1961 had ever resorted to an emergency proclamation, not even Prime Minister Kishi during the 1960 demonstrations and riots in Tokyo against the security treaty with the United States.

It seems apparent, then, that the return to the hands of the executive branch of some control over the administration of the police has not resulted either in an erosion of the freedoms of the people and their rights before the law or in a return to police oppression.

The Defense Establishment

The establishment of the Defense Agency and of the Self-Defense Forces under its control and direction followed a pattern roughly similar to that of the National Public Safety Commission. Complete disarmament had been achieved early in the occupation, but before the occupation came to an end, the question of Japan's national security arose in view of the Korean war, the rapid growth of Communist military power in China, the Soviet Union, and North Korea, and the general state of tension in world affairs. Just after the outbreak of the fighting in Korea in June, 1950, the occupation authorized the establishment of what was termed the National Police Reserve (NPR), a paramilitary force designed to assist the police in maintaining internal security at a time when Japan was virtually denuded of occupation troops and when there was at least a possibility that Japanese Communists might coordinate a program of violence and subversion with the action in Korea. The NPR was converted into the National Security Force by law in 1952, just a few weeks after the end of the occupation, and that in turn was converted into the Self-Defense Forces under the Defense Agency in a law passed by the Diet in July, 1954. As in the case of the revised police law, the Defense Agency and Self-Defense Forces Laws were enacted only after a great controversy.

Heading the Defense Agency is a director-general, who must be a minister of state—and thus must be a civilian, since the constitution stipulates (Article 66) that all ministers of state are to be civilians; he is assisted by a civilian staff. Responsibility for operational plans and policies and for actual operations is in the hands of the chiefs of the Ground, Maritime, and Air Staff Sections, who in turn are members of a Joint Staff Council headed by a chief of staff; all these men are, of course, officers of their respective services.

Great care was taken in the laws establishing the Agency and the SDF to set up safeguards against the kind of military interference in the affairs of government that had characterized the old system. For example, in addition to assuring the dominance of civilians in the command organization of the SDF, the law provides for the isolation of officers from policy formulation, specifically prohibits political activity by military personnel, and gives the National Diet the power to control mobilization. This last point requires some expansion because of its fundamental importance in relation to the political and governmental position of the SDF. The prime minister is empowered to mobilize the defense forces in emergencies such as internal insurrection or actual armed attack from without. In addition, the director-general, with the consent of the prime minister, can order mobilization in times of disaster or natural calamity. But the law specifies that in both cases the prime minister must obtain the prior approval of the Diet; if this is not possible, then approval must be obtained as soon as feasible after the issuance of the order. The prime minister, or the director-general acting with the prime minister's consent, must also order demobilization as soon as the emergency has passed or in the event that the Diet fails to approve a mobilization order. Thus, what the law has done is to attempt a reasonable balance between the flexibility required for executive action in the event of a true emergency and the constitutional provision of legislative supremacy.

The modest size of the Self-Defense Forces also provides a useful guide to its position in the executive branch of government. In 1959, Japan's total military personnel numbered just over 230,000, with 170,000 in the ground force, about 28,000 in the maritime force, and about 33,000 in the air force. The maritime force had no ship larger than a destroyer; the air force had between 300 and 400 fighter planes, but no bombers; and of course there were no missiles to be used for offensive purposes and no nuclear weapons. Originally all war matériel was supplied to Japan by the United States. In the late 1950's, however, the Japanese began to produce small naval vessels, some jet fighters and trainers, and a few helicopters and other aircraft. As might be expected, the budgetary requirements of the military have been modest; since 1954, the budget of the Defense Agency and the forces under its control has averaged less than 10 per cent of the total budget and less than 1.5 per cent of the national income. Such a military establishment is clearly defensive in nature as well as name. Its modest role in government and its virtually nonexistent part in politics seems to guarantee a subordinate place in the affairs of the executive and consequently a limitation on its political potential. Furthermore, the controversy that persisted over all aspects of rearmament has served as a safeguard against a resurgence of the military establishment.

Thus, the Prime Minister's Office, in the two critical areas of executive responsibility—external and internal security—where the old authoritarianism reached its highest expression, seems highly unlikely to be able to apply the weight of executive pressure on the lives of the people. The fact does remain that the PMO represents a powerful concentration of executive power. But this phenomenon, characteristic of virtually every modern government, arises from the complexity of the modern national society. Japan's prewar government was a typical example of the growth of irresponsible executive authority, utilized to subordinate the individual to the requirements of the society. However, within contemporary Japan, as under other democracies, the key problem of control over the executive has been handled through the functioning of checks exercised primarily by the legislative branch of government. We have now noted the powerful constitutional, budgetary, and political reins that the National Diet has on the executive branch. As has been mentioned already and will be described more fully in a later chapter, the pressure of public opinion on the executive has also been considerable. As long as the executive is exposed to such pressures, it is reasonable to expect that even a continued concentration of power in its hands will not bring a return to the old system of the omnipotent executive.

The Judicial Branch

The first sentence of Article 76 of the constitution reads simply: "The whole judicial power is vested in a Supreme Court and in such inferior courts as are established by law." Not only are the legislative and executive branches excluded from any share in the judicial power, but the Supreme Court actually controls all judicial affairs of the country by virtue of the provisions of Article 77, which vests the court with the rule-making power "under which it determines the rules of procedure and of practice, and of matters relating to attorneys, the internal discipline of the courts and the administration of judicial affairs."

A key organization through which the court exercises its broad powers of judicial control is the Legal Research and Training Institute, established by law under the jurisdiction of the Supreme Court. Among other things, the Institute is responsible for the training of every person interested in a legal career. No one can become a lawyer, a judge, or a public prosecutor unless he has either been graduated from the Institute or, in a few cases, has undergone a course of in-service training there. This gives the Supreme Court control over entry into the legal profession and thus the power to determine over the years the nature of the entire system of the administration of justice. The Supreme Court also operates similar institutes for the training of court clerks and family-court probation officers. Judges of inferior courts, although appointed by the cabinet, must be chosen from a list of candidates nominated by the Supreme Court.

Article 81 provides that the Supreme Court is "the court of last resort with power to determine the constitutionality of any law, order, regulation, or official act." The tribunal has handed down many decisions dealing with issues of constitutionality, but, with the exception of certain laws passed in order to implement occupation orders or directives, it has never held any law, order, regulation, or official act unconstitutional.

The chief justice of the Supreme Court is designated by the cabinet and appointed by the Emperor—a procedure designed to place the chief justice on the same level of dignity as the prime minister, who is also appointed by the Emperor, but after designation by the Diet. The fourteen other Supreme Court justices are appointed by the cabinet. Neither consent nor approval of the Diet is required, but it should be recalled that the cabinet is responsible to the Diet for its acts.

The principle of popular sovereignty is applied to the Supreme Court, and thereby indirectly to the entire judicial branch, by the peculiar provision of Article 79 of the constitution: "The appointment of the judges of the Supreme Court shall be reviewed by the people at the first general election of members of the House of Representatives following their appointment, and shall be reviewed again . . . after a lapse of ten years . . ." If a majority of the voters favors dismissal, a judge is to be dismissed. While this peculiar procedure does ensure a popular voice in the selection of Supreme Court justices, it has proved to be largely meaningless; in every case of popular review, the justices involved have received 90 per cent or more favorable ballots. At best, this is a formal gesture in the direction of popular sovereignty; at worst, it might have the unfortunate effect of injecting a political bias into the decisions of some justice with an eye toward the coming approval of his tenure, or, conversely, it could be used by pressure groups to attempt to sway judicial opinions. Under the law, it is possible to rid the bench of justices who demonstrate unfitness in any way. The "popular review" provision seems, therefore, to be the most dispensable item in the constitution.

The judiciary that the Supreme Court controls is a national one—that is, all the courts are a part of a single nationwide system. There are 8 high courts (basically courts of appeal), 49 district courts (with 235 branches), 570 summary courts, and

49 family courts (also with 235 branches). Public prosecution is handled by a hierarchy of public prosecutors' offices, organized to parallel the structure of the courts (except for the family courts), arranged in descending order from the Supreme Public Prosecutor's office through high, district, and local public prosecutors' offices. General control over public prosecutors lies with the Ministry of Justice. This supervision cannot be extended to any individual case before a lower office; but the prosecutor-general, the head of the Supreme Public Prosecutor's office, is empowered to handle certain cases directly.

The judicial system has operated effectively in the protection of the many rights and privileges guaranteed to the individual by the constitution. It should be noted that the general rights granted were incorporated into the Japanese law, especially the four basic national codes: the Criminal Code, the Civil Code, the Code of Criminal Procedure, and the Code of Civil Procedure. The detail with which these codes deal with the rights of the accused and the national application thereof have resulted in a minimum of abuse of the rights of individuals, a striking change from the days of the Meiji constitution.

The Supreme Court has adhered strictly to the principle of the separation of powers but has honored equally the doctrine of legislative supremacy. It has, for example, insisted on its right to exercise the whole judicial power. In 1948, the Judicial Committee of the House of Councillors instituted an investigation of an alleged miscarriage of justice involving the imposition of a sentence regarded as too lenient on a deserted wife found guilty of murdering her three children. The Supreme Court vigorously rejected in 1949 the report of the committee as being an infringement on the independence of the courts. On the other hand, the Supreme Court has also consistently refused to declare legislative and executive acts unconstitutional. Broadly speaking, its arguments on this question are as follows: For the Court to declare such acts unconstitutional would be a violation of the principle of the separation of powers, as well as of the doctrine of legislative supremacy; the proper remedy for legislation not clearly unconstitutional is a political one—that is, the sovereign people can pass judgment on the Diet and on the cabinet by means of the ballot.

Local Autonomy

Chapter VIII of the constitution (Articles 92 through 95) establishes the principle of local autonomy. However, it also provides that the organization and operation of local public entities and their assemblies, the election of officials, and the right to manage property, affairs, and administration shall all be governed by law passed by the National Diet. In practice, a complex structure of local government has been created that includes Tokyo Metropolis, the urban prefectures of Osaka and Kyoto, the island of Hokkaido, forty-two prefectures (the equivalent of American states), and more than 3,700 cities, towns, and villages. All matters relating to these units are determined and controlled by the provisions of the Local Autonomy Law of 1947 (frequently revised thereafter). Perhaps the most important provision is for the direct popular election of all heads of local public entities and of a number of other officials. This effectively eliminated the former method of direct national control over local affairs through the power to appoint local officials held by the old Ministry of Home Affairs. There is also a considerable degree of autonomy in the administration of local affairs. However, the most serious problem confronting virtually all units of local government is that of finances. Funds for assistance to local public entities consistently make up one of the larger items in the national budget. The allocation of these funds is controlled by the Autonomy Ministry, established on July 1, 1960, after having been an agency of the Prime Minister's Office. This financial contribution gives the national executive considerable influence over local government.

The Government and the People

The constitution also deals with the general issue of the nature of the relationship between the people and their government. The people retain ultimate control over the government, which is enjoined to refrain from the infringement of any of the fundamental rights and freedoms guaranteed to the people and to act positively for their benefit.

Article 15 deals specifically with this relationship. Its key points are: the people's "inalienable right" to choose and dismiss their officials; the position of all public officials as "servants of the whole community and not of any group thereof"; and the guarantee of universal adult suffrage in the selection of these officials. In the old days, of course, public officials regarded themselves as servants of the Emperor and responsible to him alone, and as masters of the people. The provision that government officials shall be "servants" of the people was designed to undermine the entrenched bureaucracy that formed one pillar of the authoritarian structure. The bureaucracy is still powerful, and one insistent complaint of many Japanese is that the attitude of the new bureaucrats still smacks too much of that of the old. However, the fact remains that public officials, even if they do not regard themselves as community servants, are nevertheless no longer representatives of an omnipotent executive with all its authority and force behind them. They are now subject to the pressures of the legislative branch and of a diligent public opinion.

Article 25 of the constitution contains the positive injunction to the state that it "shall use its endeavors for the promotion and extension of social welfare and security, and of public health." It also states that the people have the right to "maintain the minimum standards of wholesome and cultured living." Thus, both by implication and by explicit statement, it calls for the exercise of state power for the promotion of individual welfare. In the crucially important relationship between the individual and his government, the former is given precedence over the latter—the characteristic feature of a democratic political system as contrasted with an authoritarian one.

The Individual Under
Japan's Democracy

The individual living under Japan's constitutional democracy occupies a position unprecedented in the history of the country. He has been released from the crushing weight of authoritarianism through the destruction and modification of many elements of the old system; he enjoys an impressive battery of rights and freedoms granted to him by the 1947 constitution; his role as a responsible, free citizen has been fostered by the free flow of information and an educational system no longer under government control; and his basic physical and psychological needs find greater satisfaction because of striking economic advances and the attempt of the state to enable each individual to share broadly in the benefits flowing from the economic activities of the society.

The abstract concept of the importance of the individual under democracy may not be as widely accepted—or even recognized— throughout Japan as it is in Western societies. But by any reasonable contemporary standard, the individual enjoys a full measure of all the political, economic, social, and psychological benefits that should ideally be those of free citizens under a system of democracy in which the idea of individualism is well developed. How this has come about is the subject of the present chapter.

The Replacement of State Supremacy

One of the crucial problems of the democratic revolution was the replacement of the concept of state supremacy with the concept of the worth and dignity of the individual. State supremacy had been rooted in Japanese thought and action by two generations of indoctrination and given further strength by the support it received from history, culture, and tradition. The individual, by custom, attitude, the subtle influence of tradition, and the obvious coercion of the state, was forced to think of himself in terms of the contribution he could make to his society. He was the means by which the ends of the society could be achieved. Those who wished to achieve their own private goals by their own means were not only rebels against society but agents of political and social subversion. In Japan, as in every other modern authoritarian or totalitarian state, the individual was told that the achievement of the goals of the society would ultimately mean his own perfection.

Although the individual was under strong constraint to conform, the authoritarian state did not by any means neglect those considerations important to the development of the person in a modern society, democratic or otherwise: the guarantee of reasonable economic well-being (food, clothing, shelter, and the means to acquire them); the stress on the physical development of the young; compulsory education, which led not only to literacy but also to specialized training for the range of professional careers available in a modern industrial society; and the provision of the means to satisfy cultural and recreational needs. These benefits for the individual naturally flowed from the process of the creation of the institutions of a modern nation. But the government tried to maintain the "proper" sociological, political, spiritual, emotional, and psychological attitudes in the individual —those that subordinated him to the family and the state—while simultaneously developing him physically and mentally to make him more useful. Sound bodies meant greater capacity to work and more and stronger parents to produce more male children to become better soldiers. Properly indoctrinated minds meant unquestioning support of the goals and policies of the nation and more effective execution of individual duties and responsibilities. The great, unrecognized irony was that many of the things that prepared the individual Japanese to be an obedient, efficient tool of the state were precisely those that were also preparing him to become, someday, a responsible citizen in a free society.

Elimination of the Emperor as an Authority Symbol

The elimination of the worship of the emperor as a semi-deity of allegedly divine ancestry was a major step in the transition of the Japanese individual from subject to citizen because the emperor was at the core of the enormous weight of omnipresent authority that forced the individual into the mold of conformity. Under the old system, the fundamental measure of the subject's loyalty and usefulness to his society was the degree of his devotion to the emperor and, consequently, of his willingness either to subordinate or to sacrifice his own goals to those of the state.

Politically, the Emperor was the supreme ruler and the object of the unswerving loyalty of his subjects, a loyalty that was sedulously developed by the agencies of government, by the media of mass communications directed or controlled by the government, by the state-operated educational system, and by the whole pressure to conform that was exerted directly by patriotic organizations and indirectly and equally effectively by the whole atmosphere of the society. The aim was to make each person a faceless unit in a mass of loyal subjects, not to lead him to adopt the correct attitude as a matter of free, individual choice.

Culturally and socially, the Emperor played an equally important role. He was the supreme symbol of the whole hierarchy of social relationships to which the individual was thoroughly subordinated. The Emperor was to the nation and to the mass of the people what every other symbol and holder of authority was throughout society: the father to the family, the older brother to the younger brother, the brother to the sister, the male to the female, the husband to the wife, the old to the young, the teacher to the pupil, the government official to the subject, the policeman to the public, the boss to the henchman. The conforming Japanese, in his blind loyalty to his ruler, was merely manifesting toward the supreme symbol of the nation his relation to other figures of authority and thus his subordinate position in society.

The enormous pressures exerted on all Japanese subjects from early childhood to develop and maintain the proper attitudes toward the Emperor cannot be overemphasized. For example, near the entrance to every schoolyard there was a small shrine in which were enclosed pictures of the Emperor and Empress. Every schoolchild had to uncover and bow before this shrine each time he entered or left the schoolyard. On national holidays, usually at 10 A.M., all Japanese inside or outside the country were supposed to bow respectfully in the direction of the Imperial Palace in Tokyo. It was a custom, not rigidly enforced, for Japanese to bow each time they passed the main entrance to the palace grounds. In photographs, in the press and otherwise, the Emperor was always shown in ceremonial dress, whether in ancient court costume or military uniform. All references to him and his activities were written in stilted, archaic Japanese—another indication of the reverence in which he was to be held. In schools, the myths of his allegedly divine origin were taught as history that could not be questioned. He was, of course, the center around which chauvinistic propaganda was built. He was the supreme symbol of authority, to which all, both literally and figuratively, bowed. The importance of his role lay not in the fact that all Japanese believed everything they were told about him and his imperial ancestors, but that the vast majority accepted as both right and proper his all-dominant position as well as their subservient one.

Today, the situation is vastly different. Details about the Emperor's personal life and his daily routine are far more widely known by his people than ever before. Thousands of citizens throng the grounds of the Imperial Palace each New Year's Day to pay their formal respects. He appears as a man not much different from millions of his subjects in dress, in appearance, in daily life, and in his avocations. He is now an individual among individuals, highly respected, but in and among his people, not a demigod above them. The Emperor is barely mentioned in textbooks.

The new status of the Emperor is the result of the humanization campaign already described. Remnants of the old attitudes undoubtedly survive, particularly among the older and less critically inclined Japanese, but it is safe to say that if the Emperor now enjoys a secure place in the affections of his people, it is the result of choice, freely arrived at. Simply the elimination of the constant indoctrination and pressure—indeed, of the inescapable presence of the symbol of the emperor in daily life—has meant that the individual is no longer subjected to the unremitting demand that he conform, that he bow before the supreme symbol and therefore to all symbols of authority.

The Family

Concrete examples of the new position of the individual in relation to his state have already been observed: the removal from the hands of the police of excessive powers of control and coercion; the creation of a new position for and new attitudes toward civil servants; and the elimination of mass conscription. Another area in which the pressure of authority on the individual has undergone an important degree of relaxation is within the family, with the reduction of the power of the head of the family over its members. Closely allied with this is the slow emergence of the attitude that the rights of the single member must at least be weighed against the demands of the family, if not given precedence over them.

To assess the degree of change in this vital area is much harder than in the case of the Emperor, since overt and observable means for judging it are generally lacking. Although the constitution says nothing about the abolition or even the reduction of the power of the male head of the family, the provisions regarding respect for all people as individuals, equality under the law, marriage based "only on the mutual consent of both sexes," equality of rights of husband and wife—as well as the enactment of laws treating marriage and the family on the basis of "individual dignity and the essential equality of the sexes"—all involved an attack on the concepts of the omnipotent paternal family head and of family supremacy over the individual. Under the family system that prevailed in modern Japan after the fall of the Tokugawas, both concepts were studiously cultivated by the government as the core of an ideal and purely Japanese family system that would serve as the foundation for a national authoritarianism. Subservience to the will of the male head of the family was one basis for unquestioning obedience to the Emperor; primacy of the family over the individual paralleled and reinforced the primacy of the state over its subjects. Thus, to free the individual from the domination of the state required freeing him from the domination of the family.

The constitutional guarantee of freedom of selection of spouse, by opening the way for individual choice, struck a blow at paternal authority. Of course, the result of this has not been complete freedom for all young people to choose their mates, or an elimination of the arranged marriage. What has happened, however, is that a number of young couples do make their own decision to get married and then go to their parents to obtain their consent, after which the traditional form of arranging the marriage by the families through a go-between is observed. The existence of such an alternative means that the will of the paternal head and the requirements of the family are no longer in an unchallengeable position.

The present Civil Code, as amended to conform with the 1947 constitution, does recognize parental authority, but it is to be exercised jointly by the father and the mother. The old Code provided that children had to submit to the will of the father, and that parental authority could be exercised by the mother only if there were no father in the family, in which case she had to obtain the consent of a family council regarding certain matters. The granting of new rights to the wife, in respect to divorce and property particularly, have resulted in a further reduction of the legal powers of the male head of the family.

Primogeniture has been abolished as a result of the constitutional doctrine of the equality of individuals under the law. This has had the consequence of further diluting the authority of the family head. Although children have equal rights under the law to inherit property, the practice has grown up in farm areas of having the oldest son become heir to the family land. The other heirs arrange to surrender their rights in return for financial assistance for higher education or the establishment of small businesses. This has meant that the younger sons have tended to move to the cities and towns and to establish their own households, which are at least removed from the constant physical presence of the head of the family.

Thus, in a number of ways, the individual in his relations with his family enjoys a greater degree of individual freedom, if not complete emancipation from parental authority.

In the public hearings held by the Commission on the Constitution (see Chapter 9), a number of witnesses, old and young, male and female, expressed uneasiness over the impact of the new basic law on the family and even said that a return should be made to at least some of the old customs. But they were unanimously agreed that what should be avoided at all costs was the concentration of authoritarian control in the family head.

The Emancipation of Women

Another development, though quite different in nature, has been the emancipation of women. The foundation for this was a constitutional guarantee against discrimination in political, economic, or social relations on the basis of sex. The constitution also went into specific detail by providing (in Article 24) for new legislation "enacted from the standpoint of individual dignity and the essential equality of the sexes" in respect to such socially and legally important matters as "choice of spouse, property rights, inheritance, choice of domicile, divorce and other matters pertaining to marriage and the family laws."

This constitutional injunction was followed in the revision of the Civil Code, which completed the legal emancipation of women. As a consequence of both the constitutional and legal provisions, there has been a significant shift in women's social position. Although women for the first time were granted equal rights to institute divorce proceedings, the divorce rate has remained low. The largest number of divorces in Japanese history, 83,689 (a rate of 1.0 per 1,000 population), occurred in 1950; in 1957, there were 71,316 divorces (.78 per 1,000). Family planning through the widespread practice of birth-control techniques and the legalization of abortion for eugenic reasons, with a resulting drop in the average number of children per family, are other important indications of a changed role for women.

There has also been a significant widening of educational and professional opportunities for the female sex. Under the previous government, boys and girls studied in the same classroom only through the sixth grade. The entire educational system is now on a coeducational basis, and, although the number of girls and women in institutions of higher learning is still comparatively small, there has been a substantial gain. In 1958, female university students numbered 73,416 out of a total of 578,060 students. In the past, there were no legal barriers against the entry of women into the professions, yet custom kept their number extremely low. While there has been no flood of women into the professions, their number has increased significantly. Numerous articles in major newspapers and magazines by and about professional women are an indication of their new status, as well as of the new importance of the woman's angle in the news.

The granting of the franchise to women has been a matter of immense political moment. Japanese women, although their voting rate has been consistently, but only slightly, lower than that of men, play a major role in elections. The criticism is frequently voiced that as a group they still do not exercise the franchise as free, responsible voters, being unduly influenced by husbands, fathers, and brothers. The charge is undoubtedly well founded, especially in rural areas, but it is also true that they constitute a bloc of voters not to be alienated or ignored by politicians. All political parties have special women's bureaus, and women are put forward as candidates by the major parties.

Indeed, it has been said that no Japanese politician dare campaign against any of the postwar gains made by women. During the intervals between campaigns, it is true, politicians may speak in abstract terms about the desirability of returning to a social order more similar to that existing prior to the surrender. But it is politically unwise, to say the least, to discuss even the possibility of depriving women of any of their specific rights or of returning them to their previous inferior status. The mere existence of an enfranchised female sex is thus not only a political fact of great importance but also a major barrier against a return to the old ways.

Another significant development in regard to women has been the great expansion in the number and nature of women's organizations. Such organizations had been established during the Meiji period, when they fell into two major groupings: first, patriotic or service associations, organized by the government or the military and really mass organizations (especially after the early 1930's) constituting an effective element in the system of authoritarian control; and second, private organizations designed to serve the interests of women's rights but without official support, in some cases without official sanction, and, in any event, under greater and greater restrictions by the government. Currently, there are tens of thousands of organizations with a membership running into the millions. In the mid–1950's, the Ministry of Labor estimated that total membership in women's organizations was more than 10 million, representing 40 per cent of all female voters and half the women in the twenty–fifty age group. There are women's organizations in all the political parties; women's auxiliaries of agricultural cooperatives had an estimated membership of 3 million in the late 1950's; parent-teacher associations, of course, have a large female membership; there are even associations of war widows; and there are such special groups as the YWCA, the WCTU, the Japanese Association of University Women, the Japanese League of Women Voters, and the Women's League for the Protection of Human Rights. Women's organizations, besides attending to their own special concerns, play a prominent part in public affairs. For example, in the controversies over rearmament, the security treaty with the United States, and the attempt in late 1958 to enact legislation extending the powers of the police, women's groups took part in large-scale public demonstrations. Women have also played an effective role of protest in campaigning against such problems as the sudden growth of pornographic weekly magazines, the rise in fares on private suburban railroads, prostitution, and various issues involving schools and juvenile delinquency. The scope of this activity, much of which may have been directed by other organizations (including political parties), demonstrates the tactical desirability of winning the support of women on controversial issues.

Japan's 47.5 million women are not all equally emancipated or enjoying the social, economic, and political benefits of their new status. Undoubtedly a substantial minority are not even fully aware of their new position; undoubtedly, too, the status of millions of women, especially in the country and the economically underprivileged sections of the cities, has undergone no real social or economic change, although the majority may vote regularly and a few may even have recourse to the newly established family courts. Nevertheless, it remains true that in Japan, as in other democracies, a substantial, active, and vocal minority has been able to take advantage of the new rights, has found them good, and is ready and willing to fight for their preservation both as something concrete that they as individuals enjoy and as something abstract that, ideally, their entire sex should share. It is also clear that there is substantial support in public opinion—both male and female—for the preservation and strengthening of the new status of women. It is inconceivable that they can ever be forced back into their position of so-called "feudal inferiority."

The Educational System

If the individual in a democratic society is to enjoy his rights, it is obviously not enough to write his role into the fundamental law of the land or to establish a system of political and social relationships that permits a maximum of potential freedom in his activities. It is also not enough for him simply to enjoy the negative advantage of being free from the coercions and compulsions typical of authoritarian societies. To be truly free in any democratic society, the individual must be able and willing to take advantage of the benefits that democracy bestows on him and to defend them in a responsible manner.

Two institutions in democratic Japan that have contributed and will contribute tremendously to the working out of the new patterns of sociocultural relationships and attitudes are the educational system and the mass-communications media. In the old Japan, both were used to stifle the free development of the individual, and to subordinate him to the demands of the state. Conformity to unchallengeable standards and blind obedience to the orders of the government were the goals of those who controlled the instruments of mass persuasion. Yet, it was these same instruments that were quickly and easily converted to the task of educating the individual in the nature of his new rights and freedoms, his new role in politics and society, and his new responsibilities under democracy.

The part played by education in the creation of democracy in Japan has been of great consequence. Young Japanese today grow up under the democratic constitution. They live under its provisions, whether or not the relationship between daily life and the constitution is fully understood and appreciated by every boy and girl. And they are being taught the meaning not only of the instrument itself but of the freedoms and responsibilities that are its essence. The school system and the mass media, once the tools of indoctrination and propaganda, have been turned to the purposes of education and the free dissemination of information, which are their basic functions under democracy.

The role of universal education in Japanese life in the late 1950's could be measured in gross quantitative terms quite accurately. In 1958, more than 23 million children and young men and women were regularly enrolled as full-time students in Japanese schools on all levels, including almost 675,000 in kindergartens. Primary schools (the first six years) had a total enrollment of 13.5 million, of whom 6.88 million were boys and 6.6 million girls; middle schools (the next three years), a total of 5.2 million, of whom 2.64 million were boys and 2.56 million girls; higher schools (ninth through twelfth years), 3.05 million, with 1.69 million boys and 1.36 million girls. As of May, 1958, total enrollment in universities was 578,060—504,644 men and 73,416 women. A noteworthy fact not revealed in these statistics is that all the grade-school and middle-school students and the great majority of higher-school students had received all their schooling under the postwar system. The great majority of university students had gone through all but the initial years of grade school since the war.

Japan did not have to initiate a campaign of universal education in 1945. Instead, the occupation's job, increasingly taken over by the Japanese themselves, was to reorganize the educational system and to change its content. In the initial, negative stages of the occupation, the principal task was that of censorship—to eliminate all that had been so effectively used in the chauvinistic, ultranationalist propaganda program of authoritarian education. Pages were torn out of books or passages inked out, verbal admonitions were issued simply not to read certain sections of textbooks—such were the procedures of that confused period. There was nothing else to do, if objectives were to be achieved at a time when paper supply and printing facilities were limited. The Japanese soon responded to the challenge of supplying new textbooks. By the mid–1950's, the change in content and appearance of textbooks was amazing. Gone, of course, were the themes of reverence for the Emperor, of the uniqueness of the Japanese nation and its mission, and of the necessity for subservience to authority.

A typical set of primary- and secondary-school textbooks that I have examined reveals what is from the democratic point of view an admirable balance of emphasis on the development of the individual and on his relations with others in the family, in the classroom, and at play. Beginning at the level of the third grade, there is also an introduction to the ideas and institutions of Japan's democracy. In subsequent years, there is consistent emphasis not only on the development of democracy in post–1945 Japan, but on the events in previous Japanese history that prevented the appearance of democracy.

A striking example of the new textbooks is the second volume of a two-volume set for use in the seventh, eighth, and ninth grades entitled *Shakai no Shikumi* (*Social Organization*). The first two-thirds of this volume, "Democracy and Human Rights," is devoted to the problem of democracy. The remaining third deals with daily life and culture, but throughout this section, too, there is a strong current of democratic thought. Of particular relevance to the problem of social change under the new democracy is the manner in which the family is depicted. Not only is the old system (labeled "feudalistic") described in a most unfavorable light, but the new one is described in detail and its contribution to the growth of democracy praised. For example, the old way is shown as one in which the head of the family was all-powerful and those under him had absolutely no independence, while the new system is described as one in which each member has the right to express his thoughts and the whole family discusses its problems together. It is also stressed that although the parents, simply as parents, do not have the right to suppress their children's opinions, the children at the same time cannot, simply because they are free individuals, defy their parents. The textbook also emphasizes the importance of the interrelation between the democratic family and the democratic society. The text was, incidentally, approved for use by the Ministry of Education.

Since the end of the occupation, some Japanese political leaders and government officials have been consistently attempting to turn the clock back by having the government take a more active hand in the supervision of textbooks, their publication and distribution. This development is another manifestation of conservative discontent with both the occupation and at least some features of the democratic society. The leaders of this movement claim that their aim is to restore to the textbooks a fuller treatment of the essentially Japanese aspects of their society and culture. They have been vigorously opposed by many who claim that the real goal of the educational-reform movement is to undermine the new democracy. However much some conservatives may want to change education, especially in regard to social affairs (including the family), it is difficult to see how they can effectively approach what they regard as the ideal in view of the already great changes that have taken place in their society, not to mention what has been happening in the schools.

It is difficult to measure in any meaningful manner the impact of the new educational system on the young people of democratic Japan. However, Professor Kawashima Takeyoshi of Tokyo University, a specialist in legal sociology, made a wise observation on this problem several years after the occupation ended. In the course of a round-table discussion, he and his colleagues turned to the apparent indifference of many young people to what the discussants regarded as the crucially important issue of constitutional revision. Said Professor Kawashima: "We are all extremely sensitive to this problem of constitutional revision, because we lived under the old system and we know what it is not to have the freedoms that we now enjoy under the new constitution. But all young people have really known nothing but freedom. They accept it merely as a matter of course, and how can you expect them to get excited about it?"

The greatest single problem in Japanese education for many years has been the examination system. From about the fifth grade of primary school until entry into a business firm or a profession after graduation from a university, the Japanese student is confronted with a series of difficult entrance examinations. A grade-school pupil must try to pass the entrance examination of a good middle school, because a good middle school will increase his chances of entering a good high school, which in turn will increase his chances of getting into a good university, and, finally, if he is graduated from a good university, his chances will be better of passing an examination for entry into a good business firm, government service, or a profession.

For years, it has been charged that this system undermines the health of the student, produces too much strain on both him and his family, stresses mere memory work, creates too intense competition not only in the classroom but among schools, and places an undue premium on entry into the "right" schools. While admitting the system's weaknesses, this observer at least has come to the conclusion that the method is one solution to the problem of providing the best education for the best-qualified students. Over the decades, it has produced the corps of trained specialists in all fields necessary for the operation of the complex national society that is Japan's; it is currently producing a well-trained group of young men and women who are confronted with the complicated tasks required by an increasingly complex society; and it is providing the training necessary for financially, socially, and psychologically rewarding careers. If the faults of the examination system are ever eliminated, it will be primarily because the problem is a matter of wide public concern.

The Mass Media

The educational system is doing an excellent job of preparing the youth for their responsibilities as citizens of a democracy. But a truly informed citizenry can exist only if the media of mass communications carry out the function, by no means their sole one, of dissemination of the information (news, statements of policy, and discussion of public issues) necessary for the effective operation of the democratic process. The mass media in Japan have been developed to a high degree. In 1959, newspaper circulation totaled about 36.3 million per day, 60 per cent morning and 40 per cent evening. In 1958, there were more than 14.6 million radio sets. By 1961, there were more than 6.5 million television sets, as compared with 52,000 in 1954. In 1958, the slightly more than 7,000 motion-picture theaters had a total attendance for the year of 1.12 billion. In addition, the book and magazine publishing industries are large and flourishing. A further measure of the importance of the mass-communications media is an astonishing literacy rate of more than 98 per cent.

Thus, these media constitute an enormously powerful means for influencing the attitudes of the Japanese people. Their response to the freedom introduced by the occupation and guaranteed by the constitution was spectacularly favorable. The press and the others have played a significant role in the wide dissemination of news, political gossip and speculation, analysis of foreign and domestic policy problems, international affairs, opinion, comment, and even political theory. At the same time, the media have revealed some of the same weaknesses and blemishes present in those of other democracies—sensationalism, bad taste, and other standard ills. However, on balance, the contribution of the communications media to the development and defense of the freedoms that they have found so desirable has been outstanding.

The total process of formal and informal education in a democratic society has several interrelated goals: to train the individual as an individual; to prepare him to contribute to his democratic society; to develop his awareness of his own role as an individual and of the complex social relationships in the framework of democracy; and to contribute to his awareness of the nature of the democratic state and of its relation to him. The formal part of the educational process stresses the training of the individual; the informal part as it is disseminated through the mass media contributes to the store of information that enables him to function effectively as a responsible citizen. The over-all operation of this process in contemporary Japan has been good. In both education and mass communications, the basic freedoms of thought, speech, and expression are present beyond doubt and are being utilized; consequently, the individual has access to that great body of knowledge, information, and opinion that lies at the foundation of his fulfillment as an individual and, in turn, is the proof of the democratic nature of his society.

The Economic Situation

To understand fully the role of the individual in the new democracy, it is also necessary to examine his economic position —not merely his economic rewards and benefits, but the manner in which he is enmeshed in the economic operations of his society, the reciprocal relationship between his contribution to the economy and the returns he receives from it. Such an analysis sheds light on the social activity of the individual, and it is a matter of considerable political importance as well.

Besides the democratic revolution, the most remarkable phenomenon of Japanese society since 1945 has been the amazing economic reconstruction and subsequent development. It has had consequences for practically every aspect of the society and has thus had an important influence on the role of the individual. At the time of the surrender in 1945, Japan's economy was at a virtual standstill: Industrial installations of all types had been destroyed or damaged by bombing; plant shutdown and unemployment automatically followed the end of war production; raw-material shortages and damage to transportation facilities made it difficult to convert to peacetime production; inflation was creating financial havoc; food, clothing, and shelter were in extremely short supply; and foreign trade was nonexistent. Yet, the Japanese had made very substantial progress toward complete recovery by the end of the occupation seven years later, and by 1955, the economy was able to enter into a new and intensive phase of development. Between 1955 and 1960, the country definitely reached what the economists aptly term the age of high mass consumption. During this period, the Japanese gross national product grew at an average annual rate of about 10 per cent. One of the pledges of all political parties during the election campaign of 1960 was to maintain the annual rate of economic growth at not less than 9 per cent during the 1960's.

The effects of this dramatic economic development are to be seen throughout Japanese society, but I shall discuss only those aspects that shed direct light on the economic position of the individual. In terms of variety, nutritive value, and quantity, the Japanese are undoubtedly the best fed of any people in Asia. One effect of economic prosperity on the diet has been a spectacular increase since 1955 in the consumption of milk, butter, cheese, ice cream, and meat, all of which are becoming a standard part of the Japanese diet. Both men and women have abundant clothing for all seasons; in addition, the importance of style indicates not only a catering to fashion and vanity, but also a high level of purchasing power. Although housing remains a difficult problem in the cities, it is no longer a critical one. At the end of the war, the estimated housing shortage was 4.2 million units. By 1957, more than 5.7 million new units (separate houses and apartments) had been constructed; some 470,000 additional units were built that year, and about 500,000 in the following year, but in 1959 it was estimated that there was still a shortage of 1.8 million units, created by the increase in the number of families, and by what in Japan is normal natural disaster. Despite the shortage, the amount of new construction is impressive evidence of the degree of recovery in the vital area of housing.

Beyond having his needs satisfied in these fundamental areas, the individual enjoys many additional benefits. Families generally are able to provide for the education of their children. The public-health program is well developed. Preventive medicine, control of disease and epidemics, and a sound if not perfect program of government-operated medical insurance also contribute to the physical well-being and health needs of the individual. A striking indication of progress not only in the field of public health but also in general living conditions is to be found in the virtual elimination of tuberculosis, a disease in which Japan had one of the world's highest rates prior to World War II.

Economic security and prosperity have also given the Japanese individual the means and the time to enjoy a wide range of recreational activities. The visiting American can only be amazed at the interest in sports and physical activities in Japan. Team sports of all kinds, including baseball, soccer, Rugby, football, basketball, rowing, and track and field, are engaged in by tens of thousands of young—and not so young—people. Tennis, hiking, skiing, table tennis, and the traditional Japanese sports of judo, archery, and fencing are also quite popular—and it should be noted that most of these sports involve individual investment in equipment. The theater, touring, spectator sports, and the pursuit of hobbies—including such traditional ones as flower arrangement, the tea ceremony, and the composition of poetry—all figure prominently in the individual's use of his leisure time. Reading continues to be a major pastime. All these activities demonstrate a high level of economic well-being, provide relief from the tensions of a contemporary industrial society, satisfy the psychological and cultural needs of the individual, and, in addition, provide the opportunity for intellectual stimulation and development.

The foundation of the benefits enjoyed by the individual is an economy that provides virtually full employment. Unemployment amounts to only about 1 per cent of the employable working force. It is true that underemployment is a widespread blemish on the over-all situation. However, the underemployed are able to enjoy incomes that, however limited, still represent purchasing power. Nor has underemployment prevented general economic prosperity. Another fact worth noting is that by the 1960's all university graduates were assured of positions commensurate with their training, thus eliminating a consistent source of personal frustration and potential political discontent. At the same time, the national rate of suicide declined for the first time in years, a fact attributed to the spread of economic prosperity.

All this is not to imply that Japan is an economic paradise for everybody. It is not. There are slums, malnutrition, low wages for long hours of backbreaking labor; there are, in short, the same kinds of individual economic difficulty and suffering that exist everywhere. Yet, the fact remains that Japan's general level of economic well-being is the highest in Asia and compares favorably with that of any industrialized society. It is also true that the Japanese are keenly aware of the economic weak spots in their society and are working to eliminate or to control them.

The political implications of Japan's prosperity must not be overlooked. In a few short years, the Japanese people have come to expect all the material benefits that flow from their economy of mass consumption—not only at the current rate but at an increasing one. It is a matter of both political and economic significance that the major parties in the general election of 1960 pledged themselves to double the national income by 1970. It is clear that one of the main reasons why the conservatives continue to be supported by the majority of the people is that they have been in power during the period of economic upsurge; it is equally clear that in the event of a slump, the party in power is likely to be held responsible.

A New Role for the Individual

We need not dwell on the political aspects of the role of the individual under Japan's democracy. We have already reviewed not only his new rights and freedoms, but also his new relationship with the government. On balance, the Japanese individual has already demonstrated that he is capable of acting as a responsible citizen under democracy. He exercises his right of suffrage; he is interested in controversial issues of both politics and government; he is capable of criticizing political leaders, parties, and procedures; he is vitally concerned with the maintenance of the democratic processes and structure that have given him concrete benefits.

Socially, as we have seen, the individual stands between the old and the new. In his social relations, the family and marriage systems, and the new role of women, the weight of law and popular attitudes is definitely on the side of the new, but the traditional current still runs strong and in a parallel course. The new has certainly not replaced the old, but it is at least in a position to compete on a footing of equality. This is a matter of fundamental social significance, for the mild competition between tradition and innovation in the late nineteenth and early twentieth centuries was rigged in favor of the former, which became one of the strongest features of authoritarianism.

Again, it should be noted that the pressure of authority vested in social institutions has diminished sharply. In Japan, as elsewhere, the individual will never be entirely free of the demands and responsibilities necessarily involved in membership in society.

But in the new Japan, there is a far broader, if not complete, area for individual choice and action in social relations.

Perhaps the most significant aspect of the new role of the individual is that it is accepted by the overwhelming majority of the Japanese people. Only the rare eccentric desires a return to the old system in its entirety. Not even the most reactionary of right-wing societies advocates a renunciation of all the benefits that have been bestowed on the individual, however greatly they may detest the word "individualism." And the left wing, far from rejecting the new, urges that the individual would profit even more if it came to power and would be less likely to lose his new position.

If the general aims and aspirations of the Japanese people can be summarized briefly, it can be said that the chief goal is simply to maintain the democratic order so that the individual may continue to enjoy the social, economic, and political benefits of the peaceful democratic revolution. Only in this way can a return to the old authoritarianism be prevented; only in this way can Japan be kept out of a war that would be destructive of all the new and precious benefits of democracy; and only in this way can the new role of the individual be protected.

7

New Patterns of Japanese Society

We have already observed what a shattering effect the lost war and the occupation had on existing patterns of Japanese society. Besides the new position of the individual, there has emerged a new structure of alignments and relations among social, political, and economic groups. This new structure, perhaps more than any other single factor, has provided a foundation for the democracy built under the artificial and unpromising circumstances of a military occupation.

Dominant groups in the old Japan—the *zaibatsu*, the bureaucracy, and the military—were not completely eliminated by the occupation, though their power and influence were temporarily reduced. Business (not the *zaibatsu*) and the bureaucracy have again become power groups, but their new positions are very different. For one thing, they themselves have been altered. More significantly, other groups, under the spur of the occupation and their own desire for power or the maintenance of a new and meaningful status, have become rivals for control and influence. As we shall see later, the problem was not to create new groups, but to create a general situation in which existing ones were given or enabled to make for themselves new positions of power and influence. With the exception of the military, all groups have gained significantly as a result of the peaceful revolution, and each has found the gains worth defending. The maintenance of balance among these sectors not only lends powerful support to the position of the individual—for, in general, what serves the interests of a group also serves the interests of those who compose it—but is the essence of democratic government and politics.

The Labor Unions

Because of their crucial role in the economy and because the more militant ones have been in the vanguard of every major political controversy, the labor unions are perhaps the most important of the new power groups. The industrial worker was the natural product of the industrialization of Japan, but he was never permitted to organize freely. The government and the *zaibatsu*, fearful of the politically subversive potential and possible economic consequences of labor organization, successfully prevented the development of trade unionism, although some unions were organized. During World War II, those few that had been permitted to survive were dissolved, and a "labor front" on the Nazi model was created.

As one of its early major actions, the occupation fostered a trade-union movement—first, by ordering the Japanese Government to remove all barriers to the formation of unions and then by actively supporting their creation and activity. By mid–1946, this program had moved so rapidly, not only because of the actions of the occupation but even more because of the positive reaction of labor and some segments of political leadership, that there were some 12,000 unions with a total membership of approximately 3.7 million. An early peak in union activity was reached in 1948–49, when there were approximately 34,000 unions with about 6.6 million members. By the mid–1950's, this had declined somewhat to about 31,500 unions with approximately 6 million members, representing about 40 per cent of the eligible labor force—that is, excluding those gainfully employed but in family or other types of small enterprises not suitable for organizing. By mid–1959, however, the decline had been more than made up with some 7 million members (out of a total employable labor force of 43.3 million) in 39,303 unions, placing Japan third (behind only the United States and Great Britain) in trade-union membership in the free world.

The union movement is organized on the basis of enterprises rather than crafts or industries. However, some degree of national organization and even national action is provided by two large federations, the General Council of Japanese Trade Unions (Sohyo) and the Japan Trade Union Congress (Zenro). The former, organized in 1950, is by far the larger, the membership of its constituent unions comprising just over 50 per cent of total union membership in 1959. Almost three-quarters of its membership is composed of government and public workers, including those from government-operated corporations such as the national railways, the national telephone and telegraph system, and the monopoly corporation that includes both a tobacco and a salt monopoly. It leans strongly to the left and is closely associated with the Socialist Party; in fact, it is commonly believed that the party is often only a tool of the union. It has been in the forefront of every controversy that has developed since the end of the occupation, playing a leading role in engineering and leading political strikes and public demonstrations. Zenro, organized in 1954 partly as a counterbalance to Sohyo, has less than a quarter as many members, representing only about 11.5 per cent of the total union membership. It is affiliated with the International Confederation of Free Trade Unions. The nearly 40 per cent of union membership not included in the "big two" consists of a group of much smaller nation-wide federations and a number of independent unions.

Unions have been active not only in areas relating to benefits for workers, but in purely political areas as well. They have consistently and successfully pushed for wage increases, shorter hours, improvement of working conditions, and protection of workers' jobs in certain industries, especially mining, where new techniques or poor competitive positions have led to reductions in the working force. In addition, however, they have staged political strikes, slowdowns on both national and privately operated railways, and mass demonstrations involving political issues.

As has previously been noted, these activities have raised in the minds of many the question of the desirability of a constitutional amendment that would not eliminate or modify the rights of labor to organize, bargain, and act collectively, but would specifically attach to these rights the responsibility of utilizing them without infringement of the public welfare. However, unless there is a decided shift on the part of the unions toward still greater and perhaps more violent involvement in politics or a radical change in the whole political climate away from the present atmosphere of freedom, it does not seem likely that such a modification would result in any significant impairment of the rights of labor.

Some Japanese critics are apprehensive about the close alliance between Sohyo and the Socialist Party. The principal concern is not the party's effect on the union, but vice versa. Excessive dependence on the union organization not only distorts policy on both domestic and foreign issues, many feel, but also tends to blunt the appeal of the party to nonlabor groups, which might prefer to vote for a nonconservative party that does not lean excessively in the direction of a single sector.

If the exercise of its rights and the deep involvement of its most important segment in politics create certain problems for the labor movement, they are also clear manifestations of its strong position in Japanese society in general. Trade unionism is not only an institutional development of considerable importance, but has brought to the fore a large number of new leaders—new in the sense that prior to the end of the war they had no significant role in either labor or society—who play crucial roles outside the union movement and are now members of the new and diffuse power elite. The taste of power that has come simply from the consciousness of numbers and the successful and frequent wielding of the weapon of the strike, the constitutional guarantee of its position, its negotiations with management, the government, and the political parties, and its considerable involvement in politics have all given the union movement and its leaders a strength that is unlikely to be yielded without a struggle.

The Farmers

Another group newly come to prosperity and power is the farmers, the great majority of whom became landowners as a result of the land-reform program, probably one of the most significant features of the entire democratization process under the occupation. Land reform was important in its own right because it created a new economic group with a major political role. And it was the prime example of the successful handling of the problem of the farmer, a problem the magnitude of which, in both economic and political terms, is tremendous all over Asia. The size of the program can be seen in the following figures:

	Total number of farms	*Landed (owning 90%)*	*Landed-tenant (owning 50–90%)*	*Tenant-landed (leasing 50–90%)*	*Tenant*	*Other*
1946	5,697,948	1,869,298	1,127,166	1,061,188	1,637,051	3,245
1950	6,176,390	3,821,531	1,590,582	410,851	312,364	41,062

Thus, in a period of four years, there was an increase of almost 2 million in the number of farmers who owned their own land and of more than 460,000 of those who owned at least half the land they tilled. More than 40 per cent of the total number of farms was involved in this substantial upward revision of the number of land-owning families. By 1955, there had been a significant increase in the number of landowners, the figures being 4.2 million owners, 1.3 million owner-tenants, 284,000 tenant-owners, and only 239,000 tenants.

But land ownership is only one indicator of the general prosperity of the Japanese farmer—a prosperity unprecedented in Japanese history and unmatched in the rest of Asia. In the initial postwar period, and for some time thereafter, the Japanese farmer was undoubtedly in the soundest economic position of any group. The reason was simple: Japan was confronted with a serious food shortage; the farmer produced the food; a flourishing black market developed; and the result was a great increase in cash income for farmers. But even in that semi-emergency situation, other developments were beginning in both the economy generally and agriculture itself that were to have a striking effect on the farmer's position. The phase of general economic reconstruction and recovery was completed by about the mid–1950's, and simultaneously Japan began to enter into its period of rapid and sustained economic growth. This alone gave the farmer a new and more stable prosperity. But the farmer was not the passive beneficiary of this development. Farm productivity reached record high levels; farm income increased; land ownership expanded;

mechanization in the form of small machinery spread rapidly; the use of chemical fertilizers increased; crop diversification was developed; and new scientific advances in disease and insect control, seed improvement, and growing techniques appeared. Many of these were the result of the general prosperity of the farmer, but they contributed in turn to the growth of that prosperity.

Economic well-being has been accompanied by notable social developments. The farmer has been able to purchase more and more consumer goods, with the result that his life has already begun to undergo considerable change. In 1960, it was estimated, for example, that 10 per cent of farm families owned television sets, slightly fewer had electric washing machines, and almost 25 per cent had electric, gas, or kerosene stoves for cooking. Even these figures indicate that old-fashioned frugality and thrift are no longer necessary virtues of the Japanese farmer. Factors such as the increasing use of farm machinery, greater demands for labor in the expanding industrial sector of the economy, and more opportunities for jobs of all kinds in the cities (as a result of general economic expansion) have resulted in an accelerated flow of the people from the land. In 1960, the average number of persons per farm household was 5.7, as compared with 6.1 in 1950; and in 1959, only about a third of the total work force was in agriculture and fisheries, as compared with about 45 per cent in 1950. Naturally, a part of the percentage decline is to be explained by the rapid increase in the total number of employed during the decade, but the trend away from the land is unmistakable.

In spite of these significant social changes on the farm, it is still true that traditional attitudes toward such elements as the structure of the family, marriage, and the role of women have undergone less modification in the rural areas than in the cities. But change there has been. Satisfaction of hunger for land, optimum conditions (within the Japanese framework) for the pursuit of his occupation, an income sufficient not only to satisfy basic needs but to provide for extras in consumer goods, recreation, and education, and relatively traditional views on social matters have kept the Japanese farmer politically conservative. The voting in the countryside has been consistently and overwhelmingly in favor of conservative candidates. Only in a few isolated, unimportant areas have either the socialists or Communists demonstrated any vote-getting appeal for farmers, who have had no reason to want a change since the democratic revolution and subsequent developments have indeed favored him.

Yet, well off as he is in comparison with his own quite recent past and his fellows in the rest of Asia, the Japanese farmer does not live in an economic paradise. Despite the increased use of light machinery, he and his family must spend many hours of backbreaking labor in the fields. Many farmers must still supplement their incomes with other activities such as forestry, fishing, or work in neighboring towns or cities. But the great and insoluble problem of Japanese agriculture is the limited extent of the area of land available for cultivation, a situation perhaps most dramatically summarized by the fact that the average size of the Japanese farm is just over two acres. It is on such garden plots that the prosperity of the farmer rests. This is not a new problem, but a geographical fact that has always been with the country.

The farmer in Japan has never been the forgotten man that his counterparts in Asia have been. Since the end of feudalism in the early 1870's made possible for the first time in Japanese history the outright ownership of land by the individual farmer, the government has been interested in agricultural problems, even though it did not begin to work effectively on them until the postwar period. For some time, there had been government-sponsored experimentation to increase the yield of the land through such devices as development of better seed, more efficient utilization of land, crop rotation, and disease and pest control. During the 1920's and the 1930's, the economic plight of the farmer was a matter of serious concern to the government, though this concern was manifested more in an awareness than in any dynamic program. Governmental interest in agriculture and its problems has probably increased since 1945 because of the new importance of the farmer's political role. Thus, the economic problems of the farmer are not likely to be permitted to develop to the point where they will begin to have adverse effects on his political attitudes.

Big Business

A third economic group—much smaller than either labor or the farmers, but more influential than either—is one that might now be called "big business." Its position vis-à-vis the democratic revolution was somewhat ambiguous. At least initially, business suffered rather than benefited from the occupation, but it later emerged in a position of great influence. Under discussion here are the large firms and business organizations that operate in such diverse areas as heavy industry, electronics, precision instruments, banking, insurance, retailing (especially large department stores), electric power, petroleum, and shipping. These firms, sometimes huge, dominate their fields, so that many medium-sized and small enterprises are directly or indirectly dependent on them, which in turn increases the significance of their role.

At first glance, these large firms are reminiscent of the vanished *zaibatsu*, against which the occupation acted rapidly and with such apparent success. By the summer of 1949, General Mac-Arthur was able to announce that the program of dissolution had been completed and that the *zaibatsu* power had been broken forever. Yet, immediately after the occupation, the old *zaibatsu* firms and firm names began to be revived, and many people who had been removed from key positions began to return to new leadership and influence in Japan's business life. These developments, plus the size and wealth of the new big-business firms, have created the illusion of a return of the *zaibatsu* to power.

As has been pointed out earlier, the occupation did not liquidate all the key executives in the *zaibatsu* firms and did not destroy the system of capitalistic enterprise under which the combines had developed. The program followed by the occupation can be equated in its essentials with the "trust-busting" during the late nineteenth century and the New Deal legislation of the 1930's, which affected the position of big business in the United States. What happened in both countries was that certain large economic combines were eliminated or modified and that laws designed either to prevent their redevelopment or to keep their activities within certain limits were enacted; there was no attempt to create an economic system that in itself would prevent the development of a system of free capitalistic enterprise, characterized by very large economic organizations with great but not overwhelming privilege and power.

Certainly, the large corporations and their officers enjoy sizable profits and wield great influence, but they do not dominate the economy and control politics to the extent that the *zaibatsu* did at their height in the 1930's. Their economic development since 1952 has indeed given them a great stake in the new and democratic Japan; being a part of it, they necessarily cannot operate as the *zaibatsu* did.

In the first place, ownership and consequently profits are not narrowly controlled, as under the old system. By 1960, it was estimated by the government that more than 9 million Japanese owned more than 9.75 billion shares of stock in Japanese firms. Obviously, many held only a few shares. It was equally obvious that such wide ownership did not mean democratic control of the policies or operations of big business. What it did mean, however, was the absence of narrow control or narrowly enjoyed and excessive profits, as well as a general level of economic well-being that permitted widespread, small-scale investment.

Perhaps the most telling feature of the position of big business in Japan today is that it is confronted with the challenge of both labor and the farmer, a situation with which the *zaibatsu* never had to contend. The unions have their own position to protect and can stand as the spokesmen of labor. The farmer's economic position parallels that of business. Indeed, both industry and agriculture have a decided interest in maintaining the status quo, for both have profited very considerably from it. Naturally, the conservative bent of the farmer in political affairs coincides to a considerable degree with the attitude of the businessman.

Personal and corporate wealth, access to cabinet posts, an intimate working relationship with the conservative parties that have dominated the government, close relations with the government itself, and identification with all Japanese economic activities combine to make business extremely influential in Japanese democracy. Either of two possible developments could change drastically its role in government and politics. Its clear and unchallenged advent to power might put the Socialist Party in a position to attempt to realize its announced policy of eliminating capitalism. On the other hand, a complete shift of the political situation to the extreme right, as a result of domestic economic difficulties, would encourage the development of authoritarian economic and political devices conducive to the reconversion of big business into the old *zaibatsu*.

The Intellectuals

Another group, of a completely different nature, is the intellectuals, who enjoy a position of prestige and influence in the new society. The intellectual may be a professor or an analyst of economic, political, diplomatic, social, or world affairs, an artist or a writer, a teacher or a journalist, a bureaucrat or even a professional man. In any of these capacities, he is likely to speak to or write for a considerable public. As a communicator of information or ideas, he plays one of the classical roles of the intellectual in any society—that of molder of public opinion. He may also, of course, be simply a follower of those who are more given to public expression of their views; the intellectuals in this substratum, which supports the more active top level of leadership, are a not inconsiderable group in Japan.

The market for ideas is a broad one indeed. Books, newspapers, magazine articles, radio and television appearances, round-table discussions on radio and television and even in printed form, public speeches and conventional interviews—all these constitute a broad and continuous outlet for the opinions of intellectuals and, for the best at least, a source of considerable income. Some intellectuals may be no more than propagandists for a cause; some may seem so busy being intellectuals that they have no time for reflection; but many deal in the currency of thoughtful criticism of events, trends, and views that contributes significantly to the national understanding of domestic and foreign affairs.

The special position and the powerful influence of the intellectual in the new democracy are rooted in the history of his role in modern Japanese society, in his fierce commitment to the defense of the freedoms and rights brought by the democratic revolution, and in his important function as critic and analyst of contemporary society. The intellectual appeared on the scene early in modern Japan. Beginning in the 1870's with the establishment of the educational system and the first forms of mass communications, intellectuals made their mark on the country. At that time, they were closely identified with the process of modernization, although some of them defended the traditional aspects of the new nation. The modern, progressive intellectual reached the peak of his influence during the 1920's. However, with the rise of militarism and authoritarianism, the group naturally began to go into eclipse, partly because it was overwhelmed by the men of action—the militarists and their chauvinistic civilian supporters, who pushed the thinkers, talkers, and writers into the background —but even more because, officially and unofficially, a program of suppression was instituted against them. The intelligentsia became the highly suspect object of a campaign of calculated persecution. They were made to appear, as indeed they were, the supporters of things Western, democratic, and liberal, and consequently opposed to everything that the men of action regarded as worth while in the Japanese tradition, the theme of the propaganda and indoctrination of the ultranationalists.

Despite the government's repressive measures, the intellectuals were not liquidated, although they were thrust into obscurity. Many of them, of course, did accept—some sincerely and some as a matter of protective coloration—the new policies and slogans as well as what passed for the ideas of authoritarian Japan. But with the new freedoms brought by the occupation, it took the intellectuals very little time to begin to function as important contributing members of the democracy. By and large, it is they who have been the most vociferous defenders of democracy and the bitterest opponents of all the moves, such as rearmament and the re-establishment of a degree of governmental control over the police, that have smacked of retrogression to the predemocratic era. Their major contribution has naturally been in the area of public discussion.

As has already been abundantly demonstrated by the intellectuals themselves, they constitute a major obstacle to a return to the old order. Only by a complete denial of all rights and freedoms could the voice of the intellectual be stilled and his powerful influence in Japanese society eliminated. Perhaps only a small minority of this group would ever man the barricades in the defense of democracy. But they will continue to provide the ammunition of opinion, discussion, and controversy indispensable to the constant, bloodless political warfare that is the essence of any viable system of democracy.

The fundamental weakness of the former position of the intelligentsia was that, as critics of the existing order, their aim was to establish a Japan that never was, one that would have been non-Japanese, for it would have been cast in a liberal mold. As un-Japanese utopians, they were unable to command a hearing or to win effective support, so their position remained weak and vulnerable. The fundamental strength of the new intellectuals is that, as the nurturers of the new democracy, they are operating in an environment that supports them as much as they support it. Certainly, they find themselves consistently standing together on most issues with the other groups—women, the unions, the farmers—who have gained from some aspect of the new system and wish to retain their gains.

The Bureaucracy

The bureaucracy, like the *zaibatsu*, was a target of the occupation, but it managed to survive the democratic revolution. The bureaucrats even retained for themselves a position of major governmental influence—remaining the core of the executive branch, despite their constitutional subordination to the Diet. But, again like the *zaibatsu*, their new position is significantly different.

One of the reasons for the rapid development of a modern government in the Japan of the late nineteenth century was the creation of a modern bureaucracy. By definition, this consisted of a corps of trained civil servants skilled in such activities as policy planning, budget compilation, management of fiscal matters, intragovernmental and public liaison, general technical and scientific matters involved in governmental operations, and all those items that can be lumped together under the term "red tape." The skills of the bureaucrat are as unique and carefully defined as those of any other specialist in a modern society. It is through the possession and the utilization of these bureaucratic skills that the essentially neutral character of the profession and its practices arises.

However, the impersonal nature of the modern bureaucracy cannot exist in a vacuum. Being a part of government, a bureaucracy necessarily becomes involved in politics, but, because of its professional and impersonal character, its role is more that of a tool than an independent force. It is its function to operate the government, but under the control, direct or indirect, of those leaders, parties, or factions actually wielding political power. These considerations governed the role of the Japanese bureaucracy until 1945.

Though subordinated to the military, the old bureaucracy became a power group, the reasons being its extremely close-knit and internally well-disciplined character, the concentration of authority in the strong executive branch of the government, and the bureaucracy's automatic and willing association with the military on its advent to a dominant position in the 1930's. The key role of the bureaucracy in the old authoritarianism was clearly exemplified by its control over the police and educational systems.

The occupation concentrated on blunting the power of this faction, but, far from destroying it, worked closely with it as the only instrument by which Japan could be governed effectively. However, with the support of many Japanese, including some bureaucrats, the occupation did restrict the bureaucracy by various legal and other devices. For example, a new and detailed civil-service law, which served as the foundation for the new bureaucracy, broke down the exclusive character of the old system. Wider eligibility for entrance examinations, new standards for promotion, and more emphasis on technical knowledge and training in nonadministrative matters have operated to provide officialdom with a broader base in society. The constitution, moreover, has surrounded the bureaucracy with checks that it never knew before: the doctrine of legislative supremacy, budgetary control in the Diet, and the subordination of public officials to the people. And as a result of the arrogance and arbitrariness of the former officials, a public distrust is constantly manifested in an attitude of suspicion toward the group and toward any move designed to return it to its old power position.

The bureaucracy and its members have, however, extended their area of governmental and political influence beyond the normal boundaries of their regular activities. We have already observed how their influence on the National Diet has been brought to bear both through the committee system and through the highly important process of the drafting of legislation, in the ministries themselves as well as in the influential Cabinet Bureau of Legislation. In addition, a high percentage of Diet members have entered politics from positions in the bureaucracy. Here, according to many observers, is a dangerous infiltration of the "supreme organ of state power" by persons who are supposed to be servants of the people. The first phenomenon is an inevitable consequence of the importance of the role of the executive in any contemporary government. And though the other potentiality remains, it is also true that there is no real evidence of the domination of the Diet by the bureaucracy. As a matter of fact, as we shall see later, the Diet has succeeded in imposing its will on the bureaucracy in several important tests of strength. Whether or not the infiltration of the Diet by ex-bureaucrats has a deleterious effect on legislative supremacy depends on the degree of transformation resulting from the shift of status involved. Certainly, what a politician must do to accede to and maintain himself in power is considerably different from what a bureaucrat must do; it is equally certain that there is a substantial difference between the two activities. These differences alone could significantly affect the ex-bureaucrat turned politician, even though he might retain a full measure of sympathy for the group from which he sprang.

For reasons relating to its nature and functions and to the influence it has been able to extend into other areas, the bureaucracy is still strong, but its old power of direct control over the daily lives of the people seems safely eliminated. Such power as the bureaucrats have derives from their role as operators of the executive machinery of a government, which, far from directing the lives of the people, is positively enjoined to act for their good and is prohibited from exercising nondemocratic controls over them.

The New Military Establishment

The new Japanese military establishment is in no position to dominate or even to influence government and politics. Weak in numbers, arms, and equipment, it is hedged about with legal and constitutional restrictions that seem to stand as insuperable barriers between it and power. Indeed, what is perhaps the greatest single deterrent to a return to power by the military is the combination of international strategic and political factors that render future Japanese aggression and a consequent domestic resurgence of militarism virtual impossibilities.

In the first place, the great strategic lesson of World War II for Japan was that it is no longer possible for the country to develop and maintain the type of massive military machine that is required for contemporary offensive war and that would also be the only kind that would have the potential to dominate domestic government and politics. A supplementary factor of great significance is that Japan, in complete contrast with its earlier strategic situation, is now surrounded by countries possessed of military capacities that make any thought of Japanese offensive action highly unrealistic. It would be national suicide for Japan to undertake an attack against the Soviet Union, though such an attack was certainly a possibility between the early 1930's and the early 1940's. Communist China, no matter how much it may still lag behind the two great military powers, possesses a capability that completely eliminates the possibility of a renewed invasion from Japan. The two Koreas, Taiwan, and the Philippines—to mention only those nations within possible striking distance of Japan—however limited their own domestic military potential may be, have military establishments backed by one or the other of the great powers. Furthermore, the United Nations has demonstrated its ability to handle limited military ventures and could undoubtedly apply sufficient pressure, political if not military, to prevent Japan's recourse to force in its relations with its smaller neighbors.

The final factor standing between the new defense establishment and political power is the great popular revulsion against war and militarism in any form. This attitude is certainly one of the most important facts of Japanese politics and foreign policy. The enormous destruction, devastation, and dislocation resulting from the great fire raids and the atomic bombs were only the fiery climax of a process that had started in 1931. The ultimate conflagration into which the old imperial military establishment drove the people brought with it a terrible material toll matched by the less visible but perhaps more enduring burden of personal suffering accompanied by emotional shock. Thus, no one paused to regret the collapse and elimination of the old military establishment and the tradition on which it was founded, and virtually all Japanese have found something good in the democratic order that has been built on the ruins left by the old regime. All politically conscious Japanese are alert to the danger of a resurgence in government, in politics, or in society of any military organization that might simultaneously mean a return to a hated past and the loss of a cherished present. Such a state of alertness and such an atmosphere of public sentiment are not guarantees against a rebirth of militarism, but they do mean that no Japanese public, now spearheaded by militant political groups and organizations, will be brought unknowingly under a new form of militaristic subjugation.

Japan's new defense establishment does not have the support of an honored tradition or of a spectacular victory; it is isolated from the seat of executive power in the cabinet; budgetary and organizational limitations close its way to the development of influence inside the government; it cannot embark on a new and independent policy of overseas aggression because of the nearby existence of strong external military forces; it has no prestige or propaganda appeal comparable to that of its imperial predecessor; and it is surrounded by a solid triple wall of public indifference, antipathy, and suspicion. Consequently, it is not surprising that it has no policy, program, or discernible aspirations for either external aggression or internal political power. It is safe to predict that this group will remain a servant of the state and of the people, and that it could again become the master of its society only if there were massive changes in conditions both inside and outside the country.

The Problem of Leadership

Discussion of these various groups inevitably raises the question of leadership. Perhaps the two outstanding characteristics of Japan's leadership corps since 1945 have been, first, the absence of men and women likely to go down in history as great leaders and, second, the small army of lesser leaders, ranging from competent to brilliant, who have contributed greatly to their society by providing the skill, the intelligence, and the knowledge necessary to build the new democracy and give it sound and effective guidance. And this situation, rather than representing any defect, can be considered another telling indication of the nature of Japanese society and its readiness for the democratic revolution.

Certainly, one of the more striking features of the new Japan is the absence of figures who will be remembered as either the architects or the symbols of the democratic revolution. This fact, of interest in itself, gains by contrast with the earlier Japanese crisis, that of the emergence of the modern national society, when great leaders abounded. One searches in vain in the first years of Japanese democracy for names to match those of the great leaders of Meiji Japan: Ito Hirobumi, the principal drafter of the Meiji constitution and the man responsible for the greatest number of governmental and political reforms; Fukuzawa Yukichi, who made perhaps the greatest contribution to the introduction of Western thought into his country; Shibusawa Eiichi and Iwasaki Yataro, two of the great business leaders; and, of course, such military men as Admiral Togo Heihachiro and General Yamagata Aritomo.

Pallid indeed, by contrast, are such postwar figures as Yoshida Shigeru, even though history may establish him as the leading political figure of the period; Katayama Tetsu, the first Christian and socialist prime minister in Japanese history; Hatoyama Ichiro and Kishi Nobusuke, the political successors of Mr. Yoshida; Nosaka Sanzo, the astute leader of the Communist Party; and Shidehara Kijuro, prime minister during the crucial initial months of the occupation. Hirohito cannot be ranked as a great leader, significant as his symbolic and psychological contribution to the new Japan has been. These and others less in the limelight—such as Professor Yukawa Hideo (the physicist and Japan's first Nobel Prize winner), Dr. Tanaka Kotaro (chief justice of the Supreme Court and later a judge of the International Court of Justice), and Professor Miyazawa Toshiyoshi (the constitutional theorist) —are leaders who have made positive contributions to their country, but they are certainly not to be ranked with their predecessors, who truly built the modern Japanese nation.

Yet, the lack of giants has proved no handicap to Japan. The task of leadership was assumed by the large number of thoroughly competent men and women who had been trained by having been the products as well as the activating forces of the modern national society. These people became the leaders in the new government, political parties, judicial and legal systems, business organizations, unions, farm organizations, educational system, and mass-communications media—all the groups and organizations that not only built but operated the new democracy. It was these men and women also who—as beneficiaries of the system of universal education and of all the professions that had contributed to the operation of Japan as a going national society in earlier decades—found freedom desirable not only for themselves but for their society. Their numbers, their high level of competence, their reaction to the democratic revolution, and their devotion to individual and social goals combined to make them into an amazingly effective corps.

The overpowering weight of the occupation and the nature of the general response to it were undoubtedly the two factors that had the greatest inhibiting effect on the appearance of great leaders. In the first place, and this is fundamental, occupation policy and action dealt with every issue that might have served as an opportunity for a Japanese to assume a position as a great leader: land reform, emancipation of women, the labor movement, the guarantee of freedoms, the elimination of the hated military leadership and its chauvinistic supporters, the revival of political parties, and the opening of new cultural windows to the outside world. In a very real sense, no Japanese, however prominent, could help becoming a follower of the occupation. In addition, the swift implementation of reforms meant that even after the occupation there was precious little to fight for in order to bring them into existence. Even the struggle to defend the new democracy has not required enough vigor to call forth great leadership.

A specific act of the occupation that had a considerable but temporary effect on the leadership corps was the purge. It resulted in the removal from public life of some 200,000 individuals (the majority of them career military men) who had been ultranationalist, authoritarian leaders in governmental, political, economic, and propaganda activities between 1931 and 1945. But the purgees were not liquidated, imprisoned, or ostracized. As a matter of fact, all were depurged by the end of the occupation, and a number have regained positions of influence because of their demonstrated capacity for leadership. Many Japanese intellectuals regard such depurgees, now returned to power, as perhaps the greatest single threat to the new democracy. But it seems unlikely (for a number of reasons that will be discussed later) that they will ever be able to turn the clock back. There is also the fact that most of the depurgees, especially those who held high positions prior to 1945, are being rapidly overtaken by age.

The political leaders most prominent during the 1945–60 period were Yoshida Shigeru and Kishi Nobusuke, two prime ministers who dominated government and politics during their tenures in power. But these men, vastly different in character and in achievement, both lack those qualities or records of achievement likely to make them loom large in history.

Mr. Yoshida emerged into prominence soon after the surrender. As a career diplomat, he had risen to the key post of Ambassador to Great Britain between 1936 and 1939, but had then gone into retirement and eventually been placed under arrest in June, 1945, for allegedly attempting to open negotiations for peace through the British Government. Because of his diplomatic career, his noninvolvement in the wartime government, and his arrest, he was regarded by the occupation as free from aggressive or authoritarian taint and thus eligible for a high position. He was appointed to the first postwar cabinet and became prime minister in May, 1946. He remained a dominant political figure until his retirement from the office in December, 1954. His five appointments to the prime-ministership during the eight-year period constitute a record. He held office for seven of the eight and a half years between his first appointment and his final resignation, being out of office only during the shaky socialist coalition cabinet in 1947 and the even more shaky coalition cabinet that succeeded it briefly. His political leadership was built on his control of a key office and his astute maneuvering as the head of the former Liberal Party.

He will not live in Japanese history as a great prime minister, if greatness is to be measured in terms of eloquence as the spokesman of the new democracy, positive contributions to the construction of the new order, or a role as charismatic leader of the new society. His achievement was one that does not lead to greatness: the administration of the affairs of his country during the difficult and abnormal period of a foreign occupation and again in the two post-occupation years, when the hand of the occupation in domestic and foreign affairs was still heavy, even though the country had become independent and sovereign. As the occupation was responsible for his access to power, so it was also responsible, at least in part, for his fall. The circumstances of his tenure of office made him the all-too-natural target for the charge that he was merely an occupation puppet.

Yoshida was never accepted by the people as a true leader. His constituents elected him to the National Diet, and the members of his party in the Diet elected him to the prime-ministership, but he never became truly admired or respected by the people. This stemmed partly from his own personality. A popular appellation for him was "Mr. One Man," reflecting his arbitrary actions within party and cabinet and his disregard of public criticism of his policies and actions. He relied on his control over his party and cabinet to keep himself in power, not on the creation of either a real or a synthetic appeal to the masses. Another factor in his fall was purely political. His hold on power was finally shaken by a long-continuing struggle for mastery over his own party, to say nothing of an incessant series of attacks from his political opponents—a rival faction of his own party that split away and operated as a separate party, the socialists, and the Communists. The result was a resounding defeat for his party in the general election of 1955.

Of a far different stripe was Mr. Kishi. A career bureaucrat, he became a key leader in the economic development—or exploitation—of Manchuria under the Japanese military. He became Minister of Commerce and Industry in the first Tojo cabinet (which was in office when Pearl Harbor was attacked) and remained in it until it fell in July, 1944. He was then out of public life until the surrender. Early in the occupation, he was arrested as a suspected Class A war criminal—one who had plotted and executed Japanese aggression—but was released late in 1948 without trial after having been imprisoned for more than three years. However, he was still a purgee. With the end of the occupation, he entered politics. It is a measure of his political astuteness that within less than five years he had risen to a dominant position in his own party, won a seat in the Diet, and been elected to the high post of prime minister—despite the obvious handicap of his wartime record.

His three and a half years in office were the stormiest of any prime minister's in Japanese history. Most of his difficulties were created by himself; yet, he surmounted them all until the final one. In the fall of 1958, for example, he sponsored a bill—poorly drafted, politically unwise, and apparently unnecessary—that called for the granting of increases of power to the police to assist them in the execution of their duties, but also might have resulted in a revival of some of the abuses of the old police system. This touched off a major controversy that resulted in the withdrawal of the bill. The controversy would have toppled a less skillful and determined politician. Kishi survived. A few weeks later, he was the center of a bitter battle within his own party over its presidency. Again he won, although his position was indeed difficult. Finally, there was the titanic struggle over a new security treaty with the United States, for which he won ratification but at the cost of his own fall from power. His downfall was not lamented. Whatever claim to political skill he may have gained by his previous adroit maneuvering was emphatically cancelled by his grave miscalculations in the late spring of 1960, which seemingly, in addition to ending his career as a major political figure, produced a grave crisis in parliamentary government. The storms that he created in Japanese politics will guarantee Kishi a place in the history books, but it will not be that of a great leader.

The Balance Among Groups

Each of the groups discussed in this chapter, with the exception of the military, has gained something as a result of the democratic revolution and wishes to maintain for itself and its constituent members the position presently enjoyed. There is also a rough balance among these groups, in the sense that no single one or combination is in a position effectively to subjugate or to deprive any other group of its position. It may be true, as many Japanese assert, that singly or together business and bureaucracy constitute the real power centers and the greatest threat to the new democracy. But only the most purblind of critics or the most biased political partisan would argue that the two are operating in the kind of political, social, and economic environment that supported their predecessors.

It should be noted at this point that in Japan's democracy, as in others, control over the instruments of force is not the key political problem it is in authoritarian states. Government utilization of the police in the disturbances of 1960 did not result in political oppression. No parties were driven underground or disbanded. Resort was not made to the terror typical of authoritarian states. The police did not use firearms to clear the streets. An atmosphere of fear and oppression did not fall heavily over Tokyo once the violence had come to an end. The military establishment was kept completely out of the picture. In a larger crisis, one of an order destructive of democracy itself, force would indeed become a true political factor. But it did not in this period of lesser strain and seems unlikely to in the future.

In the final analysis, the general state of Japanese society is such that the interests of all the groups can best be served by its continuance along present lines. Economic prosperity is certainly a major contributing factor not only to the satisfaction of individual needs and desires but also for the maintenance of the generally high level of stability that permits both the individual and collective economic interests of the society to be served. The structure of government and of governmental relationships denies to no group the opportunity to make its desires known. The general atmosphere of freedom permits the kind of open discussion that leads to the peaceful resolution of conflicts of interest among the constituent groups of Japanese society. There are no potentially divisive social issues involving the family, individuals, groups, attitudes, or activities likely to produce group antagonism. This is not the picture of an ideal society; it is a sketch of an operative democracy.

8

Political Parties and Elections

The series of free elections between 1946 and 1960 demonstrate the degree to which the Japanese people have utilized the political rights and discharged the political responsibilities that are theirs under the principle of popular sovereignty, fundamental to the 1947 constitution. In all elections, a substantial majority of the eligible voters, both men and women, have consistently exercised the right of suffrage, giving no sign of the voter apathy regarded as a sign of weakness in other modern democracies. As voters have been free to cast their ballots, so have candidates been free to campaign as they wish. The elections have also shown that the political party, one of the foundations of a system of free elections, is a firmly established institution, although it has become clear that the country by no means has a stable two-party system, a highly desirable element in the effective operation of responsible government.

To what extent did the Japanese electorate choose to exercise its suffrage in the postwar elections? What were the over-all patterns of balloting? What have these elections demonstrated in terms of the political behavior, if not the political motivations, of the Japanese people? For what do the principal parties stand? What are the bases of support of the parties? These are the questions to which we shall address ourselves now.

Election Patterns

The Japanese electorate had an opportunity in thirteen national elections between 1946 and 1960 to go to the polls. Eight of them were general elections for the House of Representatives, held in 1946, 1947, 1949, 1952, 1953, 1955, 1958, and 1960; the other five were for the House of Councillors, in 1947, 1950, 1953, 1956, and 1959. Five of them were held under the occupation, and eight after it came to an end. All of them demonstrated unmistakably that Japan had a responsive and responsible electorate.

The general elections for the lower house consistently command more attention than those for the upper house, reflecting the constitutionally superior position of the former. Of five elections for the upper house, only one—in 1950, when 72.1 per cent of the eligible voters went to the polls—had a turnout comparable to those for the general elections. In 1947, 60.9 per cent of the voters turned out; in 1953, 63.1 per cent; and in 1956, 62.1 per cent. The record low came in 1959, when the voter turnout was only 58.7 per cent. By contrast, in only one general election did the percentage of eligible voters going to the polls fall below 70 per cent—in 1947, when only 68 per cent voted. In the other general elections, the turnout ranged from 72 per cent in 1946 to 76.9 per cent in 1958, the average being about 74 per cent.

It is impossible to make any meaningful comparisons between the prewar and postwar statistics because women were not entitled to vote prior to the occupation. In 1925, universal male suffrage was established for the first time, and in the six general elections held between 1928 and 1942 the voting turnout ranged from a low of 73.4 per cent in 1937 to a high of 83.2 per cent in the wartime year of 1942. Thus, it is possible to make one comparison between prewar and postwar patterns: The percentage of male voters in the postwar elections has run only slightly below the prewar figures. The over-all proportion of voters out of those eligible in the postwar figures has run lower than the prewar one, mainly because more women than men have abstained from voting. In the postwar years, the lowest percentage of male voters was 74.87 in 1947, and the highest was 80.74 in 1949. Comparable figures for female voters were 61.6 in 1947 and 72.76 in 1952.

The high percentage of voter participation in the postwar elections can be explained by a combination of factors. Elections had been an established part of Japanese political activity since 1890. The high rate of literacy made it easy for the Japanese to respond to the massive election publicity and the vigorous campaigns waged by the candidates. The contribution of the mass media to the growth of free elections cannot be overestimated. All the great metropolitan dailies and their smaller regional counterparts—as well as the radio, newsreels, magazines, and television—devote a major portion of their attention to the issues and the men involved in the campaigns. Not only are the elections themselves emphasized, but the importance of clean elections is given equal attention. Another striking feature of the press handling of elections is the detailed analyses of the results that are published.

Postwar Japanese elections have been truly free. The government and the police no longer control the administration of elections or influence the results as under the old system. There are no restrictions on the freedom of the press or of the candidates to express their views, to discuss issues, and to make whatever appeals they wish to the voters. As will be discussed below, the one time when the likelihood of official intervention seemed greatest, in 1955, it failed to materialize.

Corruption in such forms as vote buying, excessive expenditures, and excessive contributions from individuals or business firms has been present in postwar elections, but has shown no sign of getting out of hand. Offenders have been arrested, if not in all cases prosecuted with commendable zeal. Public awareness of the problem and extensive publicity on the theme of clean elections are curbs on corruption. It should be noted here that statistics on election-law violations provide no measure of corruption, for the law covers such matters as the size of posters and the number approved, prohibition of house-to-house canvassing, and post-election courtesy calls. In any event, the experience of Western societies has demonstrated that not corruption but official control and manipulation are the great dangers to free elections.

Since the first general election in 1946, popular voting has followed a consistent pattern—a slowly declining majority voting for the candidates of a succession of conservative parties, a slowly increasing minority voting for socialist candidates, and a very small minority consistently voting Communist. Minor parties and independents have not played an important role except in the abnormal election of 1946, when the chaotic conditions of the early postwar and occupation period and the fact that it was the first free election based on universal suffrage created confusion. Minor-party and independent candidates then polled almost a third of the popular vote, with minor-party candidates obtaining 11.7 per cent and independents 20.4 per cent. In subsequent general elections, minor-party candidates (excluding Communists) achieved 5.4 per cent in 1947, followed by a high of 7.1 per cent in 1949; since then, however, they have been a negligible factor, with percentages of 2.7 in 1952, only 0.4 in 1953, 1.4 in 1955, 0.7 in 1958, and only 0.36 in 1960. Independents have never approached their high of 1946, falling to 5.7 per cent in 1947 and subsequently receiving percentages of 6.5 in 1949, 6.7 in 1952, 4.4 in 1953, 3.3 in 1955, 6 in 1958 (when five out of six successful independent candidates allied themselves with the Liberal Democrats immediately after the election, making the over-all percentage deceptively high), and only 2.8 in 1960.

Only in 1946 did the conservative parties fail to win an absolute majority of the popular vote, but even then they captured 248 seats, a majority. In that year, 46.3 per cent of the voters cast their ballots for the candidates of one minor and two major conservative parties. In view of the exceptionally high percentage of minor-party and independent voters in that year, it is safe to assume that many of them would normally have voted for conservative candidates. In 1947, the same three conservative parties polled more than 58 per cent of the vote and won 281 seats. The conservative vote totaled 63 per cent (349 seats, a conservative record) in 1949 and reached a high of 65.8 per cent (but only 325 seats) in 1952. It has steadily declined since then, as shown in the following percentages: 65.4 (310 seats) in 1953, 63.2 (297 seats) in 1955, 57.8 (287 seats) in 1958, and 57.6 (296 seats) in 1960.

The popular vote for socialist candidates has revealed an erratic trend, reflecting the intraparty difficulties of the socialists. Nevertheless, there has been a consistent socialist bloc to match the conservative alignment, though it has remained a minority. In the 1946 election, the Socialist Party won 17.7 per cent of the total vote and ninety-two seats, a respectable showing in view of the fact that the party had been in existence only a few months. In 1947, the party won 26.2 per cent of the total vote—substantially below the conservative total, but enough to give it a plurality (143 seats) in the House of Representatives and thus to win for it the prime-ministership. However, in the 1949 election, the socialists won a mere 13.5 per cent of the popular vote (almost half their previous percentage), only forty-eight seats, and a total of 4.1 million votes (as compared with 7.17 million in 1947).

Since this debacle, and in spite of two schisms in the party, the socialist vote has shown a substantial upward trend. In 1952, it regained more than it had lost between 1947 and 1949, and by 1960 it had almost doubled its 1952 total. The following table shows the steady gain in socialist strength in the elections between 1952 and 1960:

	Right-wing	*Left-wing*	*Combined*
1952	4,074,136 (57 seats)	3,490,525 (54 seats)	7,564,661 (111 seats) 21.3%
1953	4,870,054 (66 seats)	4,517,597 (72 seats)	9,387,651 (138 seats) 27%
1955	5,129,584 (67 seats)	5,682,987 (89 seats)	10,812,571 (156 seats) 29.2%
1958	Social Democratic Party of Japan		13,063,210 (166 seats) 33%

	Democratic Socialists	*Socialists*	
1960	3,464,147 (17 seats) 8.8%	10,887,137 (145 seats) 27%	14,351,284 (162 seats) 35.8%

The Communist Party has played only a minor role in the general elections, as the following percentages of the total vote clearly reveal: 1946, 3.9; 1947, 3.7; 1949, 9.8; 1952, 2.7; 1953, 1.9; 1955, 2.1; 1958, 2.5; and 1960, 2.9. The highest number of seats won was thirty-five in 1949, followed by five in 1946 and four in 1947. Other totals were none in 1952, one each in 1953 and 1958, two in 1955, and three in 1960.

One of the most interesting of the general elections was that of 1955. Here, for the first time, was a dramatic demonstration of a clear-cut shift in voting preference—in the swing of almost 3.7 million votes from one conservative group, the Liberal Party, to the other, the Democratic Party. In addition, the Liberals suffered a loss of eighty-seven seats in the House of Representatives. The Liberals, who had been the dominant party since the first election of 1946—polling a plurality of the votes even in 1947 when they lost control of the House of Representatives to the Socialist Party—were decisively defeated despite (and because of) their long tenure in office.

This massive swing of voter preference can be interpreted in no terms other than that a large number of voters decided it was "time for a change" and acted accordingly at the polls. The Liberals, for all their domination of the House of Representatives, for all their control over the executive branch, for all the prestige of having been a consistent winner, could not keep themselves in power.

On the whole, the pattern of Japanese elections seems to conform closely with the longer-established patterns characteristic of older democratic political systems. The elections have certainly demonstrated that the Japanese electorate has been remarkably responsive to the challenge of the opportunity to participate directly in political affairs. High percentage of voter participation, the exercise of choice or preference in balloting (as demonstrated not only in the variations in the voting blocs, but also in the just noted dramatic shift of votes from one conservative party to another), the maintenance of the secrecy of the ballot, wide publicity in the media of mass communications, and the absence of official interference in the conduct of the elections themselves all demonstrate clearly that the Japanese have a system of free democratic elections.

As long as these features remain typical of Japanese election activity, then other possibly nondemocratic aspects of Japanese politics will remain secondary. Japanese and foreign observers alike have been concerned by the continued presence in Japanese political activity of such things as bloc voting in villages, dictated by a local political boss or by influential families; the existence of bossism, both in local politics and on the level of the national parties; the failure of women to exercise the suffrage independently; corruption, especially vote buying; and the tendency of the Japanese voter to cast his ballot on the basis of personality rather than of issues. Yet, *mutatis mutandis*, all these shortcomings have characterized balloting in other democratic societies. They should not prove to be threats to the continuation of democratic political action in Japan, so long as the more fundamental features of free elections and free speech are maintained.

The Political Parties

Although free elections seem firmly established, the political parties have been characterized by a considerable degree of instability. Only one, the Communist Party, has had a continuous existence since 1945. The Liberal Democratic Party appeared only in 1955 as a single party, the latest of a succession of conservative parties; although relatively stable, it was handicapped by internal factional strife. There has been a Socialist Party since 1945, but it has been the victim of deep factional splits that grew into party schisms, one of which lasted from 1951 to 1955 and the second of which appeared in late 1959 and early 1960. Between late 1955 and late 1959, Japan had what could be described as a formal two-party system; however, only one election, that of 1958, was held during that period, which came to an end with a renewed split between the socialist factions. Nevertheless, despite the consistent history of intraparty instability, the political party as an institution seems to be permanently established.

Political parties, as we have seen, had appeared as early as the mid–1870's, yet it had been impossible prior to 1945 for them to establish a strong position for themselves. The alien origin of the political party as an institution, the lack of a constitutionally recognized position, the domination by the government of a succession of strong political leaders who were interested in parties as instruments of power rather than viable political institutions, the absence of civic education as to the role of parties, the limitation on male suffrage until 1925 and the complete denial of the vote to women, the concentration on the emperor as the center of all political allegiance, venality and ineffectiveness of the parties themselves during the brief period in the 1920's and the early 1930's when they attained what turned out to be a false maturity, and the vicious antiparty propaganda of the militarists and their civilian supporters—all these factors prevented the parties from flowering and resulted in their abolition in 1940 in the midst of the drive to authoritarianism.

But the occupation, from its very earliest stages, encouraged the re-establishment of the parties. That they were quickly reorganized and began to operate again demonstrated that there were political leaders experienced in party operation and that parties themselves had been in existence for some decades, in spite of their unimpressive record. These were the positive contributions of the past to the operation of the postwar parties; on the other hand, much of their persistent instability can also be traced to history.

The intrinsic factor of factionalism and the extrinsic one of general voting patterns of the electorate provide the best keys for an understanding of the role and functions of the parliamentary parties. Factionalism within the Liberal Democratic Party, which has dominated Japanese politics since its formation in 1955, is a matter of personalities with few overtones of policy and none of ideology; within the socialist parties, factionalism is mainly a matter of ideology expressed in policy, with personality playing a role only to the extent that individuals serve as the mouthpieces of competing ideologies. It might be noted here that factionalism has been regarded as the bane of political parties in Japan since their first appearance in the land.

The Liberal Democratic Party and the New Conservatism

The Liberal Democratic Party was created in November, 1955, through the merger of the Liberal Party and the Democratic Party. The Liberal Party had had a reasonably coherent existence since its founding in November, 1945, by men who had been associated with the Seiyukai, one of the two dominant parties prior to the war. Its principal leader was Hatoyama Ichiro, who was purged from politics six months later but re-emerged after the occupation, becoming Prime Minister briefly in 1955–56. However, it was dominated by Yoshida Shigeru from 1946 until 1955. The party retained its title except for a period between March, 1948, and March, 1950, when it was known as the Democratic Liberal Party, but it was also plagued by internal factional strife centering around Hatoyama and Yoshida. The Democratic Party had had a much more checkered career. It also was originally founded in November, 1945—as the Progressive Party (Shimpoto)—by men who had been active as leaders of the Minseito, the rival of the Seiyukai. But it became the Japan Democratic Party in March, 1947, and then underwent the following changes: National Democratic Party, April, 1950; Japan Progressive Party (Kaishinto), February, 1952; and finally the Japan Democratic Party again in November, 1954. Meanwhile, several other minor conservative parties had developed parallel with the two large ones, but had been absorbed by one or the other. Complicating the situation still further, there were switches of individual leaders with their followers from party to party. Eventually, the two dominant conservative parties merged to form the Liberal Democratic Party in November, 1955, a month after the reunification of the socialists. As could be anticipated from its evolution, the Liberal Democratic Party has been characterized by extreme factionalism and disputes throughout its history.

The degree of internal party strife is graphically shown by the breakdown of the number of seats won by each faction in the 1960 election as published in the Tokyo *Mainichi*, one of Japan's leading newspapers. Of a total of 296 seats won by the party in that year, the factions and their seats won were as follows: Ikeda, the Prime Minister, 52; Sato, Kishi's brother, 49; Kishi himself (former Prime Minister), 50; Fujiyama, Kishi's foreign minister, 28; and the veteran politicians Ono, Kono, Miki and Ishii, 28, 32, 31, and 17 respectively. (Nine seats were listed under "other.")

This conservative factionalism is much more than a useful device to align the leaders of the party and their followers. It is clearly reflected, for example, in the annual struggle for the presidency of the party, a position that almost automatically puts its occupant into the prime-ministership. It must also be taken into account in the nomination of party members for cabinet positions. Factions also split over important matters of policy. For example, one of the sources of ex-Prime Minister Kishi's difficulties derived from the opposition of other factions within his own party to his highly controversial policies.

Yet, factionalism in the Liberal Democratic Party has neither kept it from power nor paralyzed its actions in political crises. It is conceivable that continued strife might eventually lead to a split and the creation of at least one additional conservative party. This, in turn, might lead to the establishment of a true two-party system. But such a development is inhibited by the existence of what seems to be a permanently strong minority Socialist Party. It is worth noting that the present Liberal Democratic Party appeared as a unified conservative body just a month after the Socialists had apparently solved their internal problem of disunity.

There is no question but that the Liberal Democratic Party is conservative. And it is just as clear that the majority of the Japanese electorate has consistently voted conservative, either for the present single party or for the previous combination of conservative parties. This situation raises the important issue of the nature of conservatism in contemporary Japanese politics, as it involves both conservative party leaders and the majority of the voters.

By definition, conservatism involves the maintenance of the status quo—that is, the maintenance of society as it is, including its social, economic, and political institutions and the views and attitudes appropriate for their support and continuation. The majority of the Japanese people apparently wish to maintain the following elements in their society: a democratic, responsible political system designed to contribute to the development of the rights, freedoms, and well-being of the individual; an economic system characterized by private property and free enterprise; a social system that combines harmoniously the traditional concept of the family and its relationships and the new idea of the worth and dignity of the individual; and a general world order that will directly and indirectly support these systems and enable Japan and the rest of the world to exist without the threat of another destructive war.

Thus, in the early 1960's, conservatism means something far different from what it meant only two decades earlier. It is important, therefore, to note a few of the things that the new conservatism does not stand for: the old practice of emperor worship; the subjugation of women; the omnipotence of the male head of the family; the concentration of economic power in the hands of the *zaibatsu;* a single-party system; the authoritarian state with its police suppression and denial of freedom; and, finally, militarism and aggression. All these belonged to the old conservatism. The measure of the difference between prewar and postwar conservatism is the measure of the extent of the democratic revolution.

It is within this general framework of conservatism that we can best understand the policies of the Liberal Democratic Party. As expressed by party leaders and through formal party pronouncements, the principal elements of the party's policies can be stated as follows: the preservation of the principle of popular sovereignty; respect for and protection of the worth and dignity of the individual and all his rights and freedoms; limited rearmament for the purpose of self-defense; revision of the occupation-sponsored constitution so that it will recognize the inherent right of self-defense and conform more closely to Japanese conditions; cooperation with the free world and especially with the United States; a cautious approach to the "normalization" of relations with Communist China and the Soviet Union; the fostering and strengthening of a strong labor movement while "rectifying" some of its political tendencies and working for peace between industry and labor; modifications in the educational system, particularly to guarantee the political neutrality of teachers and to strengthen the attitudes of the young toward the family; and, lastly, a battery of welfare policies, including medical and health insurance, old-age pensions, government housing (especially for workers), welfare measures for mothers and children, promotion of family planning, tax reductions, increases in real wages, self-sufficiency in food, stabilization of agricultural prices, other general measures for the improvement of agriculture and assistance to farmers, and a substantial increase in the national income.

All these are achievable within the limits of the existing order. But the difficulty lies in the fact that some of the key points—constitutional revision, limited rearmament, "rectification" of the union movement, and educational reform—are extremely controversial. What is more, they may even be reactionary, leading to a return to the old order, to the undesirable aspects of the vanished conservatism.

Another manifestation of the strong conservative cast of the Liberal Democrats is that they have had an attraction for prewar politicians—as demonstrated by the background of the founders of the original conservative parties in the immediate postwar period—as well as for bureaucrats and businessmen. All three groups, because of both their previous roles and their present positions, are strongly conservative and even have a natural tendency toward reaction, if for no other reason than that many of them enjoyed roles of leadership or influence under the old system.

According to figures released by the Autonomy Agency (now Ministry), which is in charge of the administration of national elections, the Liberal Democratic Party in 1958 had a total income of 2.38 billion yen* of which 1.29 billion yen was contributed; the Socialist Party, in the same year had an income of 434.8 million yen, of which 186.5 million yen was contributed. These figures clearly indicate that the LDP has a degree of financial support out of all proportion to the number of votes it has commanded. On the other hand, there is nothing particularly sinister about this situation, since it apparently merely reflects the fact that the conservative majority has financial assets and is willing to support the party for which it votes.

As the statistics show, Japan's electorate votes for the conservatives. Although it is frequently and accurately stated that conservative strength is really based in the countryside, it would be completely misleading to assume that the LDP or any other conservative party has no support in the urban areas. For example, in the 1960 election the LDP won the most votes in every one of the forty-six major administrative subdivisions of the country; in only four—Hokkaido, Tokyo, Osaka, and Kyoto—did the combined vote of the Socialists, the Democratic Socialists, and the Communists outnumber the LDP vote; and in only the first two did the total Socialist vote top the LDP vote. Thus, the conclusion must be that the LDP continues able to attract a comfortable majority of the electorate. This interpretation, if correct, supports the argument of ex-Prime Minister Kishi, who stoutly maintained in the face of bitter attacks from his political opposition and widespread controversy over his policies that he had the support of the "voiceless voices"—that is, of all those who

---

*360 yen to the American dollar.

took no part in the controversy but silently voted for him and his party.

Again, if it is true that the Liberal Democrats are supported because the majority of the electorate wishes to maintain the status quo, then this argument should also be useful in explaining the failure of the socialists to exert a wider popular appeal. Before examining the current position of the two socialist parties, it is necessary to take a quick look at the prewar development of socialism and of its postwar political vicissitudes.

Socialism and the Socialist Parties

Although socialism was introduced into the country during the last years of the nineteenth century, it never took firm root, primarily because the government regarded it as a subversive movement and used every means at its command to discourage it. However, in the 1920's under the title of the Social Democratic Party (Shakai Minshuto), and in the 1930's as the Social Mass Party (Shakai Taishuto), the socialists were active, though not influential. The high-water mark, as measured by the number of seats won in the old Imperial Diet, came in the 1937 general election, when 37 Social Mass Party candidates were elected in contests for 466 seats.

However, this relatively strong showing came on the eve of the war with China. The subsequent rapid development of authoritarian government meant a decline in even the apparent strength of the socialists. Actually, in the late 1930's, there was a strong current of national socialism in the movement, which carried the party away from socialism and in the direction of nationalism. Nevertheless, the prewar history of the socialist party was that of a radical group, one that consistently opposed both the government and the established order. At any rate, the last remaining organization with any socialist ties was dissolved in June, 1940, shortly before all independent parties were ended by the government.

In November, 1945, the Socialist Party was reorganized. It grew rapidly and, as has been noted, captured a plurality of seats in the House of Representatives in the 1947 general election and was permitted to organize a cabinet with Katayama Tetsu, who enjoyed the dual distinction of being Japan's first socialist and first Christian prime minister. The socialist cabinet was in power from May, 1947, to March, 1948, and failed to distinguish itself. It is widely assumed that one of the principal reasons for the failure of the socialist government was its leaders' general lack of experience in matters of administration. However, in all fairness to Katayama, his party, and his government, other contributing factors should be mentioned. As a matter of fact, the socialist cabinet was really a coalition one, backed by a total of socialist representatives in the Diet amounting to just over half the combined conservative opposition. The magnitude of the economic problems confronting Japan at the time and the apparent unwillingness of at least some sections of the occupation to work closely with a "radical" cabinet also undoubtedly contributed to the socialists' general lack of success. At any rate, this brief contact with governmental power was not turned to the advantage of the party. It had failed to establish a record of coping with Japan's problems. It had done nothing to indicate that it was primarily concerned with the issues of daily livelihood that were the greatest worry of the man in the street, whom the party claimed to represent. Thus it failed to win the confidence of a significant segment of the voting population.

The party's fall from governmental power was followed by the crushing blow of the failure in the 1949 election. Early in 1950, there was the first of the party splits that were to continue to plague the socialists. This initial division was healed in a few months, but in October, 1951, there occurred the first great schism between the right-wing socialists and the left-wing socialists, basically over the issue of the ratification of the peace treaty and the conclusion of the first security treaty with the United States. The left wing was bitterly opposed to both, while the right wing accepted them, though reluctantly. This split existed for four years, with each wing operating as an independent party, until October, 1955. The reunified Social Democratic Party of Japan continued thereafter for just over another four years. Then it again divided, producing two parties: the Socialist Party (the old left wing) and the Democratic Socialist Party (the old right wing).

The socialists' greatest single weakness—and the underlying basis of their schism—is self-imposed: an excessive preoccupation with ideological problems. Their biggest single handicap is one over which they have no control: a general economic, political, and social situation in which the majority of the people have no real grievances against their society and hence are in no mood to listen to the socialists' potentially revolutionary platform. In other words, the socialists are kept apart, disunified, and hence at a disadvantage by their own internal disputes over doctrine, and in addition they have no real audience except themselves for their ideas for changing the status quo.

The basic schism between the two wings of the party is a profound ideological one, affecting their views not only on internal politics and economics but on world affairs as well. The left wing has a strong Marxist-Leninist flavor, although at times it has gone on record as being opposed to Communism both at home and abroad. However, it insists that the source of Japan's domestic political and economic difficulties—such as revision of the constitution in undemocratic directions, rearmament, anti-labor legislation, and the failure to aid small- and medium-sized enterprises—lies in her "monopoly capitalism," while the world's difficulties—the threat of war, tensions between the Communist and free camps, and the failure to disarm—can be blamed on the "monopoly capitalism" of the United States, in alliance with that of Japan and the nations of Western Europe. The left wing argues that the solution for Japan is the elimination of "monopoly capitalism" and the establishment of full socialism—that is, the elimination of free enterprise and the establishment of full nationalization. If this is done, then the basis for the alliance between Japanese and American capitalism will have been eliminated. The Socialists argue also that Japan must have relations with Communist China and the Soviet Union in order to achieve true "neutralism." This, they maintain, would simultaneously help to reduce international tensions and place Japan in a position where it would be less likely to be drawn into a war not of its own choosing.

There is no question but that the neutralism argument is appealing in concrete terms to many nonsocialist Japanese. On the other hand, the socialist concept of the nature of capitalism and the necessity for its replacement by a socialist economy and state necessarily involve a very considerable alteration of the status quo. As we have seen, there are few Japanese individuals and fewer groups with grievances of sufficient magnitude against the present situation to make them lean in the direction of a program as drastic as this.

The leaders of the Socialist Party, with very few exceptions, are veterans of the class struggle. For many years, against odds that turned out to be insuperable, they believed in and worked for the achievement of a society that would be vastly different from the old authoritarian one and would yield political freedom and economic benefits to the worker and the farmer particularly, both of whom were economically underprivileged to say the least. With the defeat and the occupation, the Socialists were able for the first time to espouse their ideas openly and widely and even to envisage the time when they might be made the foundation of a new and different kind of society. It would be asking too much of these men to give up their long-cherished ideas—even if they were to agree that they were flying in the face of reality—and to embark on a policy of what to them must appear one of expediency.

By no means an insignificant political force, the Socialist Party is clearly the leading rival of the Liberal Democrats. In the 1960 elections, the Socialists won 10.88 million votes, 27 per cent of the total cast. But their real problem is not that of making a respectable showing, but of capturing power, the goal of any political party worthy of the name. Their only possible strategy, as long as the existing situation obtains in Japan, is to cease fighting the nonexistent class war, in which they have no one to lead except themselves, and to begin operating as a "bourgeois" party, using every means to win votes on all issues.

When the Democratic Socialist Party was formally constituted early in 1960, many observers felt that at long last there had appeared on the scene a powerful third force. Obviously, there was considerable dissatisfaction with the leadership of the Liberal Democrats and with the policies for which both leadership and party had stood. Equally clearly, the Socialists, with their preoccupation with monopoly capitalism and the class struggle were not striking a responsive chord in enough voters to become a major challenge to the LDP. The Democratic Socialists, representing as they did the right wing of the socialist movement, stood for a policy of moderation in everything. They did not admire capitalism, but they were willing to permit it under the kind of limited socialism that they regarded as ideal for their country. They did not regard close ties with the United States as essential, yet they felt that to withdraw from the security arrangement would upset the balance of power both in the Far East and in the world, and that to enter precipitately into broad relations with the Communist bloc would likewise not necessarily serve the interests of their country.

But their policy of moderation, appealing as it was in the abstract, failed them in the crisis of mid–1960 over the issue of the security treaty. In that critical situation (to be described in detail in the next chapter), it struck many as a do-nothing policy, a refusal or even an inability to take a stand on an issue of crucial importance. The results of the election at the end of the year demonstrated that the Democratic Socialists could scarcely hope to play a major political role. As respectable as 3.46 million votes (8.8 per cent) might have been, it still left them a bad third, with less than a sixth of the amount won by Liberal Democrats and less than a third of that of their socialist rivals. The results only confirmed the trend made clear during the competition between the socialist wings in the 1950's—the more dynamic leadership and greater voter appeal of the left wing, as demonstrated by its much more rapid gains made in the elections of 1952, 1953, and 1955.

The socialists' principal source of strength in Japan lies in the cities, plus Hokkaido, where their position is strengthened by the concentration of coal miners' unions. This has been true of all postwar elections. For example, 45 per cent of the total vote of the Socialist Party in 1960 came from Hokkaido; the cities of Tokyo, Osaka, and Kyoto; and the prefectures of Kanagawa, Aichi, Hyogo, and Fukuoka, in which are located the major industrial cities of Yokohama, Nagoya, Kobe, and Fukuoka, respectively. Almost 50 per cent of the Democratic Socialist vote came from the same eight areas. (Almost 70 per cent of the Communist vote also came from there.)

As might be inferred from their urban base, both socialist parties draw their principal support from industrial workers, intellectuals, young people in general, and some sections of small and medium business. As was pointed out earlier, much of the strength of the Socialist Party and its left-wing antecedent comes from the support it has received from the powerful Sohyo federation of labor unions. Intellectuals, also concentrated in the cities, tend to support these socialist parties. Apparently, the Democratic Socialists had a powerful appeal, at least initially, for a number of intellectuals who found both the LDP and the Socialists unattractive. It is widely assumed by Japanese political analysts that the main reason for the steady increase in the total socialist vote during the 1950's was the support that the voters newly come of age gave them. Both parties have made strenuous efforts to win the support of the small and medium businessman, whose problems and interests are certainly considerably different from those of big business, which supports the Liberal Democrats by and large. However, it is difficult to determine the degree of support the socialists have won from that sector of business.

This general pattern of support for the socialist parties has prevented them from appealing effectively to a broader public. The Liberal Democrats have by far the most effective national organization, with branches set up in all areas of the country, rural and urban. By contrast, both the Socialists and the Democratic Socialists, although they have national organizations as well, are confronted with a difficult task in penetrating deeply into the countryside, where the Liberal Democrats are much stronger. In turn, this means that the socialists must also continue to have a restricted financial base that limits their power to expand.

This review of the three parliamentary parties naturally raises the issue of the nature of the Japanese party system. Between 1955 and 1959, Japan had what could be described on paper as a two-party system, with the conservative Liberal Democrats facing the progressive Social Democrats. However, there was nothing about the one general election held during this period (in 1958) to make it significantly different from previous ones,

or from the subsequent one in 1960. Then the renewed split in
the socialist bloc at least temporarily ended the hope of a sound
two-party system.

What are the possibilities for the development of a strong rival
to the Liberal Democrats? The socialist prospects are not bright.
If the internal divisive forces could ever be eliminated, there might
be a chance. In 1960, the two socialist parties won slightly under
36 per cent of the total vote, or a little less than two-thirds of the
LDP vote. This presented the socialists with a difficult, but not
impossible, problem of vote-getting. But split into two parties,
they seemed far from power. The Democratic Socialists with 8.8
per cent could be considered as nothing more than a minor party.
The Socialists with their 27 per cent of the popular vote had
less than half the LDP figure, a gap perhaps more vividly represented by the amounts themselves—about 10 million as compared
with about 22 million.

The socialists cannot rely on the accretion of young voters as
a road to power. The process is too slow. In addition, there is the
likelihood of a loss at the other end of the age scale—that is,
the swing of older voters (as distinct from party members) from
the socialist ticket to the conservative side. The events of 1960
also demonstrated the difficulty of accession to power by means
of a burning political issue. The controversy over the security
treaty in May and June was as intense as a political controversy
can become. There is no question but that the weight of popular
opinion was against the treaty and consequently against its political sponsor, the Liberal Democratic Party. Kishi, the party's
leader and Prime Minister during the controversy, was undoubtedly the most unpopular political figure in recent Japanese history. His tactics and those of his party were bitterly attacked.
And yet, six months later, the LDP polled a vote less than 1 per
cent smaller than it had won in the 1958 general elections, while
the combined socialist total was less than 3 per cent greater than
two years earlier.

There are two roads open for the socialists, but, unfortunately
for them, both seem impossible. The first is a genuine unification
that would eliminate ideology-based factionalism and permit
effective operation as a party. But two basic schisms in a decade

—to say nothing of an extremely uneasy alliance during the period of unification—seem to indicate the existence of differences so fundamental that even the prospect of power cannot eliminate them. The second would be for the Socialist Party to abandon its preoccupation with an ideology based on Marxism-Leninism. But the degree of commitment to this ideology on the part of both leaders and substantial segments of the followers indicates that it is unrealistic to expect such a shift.

It would seem that the only prospect for a socialist advent to power lies in the chance of an economic depression that would affect the well-being of most individuals and groups within Japan and provide them with a real reason for abandoning the conservatives and plumping for a new approach. If, for example, the Japanese farmer loses his prosperity and is confronted with economic difficulties on the order of those he faced prior to World War II, then it would be reasonable to expect him to abandon the conservatives and swing behind a progresssive group. He would, in other words, begin to wish and work for a change in the status quo.

The Third-Party Problem

There remains the possibility, mentioned before in relation to the problem of factionalism, of the emergence of a second conservative party. This seems more likely than the adoption of an effective program by the socialists, if for no other reason than that the history of the evolution of the LDP has provided a possible pattern. The present party did appear as the result of a merger, which had been preceded by a complex series of developments. At least some of the existing factionalism is the result of this merger. In addition, the 1955 election demonstrated that the Japanese electorate was capable of shifting its votes substantially from one conservative party to another. Finally, after 1955, on several occasions the internecine warfare in the LDP reached a stage at which the formation of a new party was widely rumored.

The chief pressure against such a development is the size of the Socialist Party. Too weak to challenge a single conservative party at the polls, it is still strong enough to be a formidable rival to a divided conservative bloc. Undoubtedly, the fear of the socialists' slipping into power as the result of a conservative split is probably the greatest factor inhibiting the formation of a new conservative party.

A new party, built around a core of experienced politicians from the Liberal Democratic camp and offering the electorate a genuine alternative still within the framework of the status quo, would be in a good position to become a political force of considerable magnitude. It would probably pull a number of voters from the socialist camp, for it is reasonable to assume that a number of urban voters have gone socialist not because they support the party, but because by so doing they register a protest against the party in power. In office since 1955, the LDP has been the constant center of controversy, coming out on the winning end, it is true, but in the process doing nothing to win genuine, widespread, and positive popular support. Again, it must be repeated that it has won because the electorate is preponderantly conservative—not necessarily because it is pro–Liberal Democratic.

Although it is undesirable for one party to dominate the political scene, it should be remembered that the Liberal Democrats have not converted Japanese politics into a one-party system as that phrase is usually understood. Twice in six years it went to the people in free general elections, and twice it was returned to power. It has never acted to still the opposition parties that have consistently subjected it and its onetime leader Kishi to both verbal and physical attack. In spite of the charges of its critics, political and otherwise, it has neither stifled freedom nor made Japan into a police state. In addition, its term in office has not converted the Japanese Government into a government of, by, and for special privilege. Yet, the fact remains that the appearance of a genuine political rival would be a desirable development under the new democracy.

The Communist Movement

The Japanese Communist Party is worth examination in some detail because of its negative role in Japanese politics. It has played an extremely minor part in terms of both the popular vote and the number of Diet seats it has won. Its principal significance, in abstract political terms, derives from what its weak position tells us about the state of Japanese democracy, and the general situation in Japanese society that has provided a singularly unfavorable environment for its development. The Japanese case is interesting also because it provides a comparison of the effectiveness as barriers against Communism of pure and narrow anti-Communism on the one hand and positive action on the other.

The pattern of the Party's development prior to the surrender roughly parallels that of the Socialist Party, except for the important fact that the Communists were subjected to even severer suppressive measures by the government than were the socialists. Founded in 1922, the Party was never legal. The government from the very beginning instituted a highly effective and brutal campaign against both the Party and individual Communists. Nevertheless, it never succeeded in extirpating either the ism or its supporters. When the war came to an end, some of the leaders were in prison in Japan, and others were in China working closely with the Chinese Reds. However, there had not been an active Party organization operating in Japan for some years, even secretly, so effective had the measures of the Japanese police been.

The anti-Communist campaign of the Japanese Government included consistent propaganda stressing the dangers of Communism. The government and its spokesmen for many years bitterly attacked Communism in Japan and in the Soviet Union as a threat to the Japanese way of life and to stability in the Far East and as a menace to the world. It was ironic that throughout that time, and especially during the 1930's, Communism was virtually nonexistent in the country. Nevertheless, the government's constant harping on the theme was to be a matter of considerable subsequent importance.

In October, 1945, the occupation issued the famous "liberation" directive to the Japanese Government. Among other things, this ordered the release of all political prisoners and the abrogation of all laws and regulations prohibiting the free formation and activity of any political organization. Although this directive applied to all political prisoners and organizations without distinction, its effect actually was to give the Communists a tremendous initial advantage.

The foundation of Communist strength, then and later, lay in the nature of the Party and its members. Immediately upon their release from prison, the Communists set about organizing their Party as an open political association. Some of the refugee Communists also returned to Japan early in the occupation; foremost among them was Nosaka Sanzo, who had spent sixteen years in political exile in both the Soviet Union and Communist-controlled areas of China and was regarded as the brains of the Party. In a remarkably short time, the Party was organized and became extremely active, disseminating propaganda, staging mass demonstrations, and playing a significant role in all political activity. The chaos and the confusion of the immediate postsurrender and initial occupation period also provided ideal conditions for the effective operation of the Party. It was, at that time, far better organized than most of its competitors, worked more purposefully, and was able to associate itself in its propaganda more closely with the difficulties and the aspirations of the Japanese common man.

Another factor working greatly in favor of the Communists was the manner in which they had been permitted to begin to function under the occupation. The liberation referred to above created the impression among many Japanese that the occupation positively favored the Communists. It was only natural for many non-Communist Japanese to follow this faulty line of reasoning: Many things in the occupation's early program seemed revolutionary—although they were obviously not Communistic—from the Japanese point of view. The occupation was responsible for the release of Communists who had been thrown into jail by the Japanese Government and kept there even after the surrender. The Party was founded without interference from the occupation. No Communist activities were hindered in the early stages of the occupation. Therefore, the occupation was pro-Communist. Thus, although the occupation never in any way formally or officially favored them, the Communists were happy to foster the impression that they were operating with the occupation's blessing.

The result of this misunderstanding together with their own efforts was the development of a strong position for the Communists in the early years of the occupation. A climax was reached in the general election in 1949, when the Communists won just under 10 per cent (slightly less than 3 million) of the popular vote and a total of thirty-five seats in the House of Representatives. This was merely the political manifestation of the strength of the Communists. They were also extremely active in the labor movement, controlling or dominating some of the more influential unions, and in the field of propaganda in its broadest sense, including the publication of numerous books and pamphlets.

Yet, the Communists were at the same time working to undermine their own position. In 1947 and 1948, the decision apparently was made inside the JCP that power must be seized through force and violence, although a powerful faction inside the Party, led by Nosaka himself, continued to insist that the Party could come to power by peaceful, democratic ("bourgeois") means. Party tactics and strategy during this key period may or may not have been aimed at the immediate expulsion of the occupation army and seizure of control over the government by force, but they were clearly designed to create a maximum of confusion and chaos. Communist-inspired riots, sabotage, and extremist propaganda had an effect precisely opposite to the one intended. They were weakening, rather than strengthening, the Party's position. What happened, in effect, was that the Communists were actually doing exactly what the old official propaganda had declared—without any demonstrable foundation at the time—they would do if they were ever permitted to operate freely inside Japan. Ironically, the repressive policies of the government had never permitted the Communists to operate and hence to show themselves in their true colors.

One specific development must be mentioned because of its great impact on Japanese popular attitudes toward Communism: the repatriation of Japanese nationals from the Soviet Union in 1949. When the war came to an end in 1945, Soviet forces during the final few days had captured more than 2 million Japanese soldiers and civilians. Late in 1945 and through part of 1946, about half of them were repatriated. But then the Soviet Union halted the whole repatriation program and stubbornly refused to resume it, even though the occupation exerted great pressure through the Allied Council for Japan in Tokyo. Early in 1949, the Soviet Union finally consented to resume repatriation. Naturally, this issue had become a matter of great public concern in Japan, since a great many Japanese were still in the Soviet Union and, moreover, the Soviet Union would neither report on their situation nor permit them to communicate with their families. With the resumption of repatriation in mid-1949, the reason for the earlier suspension quickly became apparent: The repatriates had been subjected to an intensive program of indoctrination, and some had become converted to Communism. It soon became evident, however, that many of the converts had gone over simply because they realized it was the only way they could be sure of returning home. But the conduct of some hard-core converts had the effect of verifying much of the government's previously baseless propaganda.

When the repatriation ships returned to Japan with their human cargoes, Japan was excited. After years of separation and silence, thousands of Japanese were to be reunited with their families. Elaborate preparations were made for welcoming the repatriates. However, many of them came off the ships in well-disciplined groups, chanting Communist songs and slogans and ignoring family welcoming parties. Some continued to disregard their families, attending Party meetings ashore, either at the port of debarkation or at the final destinations, as the first order of business. In the highly emotional atmosphere of the repatriation, this obvious demonstration that the Party and its discipline took priority over individual and family ties shocked many Japanese. Some repatriates also became involved in violent demonstrations, again a public show of Communist reality that confirmed the suspicions of many Japanese toward the Party. Although the incidents connected with repatriation were limited in duration and number, the public effect was profound.

At the same time, other factors of even greater significance were undermining both the role and the significance of Communism in Japan. After the initial period of toleration, the occupation, and especially General MacArthur, assumed a steadily increasing anti-Communist position. Actually, in 1949, the General hinted broadly to the Japanese Government that the best course of action would be to outlaw the Party. Although the hint was not acted upon, the continued domination of the government by the conservatives contributed to the steady growth of anti-Communist attitudes within the government itself. The Cold War situation in which Japan found itself willy-nilly involved also served to affect adversely the position of the JCP. To many non-Communist Japanese, it seemed simply that as the Soviet Union gained in power, so did the potential Communist threat to Japan. The Japanese had never truly made a distinction between the Soviet Union and Communism, primarily because Russia, Imperial and Soviet alike, had long been a threat—both real and imaginary—to Japanese security. After the Revolution, the ideological threat of Communism served to reinforce the military menace that, in the eyes of Japan, the Russian Government appeared to be.

Thus, a combination of internal and external developments resulted in a severe limitation on the power of the Communists after the high-water mark of the 1949 general elections. However, the fundamental reason why the Communists have made so little headway since 1945 in Japan, in marked contrast with other areas of Asia and the world, is that they have had to operate in a general environment singularly unfavorable to them. There has not existed in Japan, even in the difficult years between 1945 and 1948, the kind of vacuum that has contributed so significantly to Communist success elsewhere.

When Japan faced its greatest difficulties, there was an operating government that had the tremendous advantage of the support of the occupation—really a government behind the government. The mere continued operation of the government meant that the Communists were never in a position to seize power, violently or nonviolently. Likewise, the Communists were always confronted with effective political rivals, including not only a predominantly strong conservative party—or succession of them—which obtained the majority of the votes of the people in free elections, but also a strong socialist party that was able to use some of the fundamental appeals of the Communists with even more effect. The existence of strong, organized political parties with their own appeals meant, again, that the Communists did not have a free field to win, by either threats or blandishments, the mass support that, at least in the initial stages, has been one of the factors in their seizure of power in other areas. Finally, Japan has enjoyed a considerable degree of economic stability even in the darkest postwar years, and an increasingly high level of general prosperity besides. Thus, the Communists have not been in a position to use poverty, suffering, general discontent, and the promise of better things to come, all of which have provided them with such effective ammunition elsewhere.

The JCP has consistently been a minority party. It is clear that it cannot accede to power by any normal democratic political means. Only internal confusion and chaos could put the Communists in a position to come to power. Such a situation would have to be marked by a collapse of government, grave economic difficulties, and the disappearance of strong political opponents. It also seems fairly certain that such a condition could be produced by only two things: either Japanese involvement in another major war that would again make the country the target of devastating attack, or an economic collapse originating out of a serious international economic depression.

Because of the clandestine nature of a substantial segment of the Party's operations, it has been difficult to ascertain its actual membership. It was generally assumed that the official membership during the 1950's was somewhere between 75,000 and 100,000 (probably closer to the latter figure). It was also estimated that there were an additional 250,000 to 300,000 so closely identified with the Party or assorted front organizations as to be considered as Party members in all but the formal sense. Voting returns in recent general elections indicated that there were also upwards of 500,000 other Japanese (assuming that all Party members and quasi members also voted Communist) who for one reason or another voted for Communist candidates. Taking the upper limit of all these estimates, the total would be about a million Party members, fellow travelers, and pro-Communist voters—a little over 1 per cent of the whole population and less than 2 per cent of the eligible voters.

The JCP is, in Japanese terms, a revolutionary party, if for no other reason than it stands for abolition of the Imperial Throne and of the system of private property. Adherence to these two principles creates an almost insuperable barrier to the development of a strong position by peaceful means as long as Japan remains reasonably prosperous and there is political stability.

The Party, of course, continues to be legally recognized. There has been no serious attempt, governmental or otherwise, to abolish it, even though government leaders and other influential Japanese have continued to be vigorously anti-Communist, both domestically and internationally. As will be indicated in the discussion of the Subversive Activities Prevention Law, it is perfectly clear that any attempt to outlaw the Party would be vigorously opposed not only by Communists and fellow travelers but by many other Japanese without such leanings, for it would involve a fundamental challenge to the freedoms guaranteed in the new constitution.

Among all the minor parties, the JCP is the only one that seems even potentially in a position to play a serious political role. The remaining splinter groups, for the most part, lie at the other end of the political spectrum. These reactionary and/or ultranationalistic groups seem to be completely out of step with their times. They have shown no significant vote-capturing strength, nothing in the way of a propaganda appeal, and no signs of effective organization. The whole political and intellectual climate of Japan is such that their prospects of playing an influential part in Japanese politics are virtually nonexistent. Their participation in the mass violence and assassinations of 1960–61 captured headlines and created a sense of uneasiness in the Japanese public, so reminiscent was it of what had happened during the 1930's. But there was no sign that these rightist groups had any wide appeal, any organization comparable in efficiency to that of the Communists, or any program that could ever effectively win public support or even acquiescence.

9

The Role of Controversy

Between 1952 and 1960, Japanese politics was the setting for a series of controversies so widespread and bitter that they were generally interpreted as disturbing indications of a still considerable immaturity of the country's democracy. However, the manner in which the nation weathered these controversies clearly demonstrated the existence of a surprisingly strong democratic system. The issues over which the controversies arose were the establishment of the Self-Defense Forces in 1954, the revision of the security treaty with the United States in 1959–60, the Subversive Activities Prevention Law of 1952, the revision of the Police Law in 1954 and the attempt to revise the Police Duties Execution Law in 1958, and the long-continuing movement for the revision of the 1947 constitution.

In each case, one side in the controversy was the government, controlled by a conservative party that seemed bent on pursuing what was once called the "reverse course," the reversion to the old authoritarianism. It was this that seemed to indicate the precarious position of democracy. The other side was represented by a surprisingly vigorous coalition which, if it did not succeed in blocking completely the reverse course, revealed a healthy alertness to its dangers and a determination to protect democracy. Both sides adopted tactics that on occasion were not only unparliamentary but seemed to be undemocratic as well.

What gave a peculiar cast to all of these problems was the fact that none was what could be described as a purely Japanese issue: A crucial element in each was the impact of external circumstance. In some instances, the outside factor was the occupation and its work, and in others it was the general post-1950 international situation as it affected Japan. Yet, however important these factors were to their origins, the controversies provided an excellent means for measuring both the strength and the weakness of the democratic system.

The Rearmament Controversy

By far the most intensive and enduring of the disputes was that over rearmament. The term is somewhat misleading because it implies a military build-up of some magnitude. Modest as the new military establishment actually was, it still aroused substantial fears; a reminder of an unpleasant past, it created the possibility of an involvement in a future war. The controversy growing out of the establishment of the Self-Defense Forces and the revision of the U.S. security treaty actually extended all through the decade of the 1950's and into the 1960's, the events of 1954 and 1960 being simply two critical climaxes. Both developments involved tense struggles between political parties inside the Diet and widespread popular political action outside it. The controversy also had major bearing on Japan's diplomacy, for it involved relations with the United States on the one hand and with the Communist bloc on the other. As we have already seen, it also touched on a major problem of constitutional interpretation. Thus, the question of rearmament went far beyond the purely military considerations involved, which were in fact of only minor consequence.

Ironically, it was the occupation, responsible as it had been for the disarmament and demilitarization of Japan, which placed the country on the road back to rearmament. That development was not, as propagandists inside and outside Japan have charged, a manifestation of the "militaristic imperialism" of the United States. It was, instead, a step regarded as vitally necessary in view of the outbreak of the Korean War, the most serious expression of the tensions between the free and Communist worlds, in the early summer of 1950. Fearful in the critical early stages of the conflict of a possible external attack on Japan as well as a Communist-fomented internal insurrection, General MacArthur, with the backing of his government, authorized the Japanese Government early in July, 1950, to establish a National Police Reserve to supplement the police. Since the occupation was still in operation, the Japanese were in no position to react strongly against this move although they did criticize it as a step backward toward the detested old order. Even when the National Police Reserve was converted into a National Safety Force shortly after the end of the occupation, tempers did not flare to the heights they were to reach two years later. The basic reason for the relative calm was that, undesirable as any armed forces appeared to the Japanese, what was involved was essentially a change in name of the existing paramilitary forces. The further fact that the Korean conflict was still raging virtually on Japan's doorstep provided the justification of pressing urgency.

The first major flare-up over rearmament came in 1954, when the cabinet acted to create a military defense establishment that was not even thinly disguised as either a police reserve or a safety force. What was involved now was more than a great stride away from disarmament. It was the creation of a military organization which, simply because it existed, seemed to most Japanese to be fraught with the possibility of a revival of all the practices of the old military establishment.

On March 11, 1954, the cabinet submitted to the Diet the two bills necessary to bring the new defense organization into existence. One called for the establishment of the Defense Agency; the other for the creation of the Ground, Maritime, and Air Self-Defense Forces. The bills were debated bitterly for almost two months in both houses of the Diet and were finally passed by comfortable (approximately two to one) margins in both houses. The conservatives, of course, supported the two measures, and the principal opposition came from the socialists. But the voting did not follow strict party lines. If it had, the two bills would have enjoyed a larger margin of Diet approval.

We have already seen in the discussion of the role of the Self-Defense Forces in government (Chapter 5) the manner in which they have been prevented from becoming involved in politics or assuming an influential role in government. Consequently, their part in the rearmament dispute has been a passive one; it has been their existence, not their activities, that has been controversial.

Of even greater moment was the long controversy over Japan's security arrangements with the United States. Its significance derived from a number of factors: its continuation in varying degrees of intensity for more than a decade; the climactic events of the first half of 1960, posing the greatest political crisis under the new democracy; and its world political overtones, which made it a matter of considerable interest to both the free and the Communist worlds.

Security Arrangements with the U.S.

The original security treaty of 1951 between Japan and the United States was signed simultaneously with the general treaty of peace in San Francisco on September 8, 1951. The peace treaty was signed by Japan and forty-eight other nations that had been at war with it or had come into existence following the war and a Japanese occupation. The provisions dealing with Japan's security were closely related to the security treaty itself. Under the peace treaty, Japan was bound to accept "the obligations set forth in Article 2 of the Charter of the United Nations," especially the obligations "to settle its international disputes by peaceful means in such a manner that international peace and security, and justice, are not endangered; to refrain in its international relations from the threat or use of force against the territorial integrity or political independence of any State or in any manner inconsistent with the Purposes of the United Nations; and to give the United Nations every assistance in any action it takes in accordance with the Charter and to refrain from giving any assistance to any State against which the United Nations may take preventive or enforcement action." These provisions were designed to prevent a recurrence of military aggression and to bind Japan firmly to the security arrangements of the United Nations. In return, however, the treaty also provided that "the Allied Powers for their part recognize that Japan as a sovereign nation possesses the inherent right of individual or collective self-defense referred to in Article 51 of the Charter of the United Nations and that Japan may voluntarily enter into collective security arrangements." It was further provided that all occupation forces would be withdrawn not more than ninety days after the treaty came into force, after ratification by the required number of governments.

The recognition of the inherent right of individual self-defense constituted Allied approval for the creation of a Japanese military establishment, thus bringing to a formal end the initially American and later Allied policy of complete disarmament. The recognition of the right to enter into collective-security arrangements gave implicit Allied approval to the security treaty with the United States.

Before turning to the treaty itself, it is necessary to observe briefly the international situation in 1951 as it bore directly on Japan's security, to say nothing of the military problem confronting the United States and the United Nations. When the peace treaty was signed, the Korean War was in its fifteenth month. Thus, the Japanese Government was confronted with a military conflict of considerable proportions raging just a few hundred miles away, with one side being by no means friendly toward Japan. There was the possibility that, should the fighting take a drastic turn for the worse against the United Nations, Japan might face the threat of a Communist invasion with nothing except its National Police Reserve for defense. The problem confronting the United States and the United Nations was much more immediate. From the beginning of the fighting in Korea, Japan had played an exceedingly important though passive role. It provided naval and air bases essential to the military effort; it was a staging as well as a rest and recuperation area for U.N. combat forces; and Japanese industry was able to service, if not produce, Allied military equipment of many types. As long as the occupation continued, there was no real problem, for the forces operating in Korea could be regarded as an extension of the occupation. With the end of the occupation and the return of full sovereignty to Japan, however, the United Nations and especially the United States needed a guarantee of the continued use of Japanese bases and other facilities. Thus, for different reasons, both the Japanese and American Governments desired a security treaty, the former half-heartedly, the latter urgently.

As for the content of the treaty, the Preamble contained a statement of the willingness of the United States Government "to maintain certain of its armed forces in and about Japan" to satisfy the Japanese desire for their presence "so as to deter armed attack on Japan." Nevertheless, the willingness of the United States was based on the expectation "that Japan will itself increasingly assume responsibility for its own defense against direct and indirect aggression." This was, of course, the formal renunciation by the United States of its earlier policy of complete disarmament. We have already seen that this reversal was regarded by the majority of the Japanese as being unfortunate, to say the least.

There were certain other aspects of the treaty that made it less than popular at the time and later on. The Japanese Government committed itself not to grant any rights relating to bases or military forces to a third power "without the prior consent of the United States of America." This was an explicit limitation on the sovereign right of Japan to enter freely into any arrangement under treaty with another power. But what became a matter of greater and greater concern to many Japanese as time went on was that the treaty dealt in no way with the very important question of consultation between the two governments on such vital questions as the manner in which U.S. bases in Japan might be used, or the type of weapons that might be stored there. For example, it was conceivable that U.S. planes based in Japan might launch attacks on Soviet territory. In the mid-1950's, there were rumors that U.S. atomic weapons were stored in Japan. Whether or not such rumors were based on fact is beside the point; the important thing is that Japanese uneasiness over them was multiplied by their experience with atomic bombs.

The restraints placed on Japanese action, together with the complete freedom of action enjoyed by the United States, made the treaty appear to be inequitable. Japan was placed squarely on the side of the United States in the Cold War. If the Cold War should ever become a hot one, U.S. bases in Japan could then be used for offensive purposes. Thus Japan would automatically become a target for counterattacks.

With the end of the fighting in Korea, there was no longer an immediate military justification for the treaty. In addition, the presence of large numbers of American military personnel in Japan constituted a constant reminder not only of the recent occupation but also of possible Japanese involvement in a future war. No nation enjoys being reminded of an occupation, even a benevolent one. It became increasingly clear that the national interests of both countries would be served by the conclusion of a new treaty that would remove at least some of the difficulties in the existing one.

In the summer of 1957, Prime Minister Kishi paid a formal visit to the United States, where he was assured by President Dwight D. Eisenhower that U.S. ground forces would be withdrawn from Japan as quickly as possible—later done—and that negotiations for a revision of the 1951 Treaty would be initiated. From the time that conversations leading to revision were begun in the autumn of 1958, the issue steadily grew more and more controversial. However, the groundwork for the looming controversy had been well laid.

In the first place, the security treaty had become a legitimate domestic political issue. The dominant conservative parties in charge of the government since 1948 had, of course, been responsible for the conclusion of the 1951 instrument. Thus, it was natural for the socialist opposition to use the unpopular treaty to attack the conservatives. In addition, the agreement and the bases authorized under it were ideal material for anti-American propaganda by the left-wing socialists and the Communists. This propaganda utilization of the situation steadily fed the political controversy and vice versa. And for both political and propaganda purposes, the Communists, the left-wing socialists, and others who preferred not to see Japan tied so closely to the United States naturally raised the whole issue in relation to the Cold War. They asserted that in the existing state of world tension it was in Japan's interest not to be tied too closely to either side, Japan's best road being to broaden relations with the Communist world and to eliminate the security treaty with the United States. The result, it was argued, would be true neutrality and thus true security for Japan. It must also be stressed that this controversy was developing against the background of the intense antiwar feeling of the bulk of the people.

The involvement in the controversy of interested groups was automatic. On the one side stood Prime Minister Kishi and his Liberal Democratic Party, and on the other a wide variety of organizations: the Communist Party, the Socialist Party, labor organizations (especially Sohyo with its close socialist ties), student organizations (principally the extremist core of Zengakuren, which was critical of the Communist Party for being reactionary), and many others, including women's groups, as well as Christians, politically unaffiliated intellectuals, and other people who were interested because of the pacifist aspects of the problem. The press, from newspapers to influential journals of opinion, were extremely critical of the Prime Minister, his party, and the security treaty. This stemmed in part from the fact that the reporters and special writers, as intellectuals, were prone to criticize individuals, groups, or actions that they regarded as conservative or reactionary. It could also be ascribed partly to the generally antigovernment editorial policy of the press, regardless of the nature of the issue involved, and partly to the obvious fact that the great majority of the readers entertained anti-war and anti-treaty sentiments.

The situation was further aggravated by a brief and bitter struggle in the fall of 1958 over the unrelated issue of the government's attempt to revise the Police Duties Execution Law. This added to the development of a general air of tension and rendered Prime Minister Kishi the object of widespread attack and suspicion. It also brought him close to a fall from power, a situation that encouraged his political rivals to apply additional pressure on the issue of the treaty.

The controversy over treaty revision mounted steadily all through 1959, climaxed late in the year by a riot during which a mob of students under Zengakuren leadership forced its way into the compound of the Diet Building. A number also indulged in mass urination on the building itself—a gesture interpreted at the time as an expression of contempt for parliamentary government, but one that could perhaps more accurately have been taken as a gauge of the irresponsibility of a group of political juvenile delinquents.

In the face of this and other more serious manifestations of political and popular disapproval, Kishi's government concluded the negotiations, and he himself flew to Washington in January, 1960, to sign the new treaty. (Because of another Zengakuren demonstration that involved the wrecking of a part of the terminal building at Tokyo's Haneda Airport, he was forced to take a circuitous route to the airfield and to sneak aboard his plane.)

The 1960 treaty was one of "mutual cooperation and security." The mutual-cooperation provisions contained a routine pledge to "contribute toward the further development of peaceful and friendly international relations" and a more concrete commitment by the parties that they "will seek to eliminate conflict in their international economic policies and will encourage economic cooperation between them." The objectionable provision concerning prior U.S. approval of a Japanese grant of treaty rights to a third power in regard to bases or armed forces did not appear, and the highly desirable item of consultation was included. But the United States still retained the right to use bases in Japan—the treaty's most controversial feature.

Kishi's victory in the field of diplomacy only served to set the stage for the truly serious phase of the controversy. As the treaty had to be ratified by the Diet, the signing threw the whole issue squarely into the arena of politics. Ratification was assured if for no other reason than that the Liberal Democratic Party commanded an overwhelming majority in the House of Representatives. But the socialists, using as their justification the many manifestations of popular disapproval of the treaty, were determined to block ratification by any means available. Their opposition was matched by Kishi's determination to push ratification through at any cost, heightened in the spring of 1960 by the announcement that President Eisenhower would visit Japan about the middle of June. Apparently, Kishi then decided that the treaty would have to be ratified and in effect before Eisenhower arrived—possibly because this would constitute a gift of welcome, but more likely because, if the visit came prior to ratification, it could be made to appear as a device used to influence the issue and thus an act of interference in Japan's domestic politics.

The Political Crisis of 1960

At any rate, the struggle inside the Diet, as well as the general controversy, became more and more tense, with neither side showing any sign of yielding. This situation ushered in what soon became known as the crisis of May 19. The opposition had adopted the strategy of attempting to delay a vote on the treaty so that the Diet session would come to an end before ratification had been secured. This raised the important question of a vote on the extension of the session. The Prime Minister and his party were determined to force a vote on extension and set the evening of May 19 as the time. However, the members of the socialist opposition adopted the tactic of sitting on the floor of the Diet building, thus blocking entry into the lower-house chamber so that a session could not be held. The government's countertactic was to call in the Diet police to remove the human barricade by force. Amid wild disorder, this was done. As soon as the corridors were cleared, the Speaker of the House and a considerable group of Liberal Democratic representatives, but by no means all, rushed into the chamber. The session was formally opened, and in less than ten minutes, just at midnight, this rump group voted to extend the session and then ratified the treaty. This was the signal for the outbreak of what can be accurately described as the most stormy period of Japan's new democracy.

Very briefly, the principal events of the period between mid-May and mid-June were these: a series of demonstrations in Tokyo mainly concentrated around the Diet Building; an unprecedented degree of violence, resulting in injury to hundreds of demonstrators, police, and bystanders (but only one death, that of a girl student who was apparently trampled in the course of one outbreak); demonstrations against Kishi and an intensive anti-Kishi campaign in the press that had the ultimate result of driving him from office; a mass demonstration at Haneda Airport against Douglas MacArthur III, the United States Ambassador, and James Hagerty, then White House Press Secretary; and the cancellation of President Eisenhower's visit. Yet, in accordance with the Japanese constitution, the Diet ratification of the treaty was completed automatically on June 19 when the House of

Councillors had still failed, after the thirty-day period provided, to act on it.

Could this series of happenings be described as an example of democracy in action? The principal features of the crisis that provided grounds for doubts about the future of Japan's democracy can be readily enumerated: arbitrary and therefore irresponsible action on the part of the Prime Minister in attempting to ram ratification through the Diet; the socialist attempt through the sit-down strike to prevent Diet action, a device clearly outside the pale of parliamentary government; the equally unparliamentary conduct of the Liberal Democrats in voting the extension of the session and ratification in the absence of the opposition and under decidedly irregular circumstances; and the resort to violence inside and outside the Diet in an attempt to resolve a political issue. Any one of these provides ample grounds for wondering how far Japan still may be from an operable system of constitutional government. Indeed, grave doubts were raised in the minds of the Japanese themselves. However, it is a matter of considerable interest to note that many responsible Japanese observers were, contrary to the most widespread foreign reactions, more concerned with the parliamentary crisis of May 19 than they were with the subsequent violence. It is not that they condoned violence, but they recognized more clearly than outsiders that it was the symptom rather than the disease.

Despite these events, it could not be said that Japan's democratic experiment was on the verge of failure; an analysis of some of the less visible aspects will make this more apparent.

First of all, the drama of the situation obscured certain aspects crucial to an understanding of the total picture. Initially, it should be noted that, for all its intensity, the violence was concentrated in the area immediately around the Diet building. With the exception of the restricted but harassing disorder around Kishi's private residence and the demonstrations involving Ambassador MacArthur and Hagerty, violence occurred nowhere outside the Diet area in Tokyo and certainly did not spread afield, although orderly mass demonstrations did take place in many parts of the country. The restricted nature of the violence suggests that it did not involve a revolutionary plan either to overthrow or to seize control of the government. No attacks were made, for example, on important government offices concentrated in the general area of the Diet building, or even on Tokyo Metropolitan Police Headquarters, just a short distance away and a natural target of any truly revolutionary group.

There is also the problem of the nature of the Communist involvement in the outbreak. First, it should be noted that the entire situation—the anti-Kishi movement, the anti-American and anti-Eisenhower overtones, the furor over the treaty itself, the role of the police (made to appear as another manifestation of the movement back to authoritarianism), and, of course, the position of the Liberal Democrats—redounded to the benefit of Communism, both domestic and foreign. It is also undoubtedly true that Communists played an active role in keeping the crisis alive, simply because its continuation favored their cause. Communist organizations were active; Communist funds were probably used to encourage active participation by some non-Communist students; and clearly the Communist tactic of violence was being closely paralleled, if not followed. Indeed, it would have been strange if the Communists had not played an extremely active role in the entire controversy.

But the leap from these facts to the conclusion that the whole operation was Communist-inspired and Communist-managed is completely unjustified. The complex background of the controversy, as described above, demonstrates that far more than a Communist minority was interested in the issue. The point is further illustrated by the wide participation of a number of obviously non-Communist groups in the peaceful phases of the demonstrations. As far as the reaction in the United States was concerned, what the Japanese resented most was the seeming impression that only Communists were involved in the demonstrations and protests against the treaty.

It is also worth noting that with the death of the girl student on the evening of June 15, the mass violence came to a sudden end. This single death had, as did nothing else, a sobering effect not only on those who were participating in the outbursts, but also on the general public, which had apparently accepted violence, at least up to that point, as a necessary element of the controversy. And it should be pointed out that the violence was not ended by an application of overwhelming counterforce by the government. The streets were not cleared by gunfire; troops were not mobilized; and there was no patrolling by armed guards afterward. As a matter of fact, the subsequent revulsion against the use of force in politics was a matter of at least as much political significance as the violence itself.

Within a month after the end of the episode, Prime Minister Kishi had resigned from office. He was succeeded by Ikeda Hayato, a fellow member of the Liberal Democratic Party. Although it is clear that Kishi left office as a result of enormous pressure, it should be emphasized that he and his party were not ejected by a *coup d'état* and that the transfer of power—as distinct from the pressures that brought it about—was peaceful and orderly. Even the most extreme of the Kishi critics did not resist by demonstrations (peaceful or otherwise) the advent to office of his successor from the same conservative political party. With the beginning of the Ikeda prime-ministership, the political situation had returned to normal.

Another means of measuring the nature of the crisis of 1960 and, consequently, the strength of the democratic system was the election of November, 1960. It was a peaceful, orderly, and free election resulting in the confirmation in power of the Liberal Democratic Party with a popular vote only a fraction of a percentage point less than the one it had won two and a half years earlier. The Socialist Party won about twenty seats more than it had held prior to the election, but the Social Democrats lost a number of seats, with the result that the total seats won by both socialist parties was less than that won by the unified party in the 1958 general election, despite the larger 1960 socialist popular vote.

Thus the crisis of six months earlier was not reflected in the results of the election. The Liberal Democrats were not rejected for their leader's insistence on getting the treaty ratified or for his unparliamentary tactics, and the socialists were neither given rousing support for their opposition to the treaty nor rejected for their own unparliamentary actions. Perhaps of greater significance, the voters gave no sign of disillusionment with the democratic process as a result of the crisis. The voter turnout was only slightly under that of the previous national election, a decline adequately accounted for by the fact that the day of the election was a beautiful Sunday. Slightly less than three-quarters of the eligible voters went to the polls after a campaign in which the candidates and their parties were able to state their positions in the press, on television, on the lecture platform, and in street-corner appeals. In addition, there was neither pressure nor coercion on the part of the government for the voters to support the government party. And all three major parties stressed that they stood for the protection of parliamentary democracy and against violence in politics.

The developments subsequent to May–June, 1960, would seem, then, to demonstrate the basic stability of the democratic system. Had it been weaker basically, the disturbing events of the first half of the year would have made impossible the peaceful shift of power from Kishi to Ikeda and would certainly have had grave inhibiting effects on the free election that took place. Only a healthy political system could have absorbed such violence and operated as normally as Japan's democracy later did.

The 1960 controversy over the security treaty also produced a situation in which it was possible to measure the strength of the ultrarightist movement in Japanese politics. The principal rightist organization involved was the Great Japan Patriotic Party under the leadership of Akao Bin, a rabidly anti-Communist political eccentric who is the apparent recipient of sizable financial backing, judging by the number of propaganda posters his party spreads around Tokyo and his consistent campaigning for a Diet seat. His own political following is minute; in the 1960 election, for example, he polled barely over 6,000 votes in his election district (Tokyo's Sixth), which cast a total of 671,311 votes. However, his party was much in the political limelight throughout the year. Its political toughs were held responsible for the violence at Haneda Airport during the anti-Hagerty demonstrations and for some of the worst rioting around the Diet. The charge was that they touched off the trouble by attacking other groups. In addition, young Yamaguchi Otoya, the eighteen-year-old assassin of the socialist leader Asanuma Inejiro, had been a member of the party until shortly before the crime. Although the police carried out an exhaustive investigation, they were unable to establish a definite connection between Yamaguchi and Akao, though the latter apparently approved of the assassination.

What was significant about the actions of the ultrarightist organizations and individuals was that they had no apparent active support and certainly no popular sympathy. This was completely unlike the situation of the 1930's, when the rightist groups, encouraged by the politically powerful army and even actively assisted by the so-called "young officers" movement, were able to win considerable popular support; their members who resorted to violence and assassination were regarded as national heroes. It was demonstrated in 1960 that the ultrarightists are still capable of ugly violence, but also that under the present balance of political forces they are not significant.

The likelihood is that rearmament will continue to be a center of controversy so long as the international situation demands the maintenance of a defense establishment for the national security. However, the reaction to the 1960 crisis makes it seem unlikely that this question will flare to similar heights in the future, assuming the absence of a serious international crisis involving Japan or of a domestic political crisis that would encourage the use of the rearmament controversy as a means of creating additional tension.

Controversies over the Police

The police have been the center of two major controversies: the first, in 1954, when the government succeeded in effecting a reorganization of the police system (see Chapter 5) under which a degree of administrative control was returned to the hands of the central government; the second, in 1958, when the Kishi cabinet failed in an attempt to push through an amendment to the Police Duties Execution Law that could possibly have placed the police in a position to interfere once more in political affairs.

The 1954 dispute resulted in a clear victory for the government, but it also created a parliamentary crisis. When the socialists, the permanent minority, saw that they would be unable to prevent the passage of the proposed law, they boycotted the Diet session at which the vote was to be taken. As a result, the con-

servative parties alone voted the measure through. But the socialists soon saw the error of their ways and, after some days of
negotiation, rejoined the Diet session and promised to follow
regular parliamentary procedures. The crisis demonstrated weakness in the parliamentary system, but it did not inflict a grievous
wound. Nor did the new measure result in a return to the police
state, as the opposition had predicted.

In 1958, the troubles centered around a different and potentially more dangerous issue. Throughout the 1950's, the police
were confronted with two major problems of law enforcement:
the control of criminal gangs, some with large membership, that
on occasion conducted minor warfare among themselves; and
the maintenance of order during outbreaks of labor strife or of
mass political demonstrations. In addition, there were the more
routine but vexing problems attendant with a marked rise in the
rate of juvenile delinquency that seemed to be a legitimate justification for the expansion of certain police powers.

The Kishi cabinet decided to attempt to strengthen the police
by introducing a bill calling for the amendment of the Police
Duties Execution Law, which deals with the powers of the police
and the manner in which they are to be exercised. The principal
and most controversial items in the bill were: a grant of considerably broader discretion to the individual policeman in the seizure
and search of persons for weapons if he had reason to suspect
they were contemplating the commission of a crime; the right to
detain mentally deranged or drunken persons who might cause
injury to themselves or others or who might "cause serious annoy-
ance to the public in a public establishment or place" (which
might include participation in political demonstrations); the
power to detain persons suspected of planning suicide, a device
used by the former police to detain individuals suspected of
political crimes; and the application of the above powers to
minors who were defined as "those not having attained twenty
years of age," which might possibly include not only true delinquents but student demonstrators and young union members.
These and similar measures could obviously have been of assistance to the police in the execution of their proper mission of
controlling crime. But, as the critics of the bill unceasingly and

correctly pointed out, there was no guarantee that these new powers would not be applied as readily to situations involving labor-union or political activity.

There were no references in the cabinet's bill to the necessity or desirability of preventing such application, or even to keeping the new powers within the limits imposed by the constitutional guarantee of fundamental rights and freedoms, as was done in the Police Law of 1954. Either this was an outstanding example of careless drafting by the normally meticulous Bureau of Legislation, or else the fears of the critics of the bill were well founded.

At any rate, the ensuing uproar resulted in a withdrawal of the bill before it came to a vote. Again, there was a parliamentary crisis caused by the socialists in response to what they regarded as arbitrary action by the government. In addition, however, the press almost universally attacked the bill, and there were widespread public demonstrations against it, staged (as in the case of the later demonstrations over the security treaty) not only by leftists and their sympathizers, but by many other groups that could be accurately described as nonpartisan. During this controversy, a strong anti-Kishi movement developed, but the Premier was able to ride out the storm.

The 1958 dispute over the police bill was the outstanding example of the manner in which the combination of parliamentary opposition and an aroused public opinion was able to prevent a step being taken by the executive to create through legislation a situation that seemed to harbor a serious threat to the new democratic order.

The Subversive Activities Prevention Law

Another major controversy involved the passage by the National Diet of the Subversive Activities Prevention Law. This matter arose almost simultaneously with the end of the occupation in the spring of 1952 and seemed to entail a direct frontal attack on fundamental human rights. As was the case with rearmament, the initial steps toward the Subversive Activities Prevention Law were taken under the occupation, but the legislation was not introduced until mid–April, 1952, when the occupation had only two weeks to run.

Partly because of the campaign of violence and terror that had been waged by the Communist Party several years earlier, partly because of the development of Communism in both China and Korea, and partly because of the anti-Communist attitude of the occupation, the Japanese cabinet early in 1951 began to investigate the possibility of enacting a law that would enable the government to control the activities of potentially dangerous organizations devoted to subversion. The issue (one that has confronted some Western democracies) was both delicate and explosive, involving as it did the limitation of at least the constitutionally guaranteed freedom of association. Almost two months of bitter debate and public discussion and demonstrations followed the submission of the bill to the Diet. It was finally passed on July 4, 1952, and became effective on July 21.

The necessity for the law was stated in an official release at the time it went into effect. Here is a key passage:

> The reason [for the law] is that dangerous terroristic subversive activities are being carried out by certain elements in organized groups in our country. Regrettable as it may seem, dangerous activities have been revealed which proclaim in various kinds of documents the propriety and necessity for the overthrow of the Constitution and of the government established under it. These activities also seem about to move toward the realization of those aims by means of armed terrorism and guerrilla warfare. Moreover, they seem to be carried out by organized groups with international connections and appear to be strong and widely developed.

This statement was almost as controversial as the law itself. Many Japanese felt that the threat described therein was, if not nonexistent, at least considerably more remote than the official language indicated. The basic problem here was whether the degree of the danger was sufficient to justify the passage of a law whose provisions constituted threats to a constitution that the law was expressly designed to protect.

The measure's principal provisions dealing with prevention are as follows: the limitation of its application to the activities of organizations (individuals could be prosecuted under the Criminal Code); the application of the law only after an organization had engaged in proven terroristic subversive activities, and only if there was clear danger that it would resort to such actions in the future; the limitation of subversion to such acts as treason, insurrection, and ordinary crimes committed for political motives; and, finally, the inclusion in the category of subversive activities of "preparation for, plotting of, aiding and abetting, incitement, attempted incitement and instigation" of subversive activities. The final provision was perhaps the most bitterly attacked because it created a broad shadowland of interpretation that could conceivably be used to extend its application far beyond the apparently necessary limits.

It was also provided that the law was to be enforced by two agencies, both in the Justice Ministry. A Public Security Investigation Agency would be responsible for the investigation of organizations charged with terroristic subversive activities and for the recommendation of action to be taken against them, while a Public Security Examination Commission would make decisions regarding the control of organizations against which the PSIA had lodged charges. Both agencies are independent of any law-enforcement bodies. They were created under separate legislation, although their establishment was called for in the Subversive Activities Prevention Law.

Thus, it can be seen that there are features of the law that might directly or indirectly suppress or limit the freedoms enshrined in the constitution; as such, they obviously constitute a potential danger to democracy. However, of far greater significance to the issue of democracy in Japan were the reactions to the proposed law and, perhaps of even greater import, the incorporation into the law of certain other features that were designed to offset the implications of its preventive and control provisions.

First of all, the reaction against the government's bill was vehement from the beginning. Not only was it fiercely attacked in the National Diet itself, but there was also a widespread public reaction. Undoubtedly, a good deal of the latter was fostered by the Communist Party, against which the law was obviously directed. However, by no means all the opposition was sponsored by or sympathetic toward the JCP. What chiefly concerned the opponents of the bill was a twofold question, both sides of the same coin: Did it represent a frontal attack on the rights and freedoms guaranteed in the 1947 Constitution? And did it presage the return to the old system of government?

Leading Japanese newspapers laid down a heavy editorial barrage against the bill. Thirty academic organizations officially proclaimed their opposition. Thirty-two cultural associations (including organizations of writers, artists, women, Christians, and newspapermen) also opposed it. Labor unions demonstrated against it. A number of distinguished Japanese, the majority of them opposed to the bill, appeared at the Diet hearings. Thus, the public clearly demonstrated not only widespread interest in the measure, but also a fear that it might positively injure the fundamental rights and freedoms of the new democracy, which were considered worth fighting to defend.

Of equal significance were the questions raised during the debate in the National Diet, in both the House of Representatives and the House of Councillors. Members wanted to know if the enactment of the law was justified by the degree of present danger involved in subversive activities. Since similar legislation had been used in the past to restrict freedom, they asked, and since the law under debate held the same possibility, might it not be best to drop the proposal entirely? Could Japanese officials be trusted to enforce the law justly, particularly in view of the government's past record in respect to similar laws? Could such a law control underground activities (perhaps the greatest danger) of subversive organizations?

Moreover, the House of Councillors made a number of significant amendments. One of the most important was an explicit linking of the law to the people's rights as stated in Article 2: "Because it has an important relation to the fundamental human rights of the people, this law must be applied only within the narrowest possible limits necessary for the preservation of public safety, and it must not be interpreted to extend beyond this in the slightest degree." In addition, the House of Councillors was responsible for the statement of a definition of incitement, designed to limit the possible extent of interpretation of this vague concept. It also wrote into the bill a provision specifically setting up as a crime the abuse of administrative authority by investigators involved in the enforcement of the law.

However, it is of equal importance to note that in spite of the additional safeguards that the Diet wrote into the law, the government had already shown its alertness to its responsibilities under the 1947 constitution. Article 3, which was drafted by the government, declares that action taken under the provisions of the law "must never deviate from the authorized limits of authority by unlawful limitation on the rights and freedoms of the people guaranteed in the Japanese Constitution, such as the right of workers to organize and act collectively and the freedoms of learning, expression, assembly, association, religion, and thought." It also provided that "there shall be no abuses nor shall there be any interference with or limitations on the legitimate activity of labor unions or other organizations." It was in spite of this apparently ironclad pledge that the House of Councillors insisted on the additional article quoted above.

Another primary consideration is that the law establishing the two enforcement agencies spells out in meticulous detail the manner in which hearings must be carried out and the way in which adverse decisions can be appealed in regular courts of law. These provisions, plus the more general ones of the constitution dealing with due process of law, seemed to be a more than adequate guarantee against arbitrary execution of the law.

It may seem anticlimactic, but in the years following its passage there has not been a single important case involving the enforcement of the Subversive Activities Prevention Law. Its critics have thus been forced into the position of charging that, although the law has not been used for purposes of oppression, its very existence constitutes a barrier to the untrammeled enjoyment of constitutional freedoms.

However, the issues raised by the law, the manner in which they were handled, the public discussion of the problems, the pressures brought to bear on the executive branch of the government, and the whole process of the enactment of this controversial legislation clearly revealed the fact that at this early opportunity in their independent existence as a democratic society, free of both the guidance and the restrictions of the occupation, the Japanese had proved their ability to act within the framework of a democratic system.

The Problem of Constitutional Revision

The controveries discussed so far have been colored by an air of excitement arising from the tensions created by actual or apparent threats to the democratic order, the drama of political struggle of party against party, and the emotional impact of both peaceful and violent mass public demonstrations. However, the dispute over constitutional revision, though lacking in comparable excitement, is a far more fundamental matter, touching directly the foundation of constitutional democracy. Such a conflict was fated to arise from the moment the draft of what became the 1947 constitution was released. It was evident from the occupation's role in the drafting that many Japanese would welcome some form of revision, if only to make them feel that their basic law was purely Japanese, without the taint of either foreign origin or foreign pressure for adoption.

About thirty months after Japan regained its sovereignty in the spring of 1952, what was then the newly organized Democratic Party in its statement of policy issued in November, 1954, urged the establishment of a commission of deliberation on the constitution. Although there had been other expressions of opinion on the issue, this can be regarded as the first serious step in the direction of constitutional revision. Two months later, Prime Minister Hatoyama, a member of the same party, in the course of his administrative speech at the opening of the twenty-first session of the Diet, called for the creation of a nonpartisan Constitution Investigation Commission. Meanwhile, the other two conservative parties of the time, the Liberal Party and the Progressive Party, had established their own committees on the constitution and had also arrived at the conclusion that a government commission should be established by law. And in January, 1954, the People's Federation for the Defense of the Constitution, composed of representatives from 144 organizations, had been established under the leadership of the socialists and their close and powerful ally, Sohyo, the labor federation. Thus, the political battle lines over the issue of revision were drawn between the conservative and socialist parties.

It would be useful here to glance briefly at the arguments that the revisionist forces have put forward and the replies of the antirevisionists. The fundamental reason advanced by the conservatives for revision is simply that Japan, as an independent and sovereign nation, should have a constitution clearly suitable for it and free from the blemish of foreign inspiration. On this last point, the arguments of the revisionists deal with both the wording and the spirit of the constitution, ranging from the criticism that certain words and phrases sound like translations from a foreign language to the statement that both institutions and attitudes set forth in the document are completely out of line with Japanese tradition. Of course, the real starting point for revision is the controversial Article 9, perhaps most reminiscent of the occupation and its policy.

It must be noted, however, that the conservatives stoutly maintain that they are interested in preserving the democratic principles of the new basic law. Here they have no quarrel with their opponents, who equally stoutly maintain that the constitution needs no revision, for it has established beyond challenge those same fundamental principles. But at least some of the conservative suggestions for revision would have the effect of significantly reducing the force of the very principles they so vehemently claim to defend.

Between late 1954 and the spring of 1956, five major conservative drafts for a new constitution were issued, four by conservative political organizations and the fifth by a group called the League for the Realization of an Independent Constitution, led by a prominent conservative politician. The conservative position has changed very little subsequently.

The two major conservative proposals deal with a modification of the renunciation-of-war provision and a more explicit connection between the people's enjoyment of fundamental rights and freedoms and the concept of the nonimpairment of the public welfare. Under a general revision of Article 9 to permit at least the establishment of a clearly constitutional position for the Self-Defense Forces, the conservatives are interested in two other points. These are a statement of the responsibility of the individual to contribute to the defense of the country (a circumlocution for the re-establishment of conscription), and the elimination of the constitutional provision that only civilians can serve in the cabinet (in order to permit a military man to become director-general of the Defense Agency). The clarification of the doctrine of the public welfare would include such specific provisions as one dealing with the responsibility of the people to abide by the law and another for them to cooperate in the development of the nation's economic life. Such provisions, as their critics point out, could easily lead to the application of pressure on the labor unions not to strike, but to observe the law and contribute to the people's economic life by continuing to work under conditions imposed by a conservative-dominated government sympathetic to management.

Another suggestion of the Liberal Democrats is for the selection of a portion of the House of Councillors not by direct election but by "other democratic means." Although the nature of such other means is not clear, it should be noted that other conservative suggestions in this field have included "recommended" (i.e., appointed) members and indirect election. While these suggestions might take some of the occupation taint off the present system, they would also, as a movement away from the purely elective method, imply a modification of the basic doctrine of the people's sovereignty.

One point on which the conservatives seem unanimous is the role of the emperor. He should, according to all conservative suggestions, no longer be the symbol of the people's unity, but the head of the state. Although some Japanese feel that this would be another step backward, it would not necessarily be so. Only a reconcentration of power in the hands of the executive, which would come about only with the abandonment of the principle of legislative supremacy, and the reconstitution of close lines between the cabinet and the throne could put the emperor into the old position of a mere political pawn.

Two other matters of concern to the conservatives are the family and the three rights of labor, which have already been touched on and will be discussed below in a different context.

It is not necessary to describe in detail the position of the antirevisionists. They stand simply for the retention of the constitution in its present form. They consider the manner in which the occupation "forced the constitution on Japan" (as the revisionists put it) to be beside the point. The only thing that really counts, they argue, is that the constitution has brought to the Japanese people the rights and freedoms and all the attendant benefits that they have found to be so dear.

The Commission on the Constitution

The first major governmental step toward revision came in June, 1955, during the twenty-second session of the Diet, when Kiyose Ichiro, famed as the principal Japanese defense counsel for General Tojo, introduced a bill for the establishment of a commission to investigate the constitution. It was passed by the House of Representatives and sent to the House of Councillors, where it failed to come to a vote before the end of the session a few days later. It was not until February 11, 1956, that Kishi, then only a Liberal Democratic representative, introduced a new bill calling for the creation of a commission. After two days of general debate and twelve debates in the Cabinet Committee of the House—which was charged with the responsibility of reviewing the bill because the commission would be established under the jurisdiction of the cabinet—the bill was passed on March 29, 1956, by a vote of 239 to 139. Following eight further days of debate in the Cabinet Committee of the upper house between April 23 and May 9, the bill was also passed by the Councillors by a vote of 106 to 65 on May 16, 1956. In both houses, the socialists voted solidly against the bill. Although it did not become the center of a major controversy, the care with which the Diet considered it shows that it was by no means regarded as an innocuous measure.

The commission established under the 1956 law agreed after consulting with the cabinet to give itself the title of Commission on the Constitution (although its Japanese title is more accurately translated as Constitution Investigation Commission). The law places it under the jurisdiction of the cabinet. This was one reason for the vigorous opposition of the socialists, who maintained that under Article 96 of the constitution only the Diet could institute constitutional amendments and that, therefore, an executive-controlled commission, even though constituted simply to study the constitution, violated the spirit, if not the letter, of the basic law. The legally stipulated duties of the commission were simple: to study the constitution, to investigate and deliberate on problems relating to it, and "to report the results to the cabinet and through the cabinet to the Diet." Thus, the law did not in any way bind the commission to make any recommendation concerning revision, although it would be astonishing if it refrained from dealing with the issue. The commission was to consist of fifty members, all appointed by the cabinet—thirty to be chosen from the Diet and twenty from among "men of learning and experience"—but it never had more than forty members.

The difficulty over the filling of the roster was a reflection of the political and controversial nature of the revision question. Initially, the cabinet's position was that the thirty memberships from the Diet would be allotted so that the Liberal Democrats would have twenty and the Socialists ten, a reflection of the proportion of Diet seats held by the two parties. But the Socialists rejected this offer and boycotted the commission entirely, a course of dubious tactical soundness. In addition, although twenty "men of learning and experience" were found to sit on the commission, the great majority of Japan's most distinguished legal and constitutional scholars refused to join it, both because of its highly partisan origin and because they felt that its mission actually was to revise. Instead, they established their own Constitution Study Society in Tokyo, with a branch in Kyoto, devoted to study alone, but its leaders declared that they would join in the fight against revision if the government actually proposed it. However, virtually all these scholars appeared before the commission as witnesses once it began its work.

It was not until almost fifteen months after the law was passed that the commission held its first meeting. But in roughly the first two years of operations it held more than a hundred meetings, both plenary and committee sessions, and published more than 5,000 double-column pages of stenographic reports of its sessions. In those two years, thirty-five plenary sessions covered subjects ranging from routine business through the origins of the constitution to discussion of all its articles. There were four committees: one on the process of the enactment of the constitution; the First Committee on the judicial and legal system and the rights and duties of the people; the Second Committee on the Diet, the cabinet, local government, and financial provisions; and the Third Committee to deal with the position of the emperor, the constitution as the supreme law, and the renunciation of war. All sessions, plenary and committee, followed a general pattern: an initial period of fairly long oral statements by invited witnesses, followed by question-and-answer exchanges between the witnesses and members.

Perhaps the most interesting, if not the most important, single aspect of the commission's work was the series of local public hearings held throughout the country. The reports on these hearings are undoubtedly the richest single source of information on the thoughts and feelings of a representative group of Japanese about the state of their society under constitutional democratic government.

Each hearing consisted of a morning and an afternoon session, averaging a total of about five hours, with six to ten witnesses appearing. Under the rules, representatives were invited from such groups as big business, small and medium enterprises, labor, agriculture, women, youth organizations, newspapers, and academic circles. Not all groups were represented at all meetings, labor and the academic world being the least often represented. In the early meetings, representatives were named by their organizations or the media of public information or were appointed from among applicants by the appropriate organ of local government. However, the system was later altered so that about half were appointed according to the original plan and half by the commission chairman, after consultation with the steering committee, from among those who applied for the privilege of testifying. Witnesses were to deal with important constitutional problems on the basis of their actual experience.

Some witnesses spoke for organizations or groups that they represented; some specifically dissociated themselves from their groups and spoke as individuals, while pointing out that their views reflected the attitudes of those with whom they were associated; and some spoke purely as individuals. Some witnesses delivered what appeared to be carefully prepared speeches, while others chatted informally. What gave the testimony its value and interest was that the great majority of witnesses were obviously convinced intellectually or emotionally that what they said was of considerable importance to themselves, their country, and the issue of constitutionalism. It is worth while to summarize briefly some of the principal themes of the testimony, for they shed light not only on the relatively restricted issue of revision, but on the more important problem of popular attitudes toward the constitution and the society under it.

Opinion was split on the origins of the constitution. Both views described above—resentment against the occupation at the one extreme, and at the other disregard of origin because of the general excellence of the document—appeared. In between, however, there were many who felt strongly neither one way nor the other, but who indicated that it would be preferable for Japan to have a constitution that was Japanese beyond any doubt. Many commented on the language, either on the difficulty of words or phrases or on the strong foreign flavor.

A large majority of the witnesses in the early hearings desired an amendment of Article 9 that would explicitly recognize the inherent right of self-defense. On the other hand, there was unanimity of opinion against involvement in any kind of war, defensive or otherwise. A few stated that armed forces contributed to the dignity of an independent nation, but even those indicated no desire for a return to the pomp and circumstance of the old imperial forces. Some expressed the view that the Self-Defense Forces should be made constitutional because the contradiction between them and Article 9 was undermining respect for the constitution as a whole.

It was obvious that no one wanted a change that would threaten the new rights and freedoms. However, a clear majority were ready to approve a more explicit statement of responsibilities attaching to rights. The most frequently mentioned problem was the three rights of labor, which many asserted were being exercised by the unions to the detriment of the public. Some, however, strongly asserted that the existing statements relating rights and freedoms to the public welfare were adequate, and that the solution to the problem lay not in amendment but in education as to the nature of responsibility.

All who mentioned the issue supported the Emperor. However, there was wide divergence of opinion on whether the Emperor should remain a symbol or whether he should be made the head of state. Although there were many who strongly supported the head-of-state concept, none—except one obviously eccentric witness—wished to see the Emperor placed in a position in which he might again become involved in politics and manipulated, as was the case under the Meiji constitution.

There was also unanimous agreement that there should be no return to the old family system, especially the concentration of authority in the male head of the household. Even those who were most dubious about some of the features of the new family were quick to deny that they wanted a return to that aspect of the old. Most women stated that their new position was a great improvement, although some were not sure of the extent of the change that had taken place or were concerned over the disruptive effects on family life of some of their new freedoms.

Two problems frequently mentioned were filial piety, especially as expressed in the support of parents in old age, and equal rights of succession to property, especially farm land. Though a few expressed the thought that there should be a constitutional provision establishing the responsibility of children toward parents, others declared that the problem could be solved either by adequate enforcement of laws presently on the books or through what was termed proper family life. In the early hearings especially, the commission was anxious to hear opinions on the right of equal succession to property, particularly because it might result in the atomization of holdings of farm land. Most of the farmers who testified on this declared that although they were concerned about the general problem of atomization of land-holdings, there was little of it resulting from the right of equal succession (which arose, it will be recalled, from the constitutional principle of equality under the law). Most said that the problem was handled by voluntary renunciation of rights by heirs other than the eldest son, cash settlements, or provisions for higher education—or, again, that the matter would be solved if the proper relationships were maintained within the family.

Men as well as women expressed concern over such social problems as lack of proper respect on the part of children toward parents, juvenile delinquency, overemphasis on individual rights within the family, and the unwillingness of some girls to become farm brides. However, the solutions generally suggested did not include constitutional amendment, but a general raising and stabilization of the standard of living, social education, legislative action by the government (especially in the economic field), and the development of attitudes of love and mutual respect within the family (or, as one witness put it, proper family life, not the proper family system).

Three governmental problems mentioned by many were local government, the role of the House of Councillors in the Diet, and popular review of Supreme Court justices. The local government issues most frequently raised were financial burdens, inefficiency because of overlapping or duplication of function with local offices of central government agencies, and the possibility of supplementing or supplanting the prefectural system with a regional system. The most common complaint about the House of Councillors was that it had become almost identical with the House of Representatives because it also had become the scene of partisan political struggle and could therefore not act as an upper chamber of wisdom and moderation. There was almost unanimous opposition to popular review of Supreme Court justices, mainly on the grounds that it seemed to be meaningless.

In the agricultural prefectures particularly, economic problems under the constitution were a constant theme. A number of witnesses stated that Article 25, which guarantees the people the right to a minimum standard of wholesome and cultured living, was not being effectively enforced by the government. Others, especially women, stressed that the government was not providing completely free education as set forth in Article 26. Several farmers declared that the constitution should contain guarantees for farmers and fishermen similar to those for workers. Representatives of small and medium business enterprises made similar suggestions.

Two general themes, also typical of the agricultural prefectures, shed considerable light on popular attitudes toward the constitution. One could be stated thus: "The constitution is good, but it is also very idealistic. Can't something be done to close the gap between this idealism and the reality of our daily lives?" The other was: "The people in this area really do not know much about or understand the constitution. They cannot support either the constitution or democracy until they have had more education in and experience with political matters." Neither of these implied either abandonment of or pessimism about the future of constitutionalism, but rather its strengthening.

If the public hearings held by the Commission on the Constitution accurately reflected public attitudes toward the nation's fundamental law, the conclusion must be that while revision would be accepted, no tampering with fundamental rights and freedoms would be tolerated and that in general the constitution required a minimum of amendment to become completely Japanese. Perhaps the most important thing about this aspect of the commission's work was that the voice of the people had been heard as never before on the issue of constitutional government. It was the voice of a people anxious to retain for itself the benefits of democracy, and prepared to debate as responsible free citizens the issues bearing on the future of their fundamental law.

Even after three years of deliberations, there was no real clue as to the nature of the recommendations that the commission was bound by law to transmit to the cabinet. The reports of the commission sessions revealed a considerable split within the body, especially among the experts, along liberal versus conservative lines, without reference to partisan politics. That could lead to the submission of a majority and a minority report, for which there was abundant precedent in the decisions of the Supreme Court, for example.

But the problem of revision would not be solved by a report from the commission. Amendment can take place only under the following procedure: Initiation through "a concurring vote of two-thirds or more of all the members of each House," and then ratification by an affirmative vote of the majority of all votes cast by the people on the proposed amendment. This procedure, especially the initiation phase, throws the issue of revision squarely into partisan politics. No single conservative party or any combination of conservative parties has ever controlled two-thirds of the seats in both houses of the Diet. Only in 1949 and 1952 (and possibly in 1953, depending on how the small number of independent and minor-party members voted) have the conservatives mustered more than two-thirds of the seats in the House of Representatives. As we have seen, the socialists seem to be doomed indefinitely to a role as a permanent minority party on the basis of the slowness with which their popular vote has been increasing; nevertheless, they still control more than a third of the seats in the lower house. And there is no indication that the socialists, for all their internal strife, and the Communists will split on the issue of revision.

Another factor operating in favor of the constitution as it stands is that the longer the people live under a fundamental law that has yielded them desirable benefits and has revealed no basic defects (if defects can be measured by the failure of the constitutional system to function according to the broad patterns laid down in the document itself), the less they will consider it in need of change. Even the unfortunate situation created by the conflict between Article 9 and the defense establishment has not resulted in a slowing down of the effective operation of the constitutional system. An optimist would argue that the longer the constitution operates effectively, the less popular desire there will be for amendment, drastic or otherwise.

The Significance of Controversy

Putting aside for the moment the obvious and potentially serious problems confronting Japan's political democracy that have been revealed by the controversies discussed in this chapter, we can see that controversy has also provided an accurate gauge for the measurement of the strength of the new system. In the first place, it reveals the degree of existing political freedom. Clearly, freedom of assembly and association, freedom of thought, and freedom of all means of expression must exist in order for democratic political controversy to flourish. Had these and other freedoms not been present in Japan, there would have been no controversy—and no democracy. As long as such disputes continue, Japan's democracy will be safe. The sole concern must be to prevent them from growing into situations leading to chaos and collapse.

Controversy has demonstrated that arbitrary action by a political leader, a political party, or by the executive arm of the government will not pass unchallenged. To the opponents of the conservative wing in Japanese politics, the record must seem discouraging: the Self-Defense Forces established, an unpopular security treaty with the United States ratified, a degree of administrative control over the police returned to the hands of the government, and a law involving possible infringement on the freedom of association passed. Yet, each was challenged, and the government was forced to struggle very hard indeed to obtain the legislation it desired. Perhaps it should be reiterated as a general point that the undesirable outcome of all these conflicts has not resulted in the erosion of rights and freedoms that seemed to be threatened. As a matter of fact, the controversy over the 1960 security treaty could never have occurred had the potential for political evil of the revision of the Police Law and the passage of the Subversion Activities Prevention Law been realized.

The controversies have also demonstrated the existence of a healthy degree of political consciousness and concern among the people. Each of the quarrels was furthered by the socialists and Communists for partisan or ideological reasons. But a variety of other individuals and groups, for their own legitimate reasons, resorted to political action—not just mass demonstrations, but participation in elections and in active following of the question in the media of information.

Directly related to the issue of public concern over problems of political democracy was the additional important consideration of widespread alertness to the danger posed by the controversies. This was clearly manifested in an awareness of the possibility of a threat to the new rights and freedoms or of a return to the detested features of the old authoritarianism, as well as in a concern over the impact of unbridled controversy on democracy itself. In 1960, the Japanese themselves saw clearly the implications of the resort to violence and of the failure of both major political parties to abide by the standards of parliamentary procedure. Western experience has demonstrated many times that the greatest defense of democracy is this alertness to internal threats.

Finally, the differences of the 1950's demonstrated the strength and resilience of democracy. The bitterness, the extent, and the content of these controversies over the years between 1952 and 1960 might have produced a return of the military to a position of power and influence, the use of the police as an instrument of authoritarian control, the imposition by the government of a series of restraints on such freedoms as those of expression, assembly, and association, either a leftist or a rightist *coup d'état*, the collapse of parliamentary government, or the ending of free elections as the result of public indifference growing from a cynical rejection of the democratic process. Yet, not one of these occurred. Indeed, the system of parliamentary democracy seemed stronger than ever before in 1960, precisely because it had survived each crisis, great or small, and because of the broad popular awareness of the necessity for solving the problems revealed.

10

Present and Future Problems

Japan's democracy today faces three broad categories of problems: There are weaknesses and imperfections in the present democratic order that can reasonably be expected to produce no serious stresses and strains. There is a core of serious political problems that could undermine the democratic order if its generally strong resilience should be weakened. Finally and most importantly, there is a complex of international economic and political considerations, wrapped in the uncertainties of the future but none the less tangible, which may become sources of danger. The first two categories are under Japanese control, and the possibility is good that they are also within the capability of the Japanese to solve. The third, however, lies not only outside Japan, but also beyond Japanese control and probably even influence.

To apply the abstract standards of an egalitarianism that may or may not be characteristic of Western democracies to the social aspects of Japanese democracy is to expose the shortcomings that we have already observed: the failure to achieve a fuller realization of equality for women, the still incomplete sense of the worth and dignity of the individual, a strong sense of social hierarchy, the influence of the leader especially in rural society, and the subordination still of individual to group requirements. All of these, in one way or another, touch upon the problem of the role of the individual under democracy. There is no reason why these issues cannot be slowly solved within the system itself as it has already been created and as it has been in operation. More importantly, perhaps, there is no indication that the continued incomplete realization of individualism in Japanese society will erode the democratic system.

Two Minority Problems

Japanese society is confronted with two problems of discrimination that are likely to remain unresolved for some years. One involves the Eta, who might loosely be regarded as a caste, and the other the Korean residents, a national minority. The Eta have for centuries been an outcast group in Japanese society, apparently because they have engaged in occupations regarded as unclean or polluting, such as the slaughter of animals and working with leather. There is no accurate account of exactly when or how this caste originated. It is clear, however, that they have been accepted as being racially Japanese, though still considered outcasts. The name Eta is rarely used, non-Eta using the term "special community" or "people of the special community," and the Eta apparently preferring the term "new common people," arising from the abolition of the legal restrictions on them in 1871.

However, in spite of the earlier emancipation and the current guarantee of the equality of all individuals under the present constitution, the Eta have remained not only discriminated against, economically and socially, but despised as well. A few have passed into the general community in recent years, but most of the people of the special communities reside in segregated areas and under conditions of extreme poverty, except for a small percentage that have been able to raise themselves to an approximately lower middle-class level. In general, they are regarded with disgust and revulsion by the rest of society, which will have nothing to do with them. One American investigator has found that the Eta themselves have tended to develop strong feelings of group solidarity, partly as a means of self-protection and apparently as a result of centuries of tradition.

The Eta probably number about 2 million, a minority so small that it is impossible for it to attempt effectively to bring about a change in its position by means of political pressure, although it is represented by an organization striving to improve its position. However, in the public hearings of the Commission on the Constitution, at least two witnesses in the early sessions referred briefly to the unhappy plight of the "special community," which is obviously being discriminated against in violation of constitutional principles. Apart from expressions of sympathy and a statement that something should be done to change their social position, no concrete plan was put forward for helping these people. Perhaps the only hope for amelioration lies in the exceedingly deliberate operation of general social change, which may in time eliminate attitudes that have existed for centuries. However, if more of the general economic well-being of the country can percolate into the special communities, there is a possibility of a speeding up of the process of the elimination of discrimination. For this would enable their members to escape from their present poverty and squalor, thus easing their passage into the general community.

The Korean national minority constitutes a dilemma of a different order. Unlike the Eta, the Koreans are foreigners. But their position has been difficult because, although most of them came into the country as Japanese subjects, they were treated not merely as second-class citizens, but as colonial subjects. The majority were imported into Japan as extremely low-paid common labor after Korea was made a Japanese colony. From the late 1930's until the end of World War II, a great many Koreans flooded into the country. The demands of the wartime economy had created a serious shortage of labor in Japan proper, and, in addition, for many Koreans the wages, low as they were, were still better than what could be earned in colonial Korea. When the war ended and Korea was liberated from its colonial status, those who had come to Japan were permitted to be repatriated and to return to Korea. Of an estimated 2 million Koreans in Japan at the end of the war, about 75 per cent returned by mid-1948. The Korean minority numbered approximately 600,000 thereafter. In 1959, a program of repatriation to North Korea for those who wished it was worked out in collaboration with the International Red Cross, over the bitter opposition of South Korea. During 1960, perhaps 75,000 returned, leaving an estimated net population of about 500,000.

Except for a few who have been able to overcome the almost insuperable handicaps of their position, the lot of the Korean minority has been an unhappy one indeed. Suffering from the circumstances of their importation into Japan as the cheapest of common labor, they have been unable to raise their general level of living. They continue to be paid low salaries because of their lack of skill, and, since they are now legally foreigners, they must compete against Japanese who are competing among themselves for jobs. It is small wonder that the majority of the Koreans have been forced to live under slum conditions. As is the case with similar minority groups in other societies, the incidence of crime among the Koreans has been high. This is due partly to their depressed standard of living and partly (especially in the early years following liberation) to a resentment of their former colonial status expressed in a defiance of the law.

To complicate the situation further, the Communist movement among Korean residents has been strong. Communists from North Korea have naturally been eager to win as much support as possible from the Korean residents of Japan. In addition, the resentments created among some by discrimination have been turned to political use by the Communists, both Korean and Japanese.

However, it is safe to assume that the majority of the Korean residents are in Japan because they have chosen to be. Formal and informal repatriation between 1945 and 1948 and the North Korea program begun in 1959 took many back to their native land. If and when normal relations are established between the Republic of Korea and Japan, another repatriation program will undoubtedly be set up. Those who remain in Japan after that will clearly have decided to cast their lot there. Such residents will probably number well under half a million and will probably opt to become naturalized Japanese citizens. It is safe to predict that this troublesome minority issue will be settled by the end of the twentieth century. In any event, it is not likely to subject the democratic system to strain, as undesirable as some of its aspects may be.

Problems of Political Democracy

By far the greatest internal strains on the system of democracy have appeared in the area of politics. Some of them are minor:

the prevalence of factionalism in party politics, with the result that personalities of party leaders have outweighed matters of principle; the prevalence of bloc voting, especially in rural villages, which enables influential local leaders to produce, through the application of legitimate social pressure, the politically undesirable result of mustering the village vote behind a single candidate, invariably conservative; and the apparent control, again in the rural areas, of the female vote by the male members of the family. Similar problems have existed in Western democracies and have gradually been solved or kept politically insignificant. There is no reason to believe that the Japanese pattern will be different, assuming that other, more serious political questions are solved.

Violence is not only a problem but a source of deep concern. Nevertheless, it is also true that the Japanese political system has proved its capacity to absorb a very considerable degree of violence without impairment of freedom, of free elections, or of its system of responsible government. It is safe to say that only under conditions of revolution, an extremely remote possibility, will violence become a real threat to democracy. Indeed, at such a point the entire atmosphere of Japanese society would have changed to the extent that the conditions for democracy would have already disappeared.

By far the most serious political issue confronting Japanese democracy lies in the continued inability to perfect an effective two-party system. The fundamental question is not the minor one of creating such a system simply because any well-ordered democracy has one, but the far more important issue of providing a means for resolving political tensions. The problem is twofold, involving, on the one hand, the frustrations of the permanent minority and, on the other, the long tenure of the permanent majority. It is out of this situation that disturbing tensions have arisen and dangerous ones may arise in the future.

Under any system of party government, the party out of power can develop a considerable sense of frustration if long kept from control of the government. The Republican Party in the United States, for example, was out of power between 1933 and 1953. This long period of frustration undoubtedly contributed to the excesses of some of its principal figures in the arenas of domestic politics and foreign policy. Japan's socialists were in control of the government for only a short period under the occupation, under circumstances that made it impossible for them to operate effectively. The brief taste of power, the perhaps unconscious desire to prove that they could do better under more favorable circumstances, and their firm belief in the rightness of their policies have undoubtedly added considerably to the socialist sense of frustration.

But there is the additional exacerbating circumstance that they seem to be doomed indefinitely to a position in which they can capture only about a third of the popular vote and a third of the seats in the powerful lower house of the Diet. How long can their patience both as human beings and as party politicians last in this situation? Is it any wonder that the socialists have been eager to resort to political strikes, to mass demonstrations, and to unparliamentary procedures, even including violence, within the Diet in a vain effort to force the government and the party that controls it to yield on both policy and political issues?

The difficulties of the permanent minority are further compounded by the fact that it is also a socialist minority. The complex of theoretical and tactical questions thus created has inhibited the party from developing as an effective opposition, able to compete for the favor of the electorate with hope of success. Some of the foremost leaders—both intellectual and political—of the party are veteran socialists. During their period of persecution and struggle, perhaps their sole comfort was refuge in a doctrinaire Marxism that seemed to them not only to explain their current plight but to hold the key to the creation of a better society in which they could play an open role. It is not surprising that they should have become firm converts to the doctrine and considered it as still applicable to Japan under post–1945 conditions. Men of this cast of thought have been at the core of the influential and powerful left wing of the party, and this has created a great tactical difficulty.

It seems almost incredible that in the Japan of 1959–60 the second major political party could become mired in a bitter, divisive argument over the theoretical question of the role of revolution in contemporary Japanese politics, when there existed no conditions at all—economic, political, or social—that could produce either an active or a passive acceptance of a revolution. Yet, precisely such a controversy occurred. The adherence of a core group of leaders to a theory that was empty in terms of the real political situation vastly reduced the appeal of the party. It is hard to conceive of a party of workers and farmers coming to power in Japan. Its leaders now realize the necessity of the party's becoming truly a "mass party" and are striving desperately to make it so, but their simultaneous adherence to a revolutionary doctrine has little more than intellectual appeal to a restricted sector of voters concentrated in urban industrial areas. Therefore, the problem that the socialists must solve, if they are to come to power as a parliamentary party, is to reconcile their theoretical preoccupation with revolution with the requirements of building a mass appeal among a population that has no reason to think or to act in revolutionary terms.

This preoccupation with revolution and the record of resort to extremist political action provide some grounds for a fear of acts of political desperation by the socialists. Yet, such acts are not likely unless there is serious economic depression, coupled with a conservative government's attempts to quell economically inspired political discontent and unrest by oppressive measures—again, a situation in which the conditions for democracy would be largely missing.

There is also the problem of political tactics. If the socialists continue as a political party, their best chance for normal accession to power seems to lie in an accommodation to the existing situation, in which the people as a whole have no pressing economic problems, there is no observable oppression growing out of class struggle, and there are no serious social tensions. They could then begin to develop a political strategy designed to force the conservatives out of power, by working within the present framework of economic, political, and social reality. If the present high level of economic well-being persists, then that fact in itself may eventually force the socialists to abandon their devotion to the cause of revolution arising out of class conflict. Indeed, signs of such a trend began slowly to emerge during 1960, but it was too early to tell whether or not there would be a change in the very character of the party.

As to the long tenure of the permanent majority, we have noted the arbitrary and irresponsible actions of the conservatives during the political controversies of the 1950's and early 1960's. Certainly, they must have enjoyed the confidence bred of an apparently secure position as the dominant party, based on a consistent and substantial support by the electorate as a whole. Perhaps this was the principal reason for Kishi's reliance on the "voiceless voices" of support, which he alleged were in his favor during the fight over the security treaty. It is true that the majority of the people have supported the conservatives. But the question can always be raised as to whether this support is a positive endorsement of the specific policies and actions of the conservative government, or whether it reflects only a general support for the status quo. At any rate, in the election of 1955 the Japanese electorate gave convincing proof that it was capable of voting for a party that was not in power, by shifting its support to a rival conservative party.

It is clear that the reigning Liberal Democratic Party wants to maintain itself in power as long as possible. We have also seen the extent of the factional rivalry that pervades it. It is difficult to imagine the LDP shifting its position substantially as long as the socialists seem determined to fight on the line of their own choosing. There remains the remote possibility of the emergence of a second conservative party as a result of further factional conflict. Once this question of political competition among parties of more balanced appeal and strength were solved, the nation's political democracy would find itself on an even keel, subjected only to the normal, ever-present strains and tensions inherent in any free political system.

International Trade

Paradoxically, the areas containing the greatest threat to the future of Japan's democracy are ones in which there has been no true crisis since 1950, yet in which the danger of crisis must always lurk. One is Japan's delicate position in international trade. The other is her equally delicate position in international politics. Anything that serves to disturb the balance of either of these is likely to have immediate and adverse effects on Japan's democracy.

We have already noted the momentous consequences to its democracy of Japan's general prosperity, unprecedented in its own history and unparalleled in the rest of Asia. A firm prop of the new position of the individual in Japanese society, it has given social and economic groups an important stake in the maintenance of the new society. We should now examine a few other economic considerations of major importance, especially as they affect the serious problem of the country's international economic relations.

The maintenance of the present level of economic well-being is a matter of considerable political gravity, if for no other reason than that the population has found it desirable and has come to expect its continuation. If the sole problem were the ability of the Japanese to maintain the economy at the level necessary for continued prosperity, there would be no problem at all. The reason for this optimistic forecast lies in the history of Japanese economic development during the past century. Since 1870, Japan has successfully performed a series of economic tasks of great complexity and magnitude: the conversion of a feudal, agriculturally based economy into a modern, industrialized one; the creation of a world-wide network of trade and other economic operations such as banking and shipping; the establishment of a structure of heavy industry, which was the foundation for one of the world's more formidable military establishments; the amazingly rapid reconstruction of a war-ravaged domestic economy and the simultaneous re-establishment of a major network of world trade; and, finally, the development of an economy of mass consumption.

Obviously Japan drew on the store of scientific and technological knowledge that had been built up in the Western world, which had actually initiated the industrial and technological revolutions. But the fact remains that, except during the initial period in the nineteenth century, almost all these economic tasks were carried out by the Japanese alone, with only the normal amount of international interchange of ideas and techniques. This could not have been so effectively accomplished had Japanese society not developed a large body of trained personnel, adept in all the economic skills that are demanded in a complex modern, industrialized economy. Top-level governmental and private financial policy-makers, bankers, insurance actuaries, engineers, designers, scientists, transportation experts, agronomists, lawyers, naval architects, aircraft designers, statisticians, technicians of all types, international traders—the list is as long as the specializations necessary to keep an industrial society in effective operation. On a lower level, but of no less importance to the economy, is the large labor force, trained to keep the highly complicated machinery of industry in effective and orderly operation. This force has been created by the mass-education program that was sponsored by the Japanese Government from the beginning of the modern period, and by an equally great emphasis on high-school–level technical and trade schools.

Nor should it be forgotten that Japan has had in operation for many decades an efficient system of national government, the kind that could not only lend specific assistance to the economic development of the society, but could also create and maintain the conditions of order within the society that are so vital to the efficient operation of the economy—if efficiency is measured solely in terms of the maintenance of the economic well-being of the society as a whole.

To put the issue in other terms, through the process of solving a series of complicated economic questions, by the development of an effective structure of government, through the accumulation of knowledge and experience in dealing with national economic problems and processes, and by building up economic expertise on all levels, the Japanese have given an impressive demonstration of their ability to cope with real and pressing economic problems. It is this history that gives assurance that they have the capacity to solve their future problems—to the extent, that is, that the problems remain relatively unaffected by external considerations.

Moreover, in dealing with these major questions as well as in other economic developments, the Japanese have confronted and overcome a series of diverse crises. The transition from feudal agriculture to modern industrialization was a major crisis, entailing not only economic tensions of a considerable order, but also social and political ones as well. The stresses and strains caused by the expansion of war industry, especially after 1937, constituted a crisis of a different order. So did the postwar reconstruction, which involved not only rebuilding of wrecked plant facilities, but the handling of an inflation that fell just short of being as catastrophic as those that visited China during World War II and Germany after World War I. The struggle to get out of the depression of the mid–1920's and the complete loss of all overseas economic interests and contacts after World War II were still others. All of them were so handled that Japan did not fall into economic disaster. The meeting of these crises with their attendant problems provided, again, a source of experience and of skill that will be an invaluable asset in the future.

What makes Japan's past achievements even more impressive, and also raises the crucial problem of the future, is the list of insoluble economic handicaps: a restricted area, about 142,000 square miles, of which only about 24,000 square miles can be tilled (which means that only about 80 per cent of the food requirements for its population of more than 90 million can be met domestically); and either an absolute lack or a grave insufficiency of almost all the basic animal, plant, or mineral raw materials for modern industry, heavy or light. Thus, Japan is dependent on foreign trade—imports of food and raw materials, and exports of manufactured goods to pay for imports—not only for economic stability and prosperity, but for economic existence itself.

Of crucial importance to Japan, then, is the maintenance of a going system of international trade on the level developed during the 1950's. Whatever the defects of that system, it was not typified by insuperable barriers that denied for economic reasons alone—as distinct from strategic or political reasons—the access of any nation to external markets and sources of raw materials. It was as an operating link in such a system that Japan was able to make its remarkable economic gains in the 1950's. But obviously the maintenance of such a system was beyond the power of the Japanese alone. This dependence on outside sources and markets had confronted the Japanese virtually from the moment the process of industrialization was inaugurated.

The Japanese have placed major emphasis on their external economic relations for many decades. In the first place, they emerged on the stage of international relations in the latter part of the nineteenth century, when most governments and most private enterprises thought in terms of the capture of foreign markets and of foreign sources of raw materials, either by direct territorial conquest or by indirect political or economic controls. Japan's early penetration of Korea and China was to a large extent cut on the same pattern as the economic imperialism of the Western powers at the end of the nineteenth century. As the pace of Japan's industrialization was stepped up—as a result of development and expansion, as well as the economic demands of the wars with China and Russia—so the Japanese came to be more keenly aware of their own deficiency in industrial raw materials and of the desirability for capturing control over foreign markets for their products. From the time of World War I until the conquest of most of Asia in 1941–42, one of the major motivations for Japan's aggression was the consuming desire to achieve autarky.

Another manifestation of the impact of external economic relations on Japan's policy was the manner in which foreign markets for Japanese goods in the late 1920's and the early 1930's were closed. The Chinese resort to the boycott as a highly effective means of protest against Japanese pressures had an immediate adverse effect on Japan. At the same time, major nations of the West began to erect tariff barriers and quota systems against the inflow of Japanese-produced goods. This phenomenon was observable not only in these nations themselves, but also in their colonies, especially in Asia and Africa. This was an expression of economic nationalism that the Western nations resorted to in an attempt to solve their own economic difficulties arising out of the world-wide depression. They must have thought that if they could sell to all and buy from none, they could end unemployment and bring back prosperity. Whatever the demerits of this policy as a means of solving economic difficulties, the result was that the Japanese were shown in no uncertain terms what the loss of foreign markets could do to their economy. It is now perfectly clear that Japan can no longer ever hope to achieve direct control over either foreign sources of raw materials or foreign markets.

Japan's dependence on international trade is obviously a major economic factor in its future, but the pattern of its foreign trade is also a matter of some significance. It can be sketched in skeleton form by the following rough figures concerning Japan's foreign trade in 1958: The United States, by far Japan's most important trade partner, provided more than a third of Japan's total imports and purchased approximately 20 per cent of Japan's total exports; all of Asia took about 40 per cent of Japan's exports and provided about 30 per cent of the imports. Thus, one nation and one geographical area accounted for about three-fifths of Japan's total trade. This situation in itself constitutes a special economic problem for Japan.

In the first place, there is the obvious fact that Japan's foreign trade, and consequently its economic stability, is dependent to an excessive degree on the economy of another nation, the United States. As long as the United States continues to buy from Japan, there is no problem. However, depressionary economic conditions in the United States would immediately have an adverse effect on such purchases. Moreover, changes in American diplomacy and politics could also have an immediate adverse effect on trade relations with Japan. The situation for Japan is not a basically sound one: disproportionate dependence on the United States, with a consequent exposure to American economic and political shifts over which the Japanese Government has no control.

The case in respect to Asia is somewhat different, yet the problem of dependence is almost as great. Economically—as well as politically—Asia is diverse and complex, yet there is a pattern of similarity in factors affecting its foreign trade. First, there is the major factor of political and governmental instability, with a consequent economic instability that is characteristic of the entire area. With the exception of Thailand, all the countries of Asia have new governments, none of which existed prior to the end of World War II. Each of these new governments is still going through a developmental stage, a situation true even of the Philippines, which had an experience of growing into self-government for far longer than the others. Most of the governments are also confronted with difficult political conditions in which there is actual or potential armed resistance to the constituted authority of the government itself, certainly a factor that contributes further to economic instability.

Moreover, all the other governments of Asia are situated in underdeveloped areas, still in the process of building economic viability with at least limited industrialization. In addition, all are plagued with other, more immediate economic matters: unstable governmental finances, poverty, unemployment, inflation, foreign-trade problems, agrarian difficulties. In general, then, the situation in Asia outside of Japan is one of advanced political and economic dislocation, instability, and uncertainty. Under the circumstances, it is remarkable that trade with the outside world, including Japan, has developed to the extent that it has. In terms of Japanese economics, this situation is unpredictable and uncertain.

However, it should be stressed that the situation is also one of enormous economic promise as far as Japan is concerned. Assuming no further deterioration in free Asia in general, which, in turn, would mean no worsening of the over-all economic situation, Japan's economic stance in the whole area could be strengthened progressively during most of the second half of the twentieth century. Japan as the only truly industrialized nation in Asia possesses the personnel, the goods, the skills, and the tools that could play a major role in Asiatic economic development, particularly in the former colonial areas. Indeed, Japan's reparations settlements with the countries it once occupied show clearly the pattern of mutually beneficial economic relations that can be worked out between Japan and its Asian neighbors. Briefly, Japan supplies goods, services, and capital loans to the areas with which it has reparations agreements. The recipient countries benefit because they obtain badly needed economic assistance; Japan benefits because of the creation of economic relations that in both the short and the long haul should prove profitable, provided the nations of free Asia can successfully solve the very pressing problems that are characteristic of their newness.

Finally, there is the difficult problem of trade with Communist China, an issue of major concern to many Japanese and a vexing world problem. In the eyes of many Japanese, Red China has an enormous economic attraction, mainly because of the history of Japanese economic relations with the Chinese mainland. The precise extent of past Japanese trade with the mainland has been a matter of much dispute. However, it is generally accepted that in what might be considered the normal prewar years, from about 1930 to 1937, the Chinese mainland took somewhat over 20 per cent of Japan's exports and provided somewhat less than 20 per cent of its imports. In broader terms, what the history of Sino-Japanese economic relations demonstrated was that China had raw materials that could be utilized in Japanese plants, and that China could purchase the manufactured goods from the factories of Japan. Thus, the prospect is attractive. Yet the economic aspects of trade with Communist China are far overshadowed by a complex of political and diplomatic issues.

First of all, there is the fact that Communist China is interested in trade with Japan for political reasons as much as for economic ones. The building up of extensive trade relations with Japan would serve admirably the diplomatic objectives of Red China and the Communist world, if for no other reason than that it would tend to draw Japan away from the United States and the free world and toward the Communist orbit. It might take a long time to make an appreciable dent in the economic relations between Japan and the United States, but the building up of trade would inevitably turn Japanese attention and consequently Japanese policy more and more in the direction of the Communist world. The Japanese must also consider the reaction of the United States to a widening of economic relations with Red China. The executive branch might take a tolerant view of it, but it is safe to predict that the Congress would not, particularly since such a move would provide a good excuse for retaliatory acts encouraged by protectionist groups that feel their interests have been damaged by Japanese imports.

Whatever the arguments for or against trade with Red China, the facts of the situation are that when limited unofficial trade existed, in the mid–1950's, it was minute, representing something well under 1 per cent of Japan's total foreign trade.

Thus, the direction of Japan's external economic relations, both current and prospective, creates difficult problems that have a direct bearing on Japan's internal economic situation. Most important is the fact that Japan's internal economy stands to be extensively and perhaps adversely affected by developments in the economies of other nations. This is perhaps the item of greatest uncertainty in the whole spectrum of Japan's economic problems.

The entire issue of Japan's economic present and future has a direct bearing on the problem of democracy, because economic factors will contribute significantly to the total environment in which Japanese political issues will be worked out. An economic crisis would inevitably bring in its wake a major political crisis, the shape of which can be easily foreseen. On the one hand, the conservative majority would immediately be challenged because it could, if still in control of the Diet and consequently of the cabinet, be held politically responsible for the country's plight. To maintain itself in power, the government would be greatly tempted to move toward the extreme right, to resort to repressive measures to silence opposition. Simultaneously, the position of the left would be strengthened; obviously, its political appeals, slogans, and arguments would carry much more weight. In such a situation, the moderate, the democratic way would be squeezed more and more between the growing extremes of both the right and the left.

International Affairs

We have noted the threat to Japan's economic stability, and ultimately to its democratic political patterns, of a dependence on external trade relations. Closely related to this issue is that of the possible influence of Japan's diplomatic role in world affairs on its internal politics. In addition to the diplomatic consequences of the foreign-trade issue, there are other diplomatic aspects of equally grave importance to the future of democracy in Japan.

For instance, the geographical location of Japan places it in an unusual diplomatic environment. To the north and to the west lies the eastern segment of the vast bulk of the Soviet Union, a traditional enemy of Japan and the possessor of a massive military striking power that makes it the leader of the Communist world. To the west and southwest lies Communist China, certainly the leader of the rest of Asia. To the west also lie the two Koreas, sworn enemies of each other and a focal point of the tension between not only the free world and the Communist world, but also between the United States and the Soviet Union. The two Koreas are united perhaps only in their common dislike and hatred of Japan—the heritage of a third of a century of colonial rule. Finally, in comparison with the rest of Asia, Japan is an island of political stability.

Two circumstances operate to prevent Japan from becoming fully integrated into the web of international relations of Asia. In the first place, significant segments of Asia are Communist: the Soviet Far East, North Korea, mainland China, and North Vietnam. Thus, with the minor exception of the Republic of Korea, the coastline of Asia, extending from far north of Japan to far south of it, is under Communist control. The history of Japanese contacts with the Soviet Union and the Chinese Communists before their accession to power and of Japanese domestic anti-Communism have made rapprochement with these Communist governments highly unattractive to the Japanese Government. In the second place, the non-Communist areas of Asia, South Korea, Taiwan, the Philippines, South Vietnam, Laos, Cambodia, Thailand, Malaya, Burma, and Indonesia all have felt the oppressive weight of Japanese occupation. As a result, all have felt it necessary to keep Japan at least at arm's length. Thus, a combination of circumstances, some of which were created by Japanese actions and some of which were not, have combined to put Japan in a state of semi-isolation in respect to the rest of Asia.

Ironically, Japan's closest, perhaps only, ally since the late 1940's has been the United States, separated from Japan by more than 4,000 miles. The role of the United States in Japan's democratic revolution has been stressed here. Of equal significance, the United States also was responsible for the economic assistance that helped to put Japan back on its feet and was the sponsor for Japan's return to the international community. From 1948 on, the United States both through the occupation and from Washington assisted Japan in its successful attempt to rebuild its international economic and diplomatic relationships. The peace treaty, signed in 1951, was American-authored and far more generous than Japan had any reason to hope for when the war came to an end. Actually, it was American insistence and negotiation that finally won the acceptance by the other allies of that generous peace. When the treaty was signed, the United States also assumed responsibility for Japan's security. Finally, the United States became Japan's sponsor for entry into the United Nations. Behind all this also lay a massive structure of cultural interchange, in the initial stages largely the one-way impact of the American occupation on Japanese society, but of greater and greater reciprocity as time went on, involving the interchange of people—tourists, businessmen, students, scholars, literary figures, politicians, athletic teams—the broad flow of news and information, translation of literary works, marriages between Japanese and Americans, and virtually every other conceivable variety of cultural and social interchange.

Clearly, the self-interests of both governments and both peoples were served by this close alliance. The Japanese received badly needed economic assistance and also the guarantee against an attack from the Communist world in the tense period between 1950 and 1953, when the Korean War was raging nearby. The United States received assurances that it could continue to use Japan as a major base during the same period and, of even greater import, could be assured of the continued cooperation of a stable and democratic ally in an Asia in which American policy had singularly few things to its credit. Beyond these considerations, there was also a foundation of mutual interest, sympathy, and understanding that made possible the wide flow of less formal influences between the two countries.

Yet, this relationship with the United States has created one of the most grievous series of political and diplomatic difficulties confronting the Japanese Government and its leaders. First of all, the very closeness of the relationship has caused many Japanese to react against it. The extremes on both the right and the left have argued that Japan is simply a colony of the United States, economically, politically, and socially. Japan is independent in name only, the argument runs. On the other hand, there is also a large body of responsible opinion in Japan that holds with equal conviction that the situation is an unhappy one: first, because it means that Japan has chosen sides and consequently has automatically made itself a potential target in the event that the Cold War becomes hot; and second, because such a close working alliance has made it impossible for Japan to have a completely independent foreign policy.

We have already seen how these close relations with the United States have influenced the development of the constitutional-revision movement and also the problem of the establishment of trade relations with Red China. There was also the vexing question of American bases in the country, strictly legal under the terms of formal treaties, and desirable and necessary from the standpoint of the security requirements of both governments. Nevertheless, as would be true in any country, there was no disguising the fact that the bases and their personnel were foreign and that their contacts with and impact on the Japanese community were not in all cases of the happiest kind.

Consequently, it was not surprising that the issue of relations with the United States became one of the centers of political controversy and debate inside Japan. The difficulty was that it had been clearly demonstrated that of all outside influences operative on Japan following the end of World War II, it was the United States that was responsible for the introduction of democracy, for the outside aid necessary to help Japan back on her feet, and for enabling Japan to re-enter the community of nations with the greatest possible speed and with the least friction.

Since the end of the occupation, Japanese diplomacy in respect to world politics (exclusive of the bilateral relationship with the United States) has been built on three basic issues: firm cooperation and collaboration with the United Nations, of which Japan became a member late in 1956; firm alliance with the free world; and what Japan has termed "economic diplomacy"—namely, the maintenance and development of trade with all the free world. I shall discuss here only the second of these.

It is almost impossible to divorce this issue from the alliance with the United States, but it is necessary to do so. As we have seen, many Japanese for a variety of reasons have been made uncomfortable by the very closeness of the ties with the United States. On the other hand, there has been no dispute—except from the Communist minority—about the desirability of the maintenance and strengthening of the alliance with the free world. Even the neutralist bloc in politics and public opinion has urged not the abandonment of the free-world alliance, but its balancing with wider relations with the Communist bloc. The free-world alliance obviously does not carry the same implications as that with the United States, mainly because the latter involves siding with one great military power, which in turn involves the possibility of Japan's being drawn into a major war. The diffuseness of the general alliance with the non-Communist world does not carry the same implication of war.

The great significance of the free-world alliance to Japan's democracy is that it represents a Japanese willingness to stand together with a group of nations built around a core of Western democracies. In other words, it is a manifestation of a Japanese ideological affinity with the world's free nations.

It is perfectly safe to say that as long as both the alliance with the United States and the alignment with the free world persist, there will be no strain on Japan's democracy induced by external influences. The continuation of this situation means an automatic barrier to the potentially erosive effect on Japan's democracy by influences from the Communist bloc. The question here is not that of Communist subversion, the chances of which are remote. Rather, the problem is one not only of possible interference in Japan's domestic politics by a foreign Communist power, but also of the creation of either a specific situation or a general atmosphere in which there would be a strong likelihood of the introduction of nondemocratic and antidemocratic tendencies from the outside.

Initially, there was the geographical proximity of the two great Communist powers, which lay either in actual sight or within a few hundred miles of Japan itself, and with whom Japan had no formal diplomatic relations. In the fall of 1956, Japan and the Soviet Union signed a "declaration of peace" under which the state of war between the two governments was brought to an end and formal relations were established. However, this declaration was not a treaty of peace, and so in that sense relations between the two governments were still not normal. On the other hand, there were no formal relations between Japan and Communist China, although the flow of people, especially from Japan to China, was extensive.

Japan's problem was how to balance its geographical position on the edge of the center of power of the Communist world with its political, diplomatic, and economic involvement with the distant United States and the free world. The balance has been in the favor of the latter, and the Japanese Government seems committed to a policy of maintaining that balance. However, it has been so heavily weighted toward the West that almost any move from or toward the Communist world may result in a shift with perhaps far-reaching consequences for Japan's democracy.

The Japanese Government and a substantial segment of the Japanese public were keenly aware of the possible untoward effects on the country's domestic politics of a broadening of relations with the Soviet Union and Communist China. The most concrete demonstration of this concern appeared in the declaration of peace with the Soviet Union. The last paragraph of Article 3 of that declaration read: "The U.S.S.R. and Japan pledge themselves mutually not to interfere directly or indirectly in each other's internal affairs for any reasons of an economic, political, or ideological nature." Given the character of the political systems of the two signatories, this provision could apply effectively only to possible future Soviet activities in Japan. The point here is not whether the Soviet Union would scrupulously honor such a commitment, but that the Japanese Government was apprehensive of such interference in its internal affairs and wished some reassurance on this point.

In the last half of 1960, when the problem of the establishment of formal relations with Communist China became a live issue, Prime Minister Ikeda and Foreign Minister Kosaka Zentaro repeatedly stated that a necessary prerequisite for institution of relations would be a firm pledge by the Communist Chinese Government that it would not interfere in Japanese internal affairs.

With the well-organized but ineffective Communist Party and at least the left wing of the Socialist Party sympathetically inclined toward the Communist bloc, it would be strange indeed if either or both the Soviet Union and Communist China did not —in spite of any formal commitments to the contrary—attempt by every means to strengthen the position of these two groups in Japanese internal politics. The returns, both political and diplomatic, would be large indeed and could conceivably be achieved by means considerably short of subversion itself.

There is, in addition, the highly "iffy" possibility of the development by the Soviet Union, if not yet by Communist China, of a newer, stronger, and more attractive position and policy that might result in a peaceful shifting of the center of political gravity clearly and definitely toward it and away from the free world. Such a shift could arise from such elements as the attraction inherent in spectacular scientific achievements, the mounting of a purposeful, persistent, and successful campaign of economic competition with the free world, and the assumption of a military posture less threatening in terms of either general war or local aggression than has been true since World War II. Such a shift, if it ever should occur, could come about without the abandonment of the ultimate goal of the Soviet Union and its leaders— the creation of a Communist world composed of a congeries of authoritarian Communist states—because it would result from a radical change in tactics, not in strategy. But such a tactical change would also have to depend on a thoroughgoing alteration of social, economic, and political conditions within the Soviet Union. The possibility is much more remote in Communist China because of the relatively little progress that it has made toward the solution of its own very difficult internal problems.

It has already been clearly demonstrated that both the real and the alleged progress that these two Communist societies have made toward a solution of their problems, in spite of threatening and aggressive foreign policies, has had a tremendous appeal for those societies of Asia that are confronted with the same economic and social problems but have progressed more slowly toward their solution and are perhaps even more desperately interested in solving them. Assuming that in the last four decades of the twentieth century the stronger, more attractive policy outlined above is developed, then the Soviet Union particularly would have an even greater appeal for a whole complex of other governments, especially those whose societies are underdeveloped. The world may not go Communist; it may be that democracy and Communism can coexist. But if the Communist states can achieve the degree of social, economic, and political stability they are striving for, then there will be created an entirely new international situation, one in which they may be able to make rapid strides toward bringing many other governments under their influence, if not their control.

What might be the impact of such developments on Japan and its democracy? The answer to this question can only be highly speculative. However, it is clear that the effect on Japan's foreign policy would be immediate and extensive. Peaceful developments of the sort described would initially create entirely new circumstances for the bilateral relations between Japan and Communist China, and between Japan and the Soviet Union. In addition, if most of the rest of Asia were affected in the manner indicated, then the whole network of Japanese economic relations with Asia would be influenced. Thus, such shifts would inevitably mean that the ties between Japan and the free world would be drastically altered.

How this would affect Japan's internal political order, its democracy, is much less easy to foresee. If, even after such drastic shifts in their own internal situations, the Soviet Union and Communist China remained as characteristically totalitarian as they were in the past, then the shift in their diplomatic position would undoubtedly have an adverse effect on Japan's democracy. It is difficult to see how it could remain unaffected by the geographical proximity, the powerful and perhaps attractive example, and the purposeful diplomacy of its Communist neighbors.

If the future does contain these palpable but unrealized international economic and political threats to Japan's democracy, the course for the free world, and especially its leaders among the nations of the West, seems clear: to devise and to execute policies toward Japan that serve to create a maximally favorable international environment for external support for democracy there. Such a course would involve no special favors for Japan and no special effort on the part of the Western democracies—only an unclouded perception of the problem and a firm resolve to act cooperatively with each other and with Japan to solve it. Thus would the nations in which modern democracy first arose serve their own self-interest in the midst of the tensions, the uncertainties, and the dangers of the second half of the twentieth century. Even more, they would serve anew the cause of democracy at a time when the strength and viability of its institutions and ideals are badly in need of reaffirmation.

Epilogue: The Lessons

Japan's experience with democracy has taught us a small number of highly significant lessons concerning not only Japan and democracy, but some important questions of government and politics in the world of the mid-twentieth century.

The most important lesson is that Japan's experiment has proved that modern democracy is of universal relevance, not, as was erroneously assumed in past decades, suitable only for some of the nations of the Western world or for other peoples sharing the same traditions and experiences. Japan had neither the history nor the tradition that could serve as the fountainhead of an indigenous variation on the theme of democracy. In the more recent decades of its history, furthermore, it had chosen to develop an authoritarian system of government and politics, in harmony with its own past and with one prevailing form of political organization on the world scene. Yet, under the proper but unusual combination of circumstances, Japan created in a remarkably short space of time its own democracy, identical in its crucial characteristics with the general democratic pattern. This was a break with tradition and with an apparently strong and enduring system of values, but it found a ready welcome in a society in which the conditions for democracy had been invisibly established over a period of decades.

If the conclusion to be drawn from this lesson is sound, then democracy must be included in the long list of social, political, and economic developments originating in the Western world but now being extended throughout the globe. The list is long: industrialization, the modern bureaucracy, the political party, the media of mass communications, modern science and technology, modern armed forces, mass literacy, and all the other institutions that are a part of the functioning contemporary national society. The time has long passed since these could be claimed as the unique products of a "genius" characteristic only of Western civilization. They were the result of a complex series of historical developments and accidents, the gradual emergence of new social, political, and economic relationships in an environment localized initially in Western Europe, and, of course, the operation in certain key instances of the individual genius of gifted human beings. But because they are the characteristic features of the modern nation-state, they are also the very tissue of the modern world. For better or for worse, the modern national society, in its beneficent operation, is the only type of social organization that permits peoples to be independent and the individual to enjoy the supports and benefits of an effectively operating society, and which, in its maleficent operation, has brought itself and humankind to the brink of ultimate disaster.

Almost alone of all the major developments of the Western world, democracy has been regarded as relevant only to the West or to peoples partaking in the Western tradition. Not one new nation has rejected industrialization, modern science or technology, mass literacy, or the modern bureaucratic state, for all their Western origin, their present complexity, the strangeness of the concepts and techniques involved, the conflict of values created when they come into societies that have never known them, or the special knowledge and skills that they require. The argument always runs that those and similar matters deal with the material and the concrete and are thus more manageable, while democracy deals with values, institutions, and attitudes vastly more difficult to understand and adopt because they are less tangible and more abstract. Yet, while accepting this significant difference between the two areas, I also urge that it is not sufficient reason for giving up on the issue of the exportability or, better, the universality of democracy.

The task of creating a democracy is not a simple one. Even

the successful Japanese experience underscores this point. It was the three-quarters of a century consumed in the building and operation of the institutions of the modern nation-state that provided the essential substructure for Japan's democracy. But it should also be noted that the necessary institutions had been created in not much more than a quarter of a century prior to 1900, and that it was the pressure of internal and external politics in the first part of the twentieth century that guided Japan in a direction opposite from that of democracy. But the possible difficulty of the task should not distract the leaders and the people of new nations all over the world from the ultimate goal of democracy, any more than the comparable difficulties involved in the creation of an industrial economy or raising the standard of living of a newly independent people have stood in the way of working toward those goals.

Another lesson, intimately related to this one, is that a society nurtured in a nondemocratic tradition need not recapitulate the entire evolution of democracy, any more than those nations striving for industrialization need to recapitulate the whole evolution of the scientific attitude that was the necessary prelude to industrialization. The achievement of democracy by a new nation may still be a matter of decades rather than years, but it is not a matter of centuries. It would not be unrealistic to assume that, in the great majority of the nations that have become independent since the end of World War II, democracy could be achieved in the lifetime of children now living. The chief requirements would be the attainment of a level of social, economic, and governmental stability sufficient to insure a viable national society (a requirement, incidentally, for an authoritarian or totalitarian state as well); the decision by the leadership of such new nations that a democratic society is both achievable and desirable; and the willingness of the older democracies—including Japan—to cooperate in the attainment of the general goal of stability and the particular goal of democracy.

A third lesson of great significance taught by Japan's democracy is the universality of the appeal of freedom. Because there was no reason to do so, no one seriously believed at the end of World War II that the Japanese would widely recognize freedom, that they would adopt and cherish it, or that they would defend it—at least not until after a considerable period of tutelage. A centuries-old history without a tradition of freedom, an even older system of social organization that had no room for the concept of either individual liberty or an atmosphere of liberty in society, two generations of indoctrination in the importance and desirability, even the necessity, of blind support of an authoritarian system, and censorship and suppression that effectively prevented either the existence or the enjoyment of freedom seemed to have created a population that neither knew nor pondered—hardly even comprehended—the meaning of freedom. And yet the response to it was instantaneous and spectacular. If the institutions of democracy were strange to Japan, many believed that liberty, an apparent abstraction, would be even stranger. Nevertheless, it was conclusively proved that freedom, too, knew no boundaries and that it was not an exclusive possession of the democracies of the West, to be won and understood only after generations of struggle.

Of less broad significance to general problems of democracy and politics, but of critical tactical importance, is the fourth lesson: that Japan's experience has proved the general strength of democracy as a system and an ideal at a time when international Communism seems to have seized the initiative on the world political scene and when a combination of achievement and propaganda exploitation seem to make it appear to be the wave of the future. In the years between 1945 and 1955, Japan had, under extremely unpromising conditions, seen its system of democracy established and put it into effective operation, and had begun to enjoy the tangible economic, political, social benefits flowing from it. No Communist state, old or new, could claim such solid achievements for its people. We do not have to stress the very real presence of freedom in Japan and its absence in Communist societies. It is impossible to ignore or belittle the great importance of the Soviet Union in world affairs or its sizable achievements in certain areas of science. But certainly the Russian people do not know freedom, and it is doubtful if they have reached the level of economic well-being that the Japanese people now enjoy. It is impossible also to detract from the significance of the Communist victory in China. The loss of China was a major setback to the free world; and the potentialities for the future are grave indeed. There are no grounds at all for any attempt—which, in any event, is not being made here—to balance the loss of China to Communism by the gain of Japan to democracy and the free world. But the fact remains that what democracy has achieved inside Japan is solid, substantial, considerable, and enduring.

The situation is different inside China. The Communist Government has yet to demonstrate that it is fully capable of handling China's tremendous internal problems or even of maintaining itself permanently in power. The future of Communism itself is still not secure, for the vexing problems of an adequate supply of food for a gigantic and growing population, the role of agriculture in the new economy, and industrialization still remain unsolved. There seems to be no net gain observable from the outside in the improvement of the economic lot of the average Chinese. And it is beyond challenge that all freedom—except the freedom to conform, which is no freedom—has vanished from the Chinese scene. Yet China has been looked to as the model for many of the world's new nations, while Japan has scarcely been noted.

I am not touching here on the problem of the power alignment between non-Communist and Communist blocs, an issue on which it is difficult to see that democracy in Japan can have any direct effect. What I am emphasizing is that the experience of Japan has demonstrated beyond question that there is life and vitality in the idea and the practice of democracy in the second half of the twentieth century. A clearer realization of this fact might provide the free world with more than a slight infusion of confidence and renewed strength in its competition with the Communist bloc.

Finally, a word of caution. The lessons of Japan's experience with democracy cannot be extrapolated into the situations of the new nations of Asia and Africa; they provide only the most general, albeit useful, guidelines for possible new approaches to action and thought regarding the relevance of democracy to them and their problems. There were too many unique factors in Japan that cannot be—or should not be—injected into the situations of other nations: the lost war and the occupation, the country's institutional readiness for democracy, a masterful policy for democracy implemented by a military occupation paradoxically dedicated to bringing freedom and democracy to the country, and the peculiar psychological posture of the Japanese people involving the rejection of war, aggression, and authoritarianism and the positive and purposeful welcome for democracy. But even this cautionary qualification does not obviate the significance of the Japanese lesson.

If the mid-twentieth century witnessed the end of an unhappy and disastrous chapter of militarism and authoritarianism in the history of Japan and the beginning of a new chapter filled with the great promises of freedom and prosperity, it also witnessed the beginning of what might become an exciting new chapter in the history of democracy itself, one in which it seemed ready to burst the chains that bound it to the civilization of the West and to demonstrate that it could bring freedom and justice to all mankind—not only to the historically favored few.

Appendix

TEXT OF THE CONSTITUTION OF JAPAN*

We, the Japanese people, acting through our duly elected representatives in the National Diet, determined that we shall secure for ourselves and our posterity the fruits of peaceful cooperation with all nations and the blessings of liberty throughout this land, and resolved that never again shall we be visited with the horrors of war through the action of government, do proclaim that sovereign power resides with the people and do firmly establish this Constitution. Government is a sacred trust of the people, the authority for which is derived from the people, the powers of which are exercised by the representatives of the people, and the benefits of which are enjoyed by the people. This is a universal principle of mankind upon which this Constitution is founded. We reject and revoke all constitutions, laws, ordinances, and rescripts in conflict herewith.

We, the Japanese people, desire peace for all time and are deeply conscious of the high ideals controlling human relationship, and we have determined to preserve our security and existence, trusting in the justice and faith of the peace-loving peoples of the world. We desire to occupy an honored place in an international society striving for the preservation of peace, and the banishment of tyranny and slavery, oppression and intolerance for all time from the earth. We recognize that all peoples of the world have the right to live in peace, free from fear and want.

*From *The Constitution of Japan and Criminal Statutes* (Tokyo: Ministry of Justice, 1958).

We believe that no nation is responsible to itself alone, but that laws of political morality are universal; and that obedience to such laws is incumbent upon all nations who would sustain their own sovereignty and justify their sovereign relationship with other nations.

We, the Japanese people, pledge our national honor to accomplish these high ideals and purposes with all our resources.

Chapter I. THE EMPEROR

Article 1. The Emperor shall be the symbol of the State and of the unity of the people, deriving his position from the will of the people, with whom resides sovereign power.

Article 2. The Imperial Throne shall be dynastic and succeeded to in accordance with the Imperial House Law passed by the Diet.

Article 3. The advice and approval of the Cabinet shall be required for all acts of the Emperor in matters of state, and the Cabinet shall be responsible therefor.

Article 4. The Emperor shall perform only such acts in matters of state as are provided for in this Constitution and he shall not have powers related to government.

2. The Emperor may delegate the performance of his acts in matters of state as may be provided by law.

Article 5. When, in accordance with the Imperial House Law, a Regency is established, the Regent shall perform his acts in matters of state in the Emperor's name. In this case, paragraph one of the preceding article will be applicable.

Article 6. The Emperor shall appoint the Prime Minister as designated by the Diet.

2. The Emperor shall appoint the Chief Judge of the Supreme Court as designated by the Cabinet.

Article 7. The Emperor, with the advice and approval of the Cabinet, shall perform the following acts in matters of state on behalf of the people:

    (1) Promulgation of amendments of the constitution, laws, cabinet orders, and treaties;

    (2) Convocation of the Diet;

    (3) Dissolution of the House of Representatives;

    (4) Proclamation of general election of members of the Diet;

    (5) Attestation of the appointment and dismissal of Ministers of State and other officials as provided for by law, and of full powers and credentials of Ambassadors and Ministers;

(6) Attestation of general and special amnesty, commutation of punishment, reprieve, and restoration of rights;

(7) Awarding of honors;

(8) Attestation of instruments of ratification and other diplomatic documents as provided for by law;

(9) Receiving foreign ambassadors and ministers;

(10) Performance of ceremonial functions.

Article 8. No property can be given to, or received by, the Imperial House, nor can any gifts be made therefrom, without the authorization of the Diet.

Chapter II. RENUNCIATION OF WAR

Article 9. Aspiring sincerely to an international peace based on justice and order, the Japanese people forever renounce war as a sovereign right of the nation and the threat or use of force as means of settling international disputes.

2. In order to accomplish the aim of the preceding paragraph, land, sea, and air forces, as well as other war potential, will never be maintained. The right of belligerency of the state will not be recognized.

Chapter III. RIGHTS AND DUTIES OF THE PEOPLE

Article 10. The conditions necessary for being a Japanese national shall be determined by law.

Article 11. The people shall not be prevented from enjoying any of the fundamental human rights. These fundamental human rights guaranteed to the people by this Constitution shall be conferred upon the people of this and future generations as eternal and inviolate rights.

Article 12. The freedoms and rights guaranteed to the people by this Constitution shall be maintained by the constant endeavor of the people, who shall refrain from any abuse of these freedoms and rights and shall always be responsible for utilizing them for the public welfare.

Article 13. All of the people shall be respected as individuals. Their right to life, liberty, and the pursuit of happiness shall, to the extent that it does not interfere with the public welfare, be the supreme consideration in legislation and in other governmental affairs.

Article 14. All of the people are equal under the law and there shall be no discrimination in political, economic, or social relations because of race, creed, sex, social status, or family origin.

2. Peers and peerage shall not be recognized.

3. No privilege shall accompany any award of honor, decoration, or any distinction, nor shall any such award be valid beyond the lifetime of the individual who now holds or hereafter may receive it.

Article 15. The people have the inalienable right to choose their public officials and to dismiss them.

2. All public officials are servants of the whole community and not of any group thereof.

3. Universal adult suffrage is guaranteed with regard to the election of public officials.

4. In all elections, secrecy of the ballot shall not be violated. A voter shall not be answerable, publicly or privately, for the choice he has made.

Article 16. Every person shall have the right of peaceful petition for the redress of damage, for the removal of public officials, for the enactment, repeal, or amendment of laws, ordinances, or regulations, and for other matters, nor shall any person be in any way discriminated against for sponsoring such a petition.

Article 17. Every person may sue for redress as provided by law from the State or a public entity, in case he has suffered damage through illegal act of any public official.

Article 18. No person shall be held in bondage of any kind. Involuntary servitude, except as punishment for crime, is prohibited.

Article 19. Freedom of thought and conscience shall not be violated.

Article 20. Freedom of religion is guaranteed to all. No religious organization shall receive any privileges from the State nor exercise any political authority.

2. No person shall be compelled to take part in any religious acts, celebration, rite, or practice.

3. The State and its organs shall refrain from religious education or any other religious activity.

Article 21. Freedom of assembly and association as well as speech, press, and all other forms of expression are guaranteed.

2. No censorship shall be maintained, nor shall the secrecy of any means of communication be violated.

Article 22. Every person shall have freedom to choose and change his residence and to choose his occupation to the extent that it does not interfere with the public welfare.

2. Freedom of all persons to move to a foreign country and to divest themselves of their nationality shall be inviolate.

Article 23. Academic freedom is guaranteed.

Article 24. Marriage shall be based only on the mutual consent of both sexes and it shall be maintained through mutual cooperation with the equal rights of husband and wife as a basis.

2. With regard to choice of spouse, property rights, inheritance, choice of domicile, divorce, and other matters pertaining to marriage and the family, laws shall be enacted from the standpoint of individual dignity and the essential equality of the sexes.

Article 25. All people shall have the right to maintain the minimum standards of wholesome and cultured living.

2. In all spheres of life, the State shall use its endeavors for the promotion and extension of social welfare and security, and of public health.

Article 26. All people shall have the right to receive an equal education correspondent to their ability, as provided by law.

2. All people shall be obligated to have all boys and girls under their protection receive ordinary education as provided for by law. Such compulsory education shall be free.

Article 27. All people shall have the right and the obligation to work.

2. Standards for wages, hours, rest, and other working conditions shall be fixed by law.

3. Children shall not be exploited.

Article 28. The right of workers to organize and to bargain and act collectively is guaranteed.

Article 29. The right to own or to hold property is inviolable.

2. Property rights shall be defined by law, in conformity with the public welfare.

3. Private property may be taken for public use upon just compensation therefor.

Article 30. The people shall be liable to taxation as provided by law.

Article 31. No person shall be deprived of life or liberty, nor shall any other criminal penalty be imposed, except according to procedure established by law.

Article 32. No person shall be denied the right of access to the courts.

Article 33. No person shall be apprehended except upon warrant issued by a competent judicial officer which specifies the offense with which the person is charged, unless he is apprehended, the offense being committed.

Article 34. No person shall be arrested or detained without being at once informed of the charges against him or without the immediate privilege of counsel; nor shall he be detained without adequate cause; and upon demand of any person such cause must be immediately shown in open court in his presence and the presence of his counsel.

Article 35. The right of all persons to be secure in their homes, papers, and effects against entries, searches, and seizures shall not be impaired except upon warrant issued for adequate cause and particularly describing the place to be searched and things to be seized, or except as provided by Article 33.

2. Each search or seizure shall be made upon separate warrant issued by a competent judicial officer.

Article 36. The infliction of torture by any public officer and cruel punishments are absolutely forbidden.

Article 37. In all criminal cases the accused shall enjoy the right to a speedy and public trial by an impartial tribunal.

2. He shall be permitted full opportunity to examine all witnesses, and he shall have the right of compulsory process for obtaining witnesses on his behalf at public expense.

3. At all times the accused shall have the assistance of competent counsel who shall, if the accused is unable to secure the same by his own efforts, be assigned to his use by the State.

Article 38. No person shall be compelled to testify against himself.

2. Confession made under compulsion, torture or threat, or after prolonged arrest or detention shall not be admitted in evidence.

3. No person shall be convicted or punished in cases where the only proof against him is his own confession.

Article 39. No person shall be held criminally liable for an act which was lawful at the time it was committed, or of which he has been acquitted, nor shall he be placed in double jeopardy.

Article 40. Any person, in case he is acquitted after he has been arrested or detained, may sue the State for redress as provided by law.

Chapter IV. THE DIET

Article 41. The Diet shall be the highest organ of state power, and shall be the sole law-making organ of the State.

Article 42. The Diet shall consist of two Houses, namely the House of Representatives and the House of Councillors.

Article 43. Both Houses shall consist of elected members, representative of all the people.

2. The number of the members of each House shall be fixed by law.

Article 44. The qualifications of members of both Houses and their electors shall be fixed by law. However, there shall be no discrimination because of race, creed, sex, social status, family origin, education, property, or income.

Article 45. The term of office of members of the House of Representatives shall be four years. However, the term shall be terminated before the full term is up in case the House of Representatives is dissolved.

Article 46. The term of office of members of the House of Councillors shall be six years, and election for half the members shall take place every three years.

Article 47. Electoral districts, method of voting, and other matters pertaining to the method of election of members of both Houses shall be fixed by law.

Article 48. No person shall be permitted to be a member of both Houses simultaneously.

Article 49. Members of both Houses shall receive appropriate annual payment from the national treasury in accordance with law.

Article 50. Except in cases provided by law, members of both Houses shall be exempt from apprehension while the Diet is in session, and any members apprehended before the opening of the session shall be freed during the term of the session upon demand of the House.

Article 51. Members of both Houses shall not be held liable outside the House for speeches, debates, or votes cast inside the House.

Article 52. An ordinary session of the Diet shall be convoked once per year.

Article 53. The Cabinet may determine to convoke extraordinary sessions of the Diet. When a quarter or more of the total members of either House makes the demand, the Cabinet must determine on such convocation.

Article 54. When the House of Representatives is dissolved, there must be a general election of members of the House of Representatives within forty (40) days from the date of dissolution, and the Diet must be convoked within thirty (30) days from the date of the election.

2. When the House of Representatives is dissolved, the House of Councillors is closed at the same time. However, the Cabinet may in time of national emergency convoke the House of Councillors in emergency session.

3. Measures taken at such session as mentioned in the proviso of the preceding paragraph shall be provisional and shall become null and

void unless agreed to by the House of Representatives within a period of ten (10) days after the opening of the next session of the Diet.

Article 55. Each House shall judge disputes related to qualifications of its members. However, in order to deny a seat to any member, it is necessary to pass a resolution by a majority of two-thirds or more of the members present.

Article 56. Business cannot be transacted in either House unless one-third or more of total membership is present.

2. All matters shall be decided, in each House, by a majority of those present, except as elsewhere provided in the Constitution, and in case of a tie, the presiding officer shall decide the issue.

Article 57. Deliberation in each House shall be public. However, a secret meeting may be held where a majority of two-thirds or more of those members present passes a resolution therefor.

2. Each House shall keep a record of proceedings. This record shall be published and given general circulation, excepting such parts of proceedings of secret session as may be deemed to require secrecy.

3. Upon demand of one-fifth or more of the members present, votes of the members on any matter shall be recorded in the minutes.

Article 58. Each House shall select its own president and other officials.

2. Each House shall establish its rules pertaining to meetings, proceedings, and internal discipline, and may punish members for disorderly conduct. However, in order to expel a member, a majority of two-thirds or more of those members present must pass a resolution thereon.

Article 59. A bill becomes a law on passage by both Houses, except as otherwise provided by the Constitution.

2. A bill which is passed by the House of Representatives, and upon which the House of Councillors makes a decision different from that of the House of Representatives, becomes a law when passed a second time by the House of Representatives by a majority of two-thirds or more of the members present.

3. The provision of the preceding paragraph does not preclude the House of Representatives from calling for the meeting of a joint committee of both Houses, provided for by law.

4. Failure by the House of Councillors to take final action within sixty (60) days after receipt of a bill passed by the House of Representatives, time in recess excepted, may be determined by the House of Representatives to constitute a rejection of the said bill by the House of Councillors.

Article 60. The budget must first be submitted to the House of Representatives.

2. Upon consideration of the budget, when the House of Councillors makes a decision different from that of the House of Representatives, and when no agreement can be reached even through a joint committee of both Houses, provided for by law, or in the case of failure by the House of Councillors to take final action within thirty (30) days, the period of recess excluded, after the receipt of the budget passed by the House of Representatives, the decision of the House of Representatives shall be the decision of the Diet.

Article 61. The second paragraph of the preceding article applies also to the Diet approval required for the conclusion of treaties.

Article 62. Each House may conduct investigations in relation to government, and may demand the presence and testimony of witnesses, and the production of records.

Article 63. The Prime Minister and other Ministers of State may, at any time, appear in either House for the purpose of speaking on bills, regardless of whether they are members of the House or not. They must appear when their presence is required in order to give answers or explanations.

Article 64. The Diet shall set up an impeachment court from among the members of both Houses for the purpose of trying those judges against whom removal proceedings have been instituted.

2. Matters relating to impeachment shall be provided by law.

Chapter V. THE CABINET

Article 65. Executive power shall be vested in the Cabinet.

Article 66. The Cabinet shall consist of the Prime Minister, who shall be its head, and other Ministers of State, as provided for by law.

2. The Prime Minister and other Ministers of State must be civilians.

3. The Cabinet, in the exercise of executive power, shall be collectively responsible to the Diet.

Article 67. The Prime Minister shall be designated from among the members of the Diet by a resolution of the Diet. This designation shall precede all other business.

2. If the House of Representatives and the House of Councillors disagree and if no agreement can be reached even through a joint committee of both Houses, provided for by law, or the House of Councillors fails to make designation within ten (10) days, exclusive of the period of recess, after the House of Representatives has made

designation, the decision of the House of Representatives shall be the decision of the Diet.

Article 68. The Prime Minister shall appoint the Ministers of State. However, a majority of their number must be chosen from among the members of the Diet.

2. The Prime Minister may remove the Ministers of State as he chooses.

Article 69. If the House of Representatives passes a non-confidence resolution, or rejects a confidence resolution, the Cabinet shall resign en masse, unless the House of Representatives is dissolved within ten (10) days.

Article 70. When there is a vacancy in the post of Prime Minister, or upon the first convocation of the Diet after a general election of members of the House of Representatives, the Cabinet shall resign en masse.

Article 71. In the cases mentioned in the two preceding Articles, the Cabinet shall continue its functions until the time when a new Prime Minister is appointed.

Article 72. The Prime Minister, representing the Cabinet, submits bills, reports on general national affairs and foreign relations to the Diet, and exercises control and supervision over various administrative branches.

Article 73. The Cabinet, in addition to other general administrative functions, shall perform the following functions:

(1) Administer the law faithfully; conduct affairs of state;

(2) Manage foreign affairs;

(3) Conclude treaties. However, it shall obtain prior or, depending on circumstances, subsequent approval of the Diet;

(4) Administer the civil service, in accordance with standards established by law;

(5) Prepare the budget, and present it to the Diet;

(6) Enact cabinet orders in order to execute the provisions of this Constitution and of the law. However, it cannot include penal provisions in such cabinet orders unless authorized by such law.

(7) Decide on general amnesty, special amnesty, commutation of punishment, reprieve, and restoration of rights.

Article 74. All laws and cabinet orders shall be signed by the competent Minister of State and countersigned by the Prime Minister.

Article 75. The Ministers of State, during their tenure of office, shall not be subject to legal action without the consent of the Prime

Minister. However, the right to take that action is not impaired hereby.

Chapter VI. JUDICIARY

Article 76. The whole judicial power is vested in a Supreme Court and in such inferior courts as are established by law.

2. No extraordinary tribunal shall be established, nor shall any organ or agency of the Executive be given final judicial power.

3. All judges shall be independent in the exercise of their conscience and shall be bound only by this Constitution and the laws.

Article 77. The Supreme Court is vested with the rule-making power under which it determines the rules of procedure and of practice, and of matters relating to attorneys, the internal discipline of the courts, and the administration of judicial affairs.

2. Public procurators shall be subject to the rule-making power of the Supreme Court.

3. The Supreme Court may delegate the power to make rules for inferior courts to such courts.

Article 78. Judges shall not be removed except by public impeachment unless judicially declared mentally or physically incompetent to perform official duties. No disciplinary action against judges shall be administered by any executive organ or agency.

Article 79. The Supreme Court shall consist of a Chief Judge and such number of judges as may be determined by law; all such judges excepting the Chief Judge shall be appointed by the Cabinet.

2. The appointment of the judges of the Supreme Court shall be reviewed by the people at the first general election of members of the House of Representatives following their appointment, and shall be reviewed again at the first general election of members of the House of Representatives after a lapse of ten (10) years, and in the same manner thereafter.

3. In cases mentioned in the foregoing paragraph, when the majority of the voters favors the dismissal of a judge, he shall be dismissed.

4. Matters pertaining to review shall be prescribed by law.

5. The judges of the Supreme Court shall be retired upon the attainment of the age as fixed by law.

6. All such judges shall receive, at regular stated intervals, adequate compensation which shall not be decreased during their terms of office.

Article 80. The judges of the inferior courts shall be appointed by the Cabinet from a list of persons nominated by the Supreme Court.

All such judges shall hold office for a term of ten (10) years with privilege of reappointment, provided that they shall be retired upon the attainment of the age as fixed by law.

2. The judges of the inferior courts shall receive, at regular stated intervals, adequate compensation which shall not be decreased during their terms of office.

Article 81. The Supreme Court is the court of last resort with power to determine the constitutionality of any law, order, regulation, or official act.

Article 82. Trials shall be conducted and judgment declared publicly. Where a court unanimously determines publicity to be dangerous to public order or morals, a trial may be conducted privately, but trials of political offenses, offenses involving the press, or cases wherein the rights of people as guaranteed in Chapter III of this Constitution are in question shall always be conducted publicly.

Chapter VII. FINANCE

Article 83. The power to administer national finances shall be exercised as the Diet shall determine.

Article 84. No new taxes shall be imposed or existing ones modified except by law or under such conditions as law may prescribe.

Article 85. No money shall be expended, nor shall the State obligate itself, except as authorized by the Diet.

Article 86. The Cabinet shall prepare and submit to the Diet for its consideration and decision a budget for each fiscal year.

Article 87. In order to provide for unforeseen deficiencies in the budget, a reserve fund may be authorized by the Diet to be expended upon the responsibility of the Cabinet.

2. The Cabinet must get subsequent approval of the Diet for all payments from the reserve fund.

Article 88. All property of the Imperial Household shall belong to the State. All expenses of the Imperial Household shall be appropriated by the Diet in the budget.

Article 89. No public money or other property shall be expended or appropriated for the use, benefit, or maintenance of any religious institution or association, or for any charitable, educational, or benevolent enterprises not under the control of public authority.

Article 90. Final accounts of the expenditures and revenues of the State shall be audited annually by a Board of Audit and submitted by the Cabinet to the Diet, together with the statement of audit, during the fiscal year immediately following the period covered.

2. The organization and competency of the Board of Audit shall be determined by law.

Article 91. At regular intervals and at least annually, the Cabinet shall report to the Diet and the people on the state of national finances.

Chapter VIII. LOCAL SELF-GOVERNMENT

Article 92. Regulations concerning organization and operations of local public entities shall be fixed by law in accordance with the principle of local autonomy.

Article 93. The local public entities shall establish assemblies as their deliberative organs, in accordance with law.

2. The chief executive officers of all local public entities, the members of their assemblies, and such other local officials as may be determined by law shall be elected by direct popular vote within their several communities.

Article 94. Local public entities shall have the right to manage their property, affairs, and administration and to enact their own regulations within law.

Article 95. A special law, applicable only to one local public entity, cannot be enacted by the Diet without the consent of the majority of the voters of the local public entity concerned, obtained in accordance with law.

Chapter IX. AMENDMENTS

Article 96. Amendments to this Constitution shall be initiated by the Diet, through a concurring vote of two-thirds or more of all the members of each House and shall thereupon be submitted to the people for ratification, which shall require the affirmative vote of a majority of all votes cast thereon, at a special referendum or at such election as the Diet shall specify.

2. Amendments when so ratified shall immediately be promulgated by the Emperor in the name of the people, as an integral part of this Constitution.

Chapter X. SUPREME LAW

Article 97. The fundamental human rights by this Constitution guaranteed to the people of Japan are fruits of the age-old struggle of man to be free; they have survived the many exacting tests for durability and are conferred upon this and future generations in trust, to be held for all time inviolate.

Article 98. This Constitution shall be the supreme law of the nation and no law, ordinance, imperial rescript, or other act of government, or part thereof, contrary to the provisions hereof, shall have legal force or validity.

2. The treaties concluded by Japan and established laws of nations shall be faithfully observed.

Article 99. The Emperor or the Regent as well as Ministers of State, members of the Diet, judges, and all other public officials have the obligation to respect and uphold this Constitution.

Chapter XI. SUPPLEMENTARY PROVISIONS

Article 100. This Constitution shall be enforced as from the day when the period of six months will have elapsed counting from the day of its promulgation.

2. The enactment of laws necessary for the enforcement of this Constitution, the election of members of the House of Councillors and the procedure for the convocation of the Diet and other preparatory procedures for the enforcement of this Constitution may be executed before the day prescribed in the preceding paragraph.

Article 101. If the House of Councillors is not constituted before the effective date of this Constitution, the House of Representatives shall function as the Diet until such time as the House of Councillors shall be constituted.

Article 102. The term of office for half the members of the House of Councillors serving in the first term under this Constitution shall be three years. Members falling under this category shall be determined in accordance with law.

Article 103. The Ministers of State, members of the House of Representatives, and judges in office on the effective date of this Constitution, and all other public officials, who occupy positions corresponding to such positions as are recognized by this Constitution shall not forfeit their positions automatically on account of the enforcement of this Constitution unless otherwise specified by law. When, however, successors are elected or appointed under the provisions of this Constitution, they shall forfeit their positions as a matter of course.

Selected Bibliography

This highly selective bibliography, organized by chapters, is designed, first, to assist the student in his search for additional material and, second, to provide the specialist with a means for tracing the sources of my information and the development of my arguments. It is neither exhaustive nor even a complete list of the works I have consulted.

Among the newspapers, periodicals, and yearbooks on which I have depended most consistently are *The New York Times*, the *Japan Times* (formerly *Nippon Times*), *Asahi Shimbun*, the *Japan Quarterly*, *Contemporary Japan*, *Japan Report* (issued by the Embassy of Japan in Washington, D.C.), *Jiji Nenkan* (*Jiji Yearbook*), *Asahi Nenkan*, (*Asahi Yearbook*), and the *Japan Statistical Yearbook* (published by the Government of Japan with the text in both English and Japanese). My principal sources of statistical information have been current newspapers, yearbooks, and *Japan Report*.

The general reader will find particularly useful the encyclopedic, 1,077-page *Japan: Its Land, People and Culture*, compiled by the Japan National Commission for UNESCO (Tokyo: Printing Bureau, Ministry of Finance, 1958).

Prologue

Democracy:

BECKER, CARL. *Modern Democracy*. New Haven, Conn.: Yale University Press, 1941.

BRYCE, LORD. *Modern Democracies*. New York: The Macmillan Co., 1921.

CRANSTON, MAURICE. *Freedom: A New Analysis*. New York: Longmans, Green & Co., 1953.

FRIEDRICH, C. J. *Constitutional Government and Democracy*. Boston: Ginn & Company, 1946.

LINDSAY, LORD. *The Modern Democratic State.* New York: Oxford University Press, 1947.

McKEON, RICHARD (ed.). *Democracy in a World of Tensions: A Symposium Prepared by UNESCO.* Chicago: University of Chicago Press, 1951.

NEUMANN, FRANZ. *The Democratic and the Authoritarian State.* Glencoe, Ill.: The Free Press, 1957.

ROSS, ALF. *Why Democracy?* Cambridge, Mass.: Harvard University Press, 1952.

SIMON, YVES R. *Philosophy of Democratic Government.* Chicago: University of Chicago Press, 1951.

SMITH, T. V. and LINDEMAN, EDUARD C. *The Democratic Way of Life: An American Interpretation.* New York: New American Library, 1953.

Nationalism:

BROWN, DELMAR. *Nationalism in Japan.* Berkeley, Calif.: University of California Press, 1955.

HAYES, CARLETON J. H. *Essays on Nationalism.* New York: The Macmillan Co., 1926.

KOHN, HANS. *The Idea of Nationalism.* New York: The Macmillan Co., 1946.

ROYAL INSTITUTE OF INTERNATIONAL AFFAIRS. *Nationalism.* New York: Oxford University Press, 1939.

SHAFER, BOYD C. *Nationalism: Myth and Reality.* New York: Harcourt, Brace & Company, 1955.

Chapter 1

General Historical Accounts:

BORTON, HUGH. *Japan's Modern Century.* New York: The Ronald Press Company, 1955.

REISCHAUER, EDWIN O. *Japan: Past and Present.* New York: Alfred A. Knopf, 1956.

SANSOM, GEORGE. *A History of Japan to 1334.* Stanford, Calif.: Stanford University Press, 1958.

———. *A History of Japan: 1334–1615.* Stanford, Calif.: Stanford University Press, 1961.

———. *The Western World and Japan: A Study in the Interaction of European and Asiatic Cultures.* New York: Alfred A. Knopf, 1949.

STORRY, RICHARD. *A History of Modern Japan.* Harmondsworth, England: Penguin Books, 1960.

Modern Political History and Problems:

BYAS, HUGH. *Government by Assassination.* New York: Alfred A. Knopf, 1942.

CHAMBERLIN, WILLIAM HENRY. *Japan Over Asia.* Boston: Little, Brown & Co., 1939.

FRIEDRICH, CARL J., and BRZEZINSKI, ZBIGNIEW, K. *Totalitarian Dictatorship and Autocracy.* Cambridge, Mass.: Harvard University Press, 1956; New York: Frederick A. Praeger, 1961 (paperback edition).

FUJII, SHINICHI. *The Essentials of Japanese Constitutional Law.* Tokyo: Yuhikaku, 1940. (The long quotation on imperial sovereignty in this chapter is to be found on pp. 124–125 of this book.)

IKE, NOBUTAKA. *The Beginnings of Political Democracy in Japan.* Baltimore: The Johns Hopkins Press, 1950.

ITO, PRINCE HIROBUMI. *Commentaries on the Constitution of the Empire of Japan.* Tokyo: Igirisu Horitsu Gakko, 1889.

MAKI, JOHN M. *Japanese Militarism: Its Cause and Cure.* New York: Alfred A. Knopf, 1945.

QUIGLEY, HAROLD S. *Japanese Government and Politics.* New York: Century Co., 1932.

SCALAPINO, ROBERT A. *Democracy and the Party Movement in Prewar Japan: The Failure of the First Attempt.* Berkeley, Calif.: University of California Press, 1953.

TOLISCHUS, OTTO D. *Tokyo Record.* New York: Reynal and Hitchcock, 1943.

YOUNG, A. MORGAN. *Imperial Japan, 1926–1938.* New York: William Morrow & Co., 1938.

Foreign Relations:

AKAGI, ROY HIDEMICHI. *Japan's Foreign Relations 1542–1936.* Tokyo: Hokuseido, 1936.

BUTOW, ROBERT J. C. *Japan's Decision to Surrender.* Stanford, Calif.: Stanford University Press, 1954.

JONES, F. C. *Japan's New Order in East Asia: Its Rise and Fall 1937–45.* New York: Oxford University Press, 1954.

TAKEUCHI, TATSUJI. *War and Diplomacy in the Japanese Empire.* Garden City, N.Y.: Doubleday, Doran, 1935.

TOGO, SHIGENORI. *The Cause of Japan.* New York: Simon and Schuster, 1956.

Economic History:

ALLEN, G. C. *A Short Economic History of Modern Japan, 1867–1937.* London: George Allen & Unwin, 1946.

LOCKWOOD, WILLIAM W. *The Economic Development of Japan: Growth and Structural Change 1868–1938.* Princeton, N.J.: Princeton University Press, 1954.

Chapters 2 and 3

There is no good history of the occupation. Harry Emerson Wildes' *Typhoon in Tokyo*—crammed with facts, impressions, opinions, and gossip—is not truly a history. Kazuo Kawai's *Japan's American Interlude* is by far the best analysis of the occupation and its impact on Japan. *Political Reorientation of Japan* can be regarded as the Government Section's official report on its work between 1945 and 1948. The second volume is filled with important documents relating to government and politics during the period. The documents quoted in the text may be found in several of the volumes listed below, especially those dealing with the early years of the occupation.

BORTON, HUGH. "Japan under the Allied Occupation, 1945–7," in JONES, F. C.; BORTON, HUGH; and PEARN, B. H. *Survey of International Affairs 1939–1946: The Far East 1942–1946*. Published for the Royal Institute of International Affairs, London. New York: Oxford University Press, 1955.

FEAREY, ROBERT A. *The Occupation of Japan. Second Phase: 1948–50*. New York: The Macmillan Co., 1950.

GAYN, MARK. *Japan Diary*. New York: William Sloane Associates, 1948.

GENERAL HEADQUARTERS, SUPREME COMMANDER FOR THE ALLIED POWERS. *Political Reorientation of Japan. September 1945 to September 1948: Report of Government Section, Supreme Commander for the Allied Powers*. 2 vols. Washington, D.C.: Government Printing Office, undated.

————. *Summation of Non-Military Activities in Japan and Korea*, Nos. 1–35 (September/October, 1945, to August, 1948). ("And Korea" dropped from title after fifth issue.)

GUNTHER, JOHN. *The Riddle of MacArthur*. New York: Harper & Brothers, 1951.

KAWAI, KAZUO. *Japan's American Interlude*. Chicago: University of Chicago Press, 1960.

MARTIN, EDWIN M. *The Allied Occupation of Japan*. American Institute of Pacific Relations, 1948.

MURAKAMI, TATSUO. *Tenno to Tohoku: 1947 (The Emperor and the Northeast: 1947)*. Sendai: Kawakita Shimpo Sha, 1947.

REISCHAUER, EDWIN O. *The United States and Japan*. Cambridge, Mass.: Harvard University Press, 1950.

STIMSON, HENRY L., and BUNDY, McGEORGE. *On Active Duty in Peace and War*. New York: Harper & Brothers, 1947.

U.S. DEPARTMENT OF STATE. *Occupation of Japan: Policy and Progress*. Publication 2671, Far Eastern Series 17. Washington, D.C.: Government Printing Office, undated.

Van Aduard, Baron E. J. Lewe. *Japan from Surrender to Peace.* New York: Frederick A. Praeger, 1954.

Whitney, Brigadier General Courtney. *MacArthur: His Rendezvous with History.* New York: Alfred A. Knopf, 1956.

Wildes, Harry Emerson. *Typhoon in Tokyo: The Occupation and Its Aftermath.* New York: The Macmillan Co., 1954.

Chapters 4 and 5

The book by Quigley and Turner is the basic work in English on postwar Japanese government and politics; it can be consulted with profit on any governmental or political problem, even though some of the factual material is dated. I have listed a few titles in Japanese that are representative of the vast literature on the 1947 constitution. *Watakushitachi no Kempo* is a beautiful children's book on the constitution, and it is interesting as an example of how children are being taught the meaning of the constitution.

General Headquarters, Supreme Commander for the Allied Powers. "Analysis of the Constitution of Japan," *Monthly Summation of Non-Military Activities in Japan*, No. 14 (November, 1946), pp. 25–40.

———. "Japanese Government's Official Commentary on Constitution," *Monthly Summation . . .*, No. 13 (October, 1946), pp. 20–22.

"Japan Since Recovery of Independence," *Annals of the American Academy of Political and Social Science*, Vol. CCCVIII (November, 1956). See especially the section entitled "Constitutional and Governmental Developments."

Maki, John M. "Japan's Rearmament: Progress and Problems," *Western Political Quarterly*, Vol. VIII, No. 4 (December, 1955).

———. "The Prime Minister's Office and Executive Power in Japan," *Far Eastern Survey*, Vol. XXIV, No. 5.

Miyazawa, Toshiyoshi. *Japan's Constitutional Problems and Her Political Chart* (in "Japan's Problems Series"). Tokyo: Public Information and Cultural Affairs Bureau, Japanese Ministry of Foreign Affairs, 1956.

Oppler, Alfred C. "Japan's Courts and Law in Transition," *Contemporary Japan*, Vol. XXI, Nos. 1–3 (1952).

Quigley, Harold S., and Turner, John E. *The New Japan: Government and Politics.* Minneapolis, Minn.: University of Minnesota Press, 1956.

Tagami, Joji. "Some Problems on the Constitution of Japan," *The Annals of the Hitotsubashi Academy*, Vol. I, No. 2 (April, 1951).

Ukai, Nobushige. "The Individual and the Rule of Law under the New Japanese Constitution," *Northwestern University Law Review*, Vol. LI, No. 6 (January-February, 1957).

WAGATSUMA, SAKAE. "The Japanese Legal System 1945–1955: Changes in Retrospect," *Monumenta Nipponica*, Vol. XII, Nos. 1–2 (April-July, 1956).

——. "Guarantee of Fundamental Human Rights Under the Japanese Constitution," *Washington Law Review*, Vol. XXVI, No. 2 (May, 1951).

WARD, ROBERT E. "The Origins of the Present Japanese Constitution," *American Political Science Review*, Vol. L, No. 4 (December, 1956).

WILDES, HARRY EMERSON. "The Postwar Japanese Police," *The Journal of Criminal Law, Criminology and Police Science*, Vol. XLIII, No. 5 (January-February, 1953).

Books in Japanese:

HOGAKU KYOKAI (JURISPRUDENCE SOCIETY). *Chukai Nihonkoku Kempo* (*Commentary on the Constitution of Japan*). 2 vols. Yuhikaku, 1953.

KOKKA GAKKAI. (ASSOCIATION OF POLITICAL AND SOCIAL SCIENCE). *Shin Kempo no Kenkyu* (*Study of the New Constitution*). Yuhikaku, 1953 (tenth printing; originally published in 1947).

MINOBE TATSUKICHI. *Shin Kempo Chikujo Kaisetsu* (*An Article-by-Article Interpretation of the New Constitution*). Nippon Hyoron Sha, 1947.

——. *Nihonkoku Kempo Genron* (*Principles of the New Japanese Constitution*). Yuhikaku, 1948.

MIYAZAWA TOSHIYOSHI. *Nihonkoku Kempo* (*The Constitution of Japan*). Nippon Hyoron Sha, 1956.

——, Kokubun Ichitaro, and Hori Fumiko. *Watakushitachi no Kempo* (*Our Constitution*). Yuhikaku, 1955.

Chapter 6

The study by R. P. Dore is by far the best work in English on the problems of contemporary Japanese society. Matsumoto's study is both interesting and valuable, but it was apparently made over a period of years, and some of the material is dated; some of his generalizations are not always relevant to Japanese society in 1961. Barbu's study has nothing to do with Japan, but many of his ideas can be applied to both pre- and post-1945 Japanese society.

BARBU, ZEVEDEI. *Democracy and Dictatorship: Their Psychology and Patterns of Life*. New York: Grove Press, 1956.

DORE, R. P. *City Life in Japan*. London: Routledge & Kegan Paul, 1958.

GENERAL HEADQUARTERS, SUPREME COMMANDER FOR THE ALLIED POWERS. *Education in the New Japan.* 2 vols. Tokyo: Civil Information and Education Section, 1948.

HALL, ROBERT KING. *Shushin: The Ethics of a Defeated Nation.* New York: Columbia University Press, 1949.

HIDAKA DAISHIRO. "An Appraisal of Educational Reforms in Japan," in *Japan's Problems.* Tokyo: Public Information and Cultural Affairs Bureau, Ministry of Foreign Affairs, 1954.

JANSEN, MARIUS B. "Education, Values and Politics in Japan," *Foreign Affairs,* July, 1957.

"Japan Since Recovery of Independence," *Annals, loc. cit.* See especially the section entitled "Social and Educational Developments."

KATO HIDETOSHI (ed.). *Japanese Popular Culture.* Rutland, Vt.: Charles E. Tuttle Company, 1959.

KAWASHIMA TAKEYOSHI. *Ideorogi to shite no Kazoku Seido (The Family System as an Ideology).* Iwanami Shoten, 1957.

———. *Kekkon (Marriage).* Iwanami Shinsho, 1954.

MAKI, JOHN M. "Japan's Commission on the Constitution: The Approach to Revision." Unpublished paper read before the annual meeting of the Association for Asian Studies, 1960.

MATSUMOTO, YOSHIHARU SCOTT. "Contemporary Japan: The Individual and the Group," *Transactions of the American Philosophical Society,* New Series, Vol. L, Part 1 (1960).

MINISTRY OF EDUCATION, GOVERNMENT OF JAPAN. *Education in Japan: Graphic Presentation.* Tokyo: Government Printing Bureau, 1959.

Shakai no Shikumi (The Organization of Society) (Volume II). Kyoiku Shuppan Kabushiki Kaisha, 1956.

STEINER, KURT. "The Revision of the Civil Code of Japan: Provisions Affecting the Family," *Far Eastern Quarterly,* Vol. IX, No. 2 (February, 1950).

STOETZEL, JEAN. *Without the Chrysanthemum and the Sword.* New York: Columbia University Press, 1955.

Chapter 7

Although there have been good books on both agriculture and labor, no book-length study of the roles of Japanese women, big business, or the bureaucracy has yet appeared in English.

ABEGGLEN, JAMES G. *The Japanese Factory: Aspects of its Social Organization.* Glencoe, Ill.: The Free Press, 1958.

BEARDSLEY, RICHARD K.; HALL, JOHN W.; and WARD, ROBERT E. *Village Japan.* Chicago: University of Chicago Press, 1959.

BISSON, T. A. *Zaibatsu Dissolution in Japan.* Berkeley, Calif.: University of California Press, 1954.

COHEN, JEROME B. *Japan's Economy in War and Reconstruction.* Minneapolis, Minn.: University of Minnesota Press, 1949.
———. *Japan's Postwar Economy.* Bloomington, Ind.: Indiana University Press, 1958.
DORE, R. P. *Land Reform in Japan.* New York: Oxford University Press, 1959.
FARLEY, MIRIAM S. *Aspects of Japan's Labor Problems.* New York: The John Day Company, 1950.
JAPAN FAO ASSOCIATION. *Agriculture in Japan.* 1958.
"Japan Since Recovery of Independence," *Annals, loc. cit.* See especially the section entitled "Economic Problems and Developments."
KURZMAN, DAN. *Kishi and Japan.* New York: Ivan Obolensky, 1960.
LEVINE, SOLOMON B. *Industrial Relations in Postwar Japan.* Urbana, Ill.: University of Illinois Press, 1958.
MAKI, JOHN M. "Japan's Military Establishment: From Master to Servant." Unpublished paper read before the annual meeting of the American Historical Association, 1960.
———. "Japan's Rearmament: Progress and Problems," *Western Political Quarterly,* Vol. VIII, No. 4 (December, 1955).
———. "The Role of Bureaucracy in Japan," *Pacific Affairs,* Vol. XX, No. 4 (December, 1947).
NAKAYAMA, ICHIRO. *Japan's Labor Problems.* Tokyo: Public Information and Cultural Affairs Bureau, Ministry of Foreign Affairs, 1956.
TANINO SETSU, *The Status of Women in Japan.* Tokyo: Women's and Minor's Bureau, Ministry of Labor, 1956.
TOBATA SEIICHI. *An Introduction to Agriculture of Japan.* Tokyo: Agriculture, Forestry, and Fisheries Productivity Conference, 1958.
U.S. DEPARTMENT OF STATE. *Report of the Mission on Japanese Combines: Part I. Analytical and Technical Data.* Department of State Publication 2628, Far Eastern Series 14. Washington, D.C.: Government Printing Office, 1946.
WAGATSUMA SAKAE and KATO ICHIRO. *Postwar Agricultural Land Reform in Japan.* Universita Di Firenze, Primo Convegno Internazionale di Diritto Agrario, 1954.

Chapter 8

By far the most penetrating treatment in a Western language of the problems of contemporary Japanese government and politics is the work by Ike cited below. The work by Quigley and Turner cited earlier is also useful on parties and elections. Although both the left wing and the extreme right wing in Japanese politics have been studied fairly extensively, it is unfortunate that there have been no good analyses of either the major conservative parties or of the nature of postwar conservatism.

CLUBOK, ALFRED. "Japanese Conservative Politics 1947–1955," in ROBERT E. WARD (ed.), *Five Studies in Japanese Politics*. Ann Arbor, Mich.: University of Michigan Press, 1957.

COLBERT, EVELYN S. *The Left Wing in Japanese Politics*. American Institute of Pacific Relations, 1952.

COLE, ALLAN B. *Japanese Society and Politics: The Impact of Social Stratification and Mobility on Politics*. Boston: Boston University Press, 1956.

DULL, PAUL S. "The Senkyoya System in Rural Japanese Communities." University of Michigan Center for Japanese Studies, *Occasional Papers*, No. 4.

IKE, NOBUTAKA. *Japanese Politics: An Introductory Survey*. New York: Alfred A. Knopf, 1957.

JANSEN, MARIUS B. "Ultranationalism in Postwar Japan," *The Political Quarterly*, Vol. XXVII, No. 2 (April–June, 1956).

"Japan Since Recovery of Independence," *Annals, loc. cit.* See especially the section entitled "Domestic Politics."

KINOSHITA, HANJI. "Rightist Movements," *The Oriental Economist*, December, 1956.

KYOGOKU, JUNICHI, and IKE, NOBUTAKA. *Urban-Rural Differences in Voting Behavior in Postwar Japan*. (Stanford University Political Science Series, No. 66.) Stanford, Calif.: Stanford University Press. Reprinted from *Proceedings of the Department of Social Sciences, College of General Education, University of Tokyo, 1959*.

LANGER, PAUL. "Communism in Independent Japan," in Hugh Borton, *et al., Japan Between East and West*. New York: Harper & Brothers, 1957.

MAKI, JOHN M. "Japan's Voting: The Conservative Majority," *India Quarterly*, Vol. X, No. 1 (January–March, 1954).

MENDEL, DOUGLAS H., JR. "Behind the 1955 Japanese Elections," *Far Eastern Survey*, Vol. XXIV, No. 5 (May, 1955).

———. "Behind the 1959 Japanese Elections," *Pacific Affairs*, Vol. XXXII, No. 3 (September, 1959).

———. "The Japanese Voter and Political Action," *Western Political Quarterly*, Vol. X, No. 4 (December, 1957).

MORRIS, IVAN I. *Nationalism and the Right Wing in Japan*. New York: Oxford University Press, 1960.

SCALAPINO, ROBERT A. "Japanese Socialism in Crisis," *Foreign Affairs*, January, 1960.

SWEARINGEN, RODGER, and LANGER, PAUL. *Red Flag in Japan*. Cambridge, Mass.: Harvard University Press, 1952.

UKAI NOBUSHIGE. "Japanese Election Results Reconsidered," *Pacific Affairs*, Vol. XXVI, No. 2 (June, 1953).

UYEHARA, CECIL H. *Leftwing Social Movements in Japan: An Annotated Bibliography*. Rutland, Vt.: Charles E. Tuttle Company, 1959.

————; Royama, Michio and Shimako; and Ogata, Shijuro. *Comparative Platforms of Japan's Major Parties.* Mimeographed. Medford, Mass.: Fletcher School of Law and Diplomacy, Tufts University, 1955.

Ward, Robert E. "Some Observations on Local Autonomy at the Village Level in Present-Day Japan," *Far Eastern Quarterly*, Vol. XII, No. 2 (February, 1953).

————. "Urban-Rural Differences and the Process of Political Modernization in Japan: A Case Study," *Economic Development and Cultural Change*, Vol. IX, No. 1, Part II (October, 1960).

Chapter 9

Inomata Kozo. "In Defense of the Constitution," *Contemporary Japan*, Vol. XXIV, Nos. 4–6 (1956).

Kempo Kaisei (Constitutional Revision). Yuhikaku, 1956.

Maki, John M. "Japan's Commission on the Constitution."

————. "Japan's Rearmament: Progress and Problems."

————. "Japan's Subversive Activities Prevention Law," *Western Political Quarterly*, Vol. VI, No. 3 (September, 1953).

Nakasone Yasuhiro. "Reasons for Constitutional Revision," *Contemporary Japan*, Vol. XXIV, Nos. 7–9 (1956).

Nihon Shakaito (Japan Socialist Party). *Heiwa no Tori de: Kempo Mondoshu (With the Dove of Peace: Questions and Answers on the Constitution)* (1956).

Sissons, D. C. S. "The Dispute Over Japan's Police Law," *Pacific Affairs*, Vol. XXIII, No. 1 (March, 1959).

Suekawa Hiroshi. *Nihon no Kempo: Naze Mamoraneba naranai ka? Naze Kaete wa Ikenai ka? (The Constitution of Japan: Why Must It Be Defended? Why Must It Not Be Changed?)*. Omeido, 1955.

Sugai, Shuichi. "The Japanese Police System," in Ward, *Five Studies in Japanese Politics*.

U.S. Department of State. "Security Treaty Between the United States and Japan" (*United States Treaties and Other International Agreements*, Vol. III, Part 3). Washington: Government Printing Office.

————. "Treaty of Mutual Cooperation and Security Between the United States of America and Japan," *Department of State Bulletin*, Vol. XLII, No. 1076 (February 8, 1960).

Ward, Robert E. "The Constitution and Current Japanese Politics," *Far Eastern Survey*, Vol. XXV, No. 4 (April, 1956).

Chapter 10

Borton, Hugh, *et al. Japan Between East and West.* New York: Harper & Brothers, 1957.

DONOGHUE, JOHN D. "An Eta Community in Japan: The Social Persistence of Outcast Groups," *American Anthropologist*, Vol. LIX, No. 6 (December, 1957).

NINOMIYA, SHIGEAKI. "An Inquiry Concerning the Origin, Development and Present Situation of the Eta in Relation to the History of Social Classes in Japan," *Transactions of the Asiatic Society of Japan*, Second Series, Vol. X (December, 1933).

WAGNER, EDWARD W. *The Korean Minority in Japan: 1904–1950.* Mimeographed. American Institute of Pacific Relations, 1950.

Index

(Note: This is a selective index designed to help the reader locate only significant topics and subjects. Therefore, it cannot be used to find every reference to every item mentioned in the text.)